D1287399

Ecstasy at the Onion

Ecstasy at the Onion

Thirty-one Pieces on Jazz

Whitney Balliett

The Bobbs-Merrill Company, Inc.
Indianapolis   New York

ML
3561
.J3 B244

The Bobbs-Merrill Company, Inc.
A Subsidiary of Howard W. Sams & Co., Inc., Publishers
Indianapolis • Kansas City • New York

Copyright © 1971 by Whitney Balliett
All rights reserved
Library of Congress catalog card number 76–161239
Printed in the United States of America

All the material in this book first appeared in somewhat
different form in *The New Yorker* magazine.

For William Shawn and Rogers Whitaker and
Robert Amussen, Marvellous Midwives

Preface

This collection is taken from the pieces I have done on jazz for *The New Yorker* during the past five years. It brings up to date the loose chronicle of the music begun twelve years ago in THE SOUND OF SURPRISE, and carried forward in DINOSAURS IN THE MORNING, SUCH SWEET THUNDER, and SUPER-DRUMMER: A PROFILE OF BUDDY RICH. It will, I suspect, be my last book on the subject. I have been writing about the music since 1947, a more than ample time to say what has to be said on any subject. And jazz itself, in its present dwindling, defenseless state, can no longer bear much critical weight—if, indeed, it ever could. The pieces, revised in varying degrees, are arranged in four sections, each of them largely in chronological order. The first, in diary form, covers the Monterey and Newport jazz festivals, and some of the high spots of the New York scene. The second is still another attempt to plumb Duke Ellington, surely one of the most elusive and brilliant men of this century. The third brings together seven critical pieces. And the last is a celebration of some of the *people* who have given us so much pleasure in the past fifty years. (Barney Josephson and Max Gordon are not jazz musicians but essential catalysts, and Bobby Short is a supper-club singer whose style is an exquisite refinement of one kind of jazz.) I don't like to think of jazz as dying. Perhaps it has simply finished what it had to say. At any rate, it cannot vanish, any more than Bach or Boswell. The recordings are there, and probably the best of them will one day enjoy an attention and acclaim that would astonish the great and mostly unsung inventors who made them.

W. B.

Contents

III
Reviews 1967–1971

IV
People 1968–1971

I
Notes: Newport, Monterey, New York

Newport   1966

July 1st: The Newport Jazz Festival, which is twelve, continues to put on weight. Festival Field, set on a slope overlooking Newport Harbor where fishermen once dried their nets, has been enlarged from twelve thousand seats to eighteen thousand. These seats, stretching almost as far as the eye can see, cover nine acres and have been enclosed in an eight-foot-high cedar stockade. There is a huge new stage supported by a forty-five-ton galaxy of steel girders, and there are a couple of new two-story Japanese-style buildings—one an administration building complete with a conference room, and the other a performers' building, connected to the rear of the stage by a fifty-foot bridge. The musicians, who once had to change and wait in gusty, musty tents, appear pleased. A press building has been promised before the end of the season.

The first concert, given tonight, breasted this institutionalism pretty well. One exception was the Dave Brubeck quartet, which, despite the ministrations of Joe Morello and the elegant aesthetics of Paul Desmond, grows paler and paler. Another was a rock-'n'-roll singer called Little Esther, who owes the late Dinah Washington everything except her tendency to sing flat. But Jimmy Smith, an organist accompanied by electric guitar and drums, sounded like the ocean, while the Newport Jazz Festival All-Stars (Ruby Braff, Bud Freeman, Gerry Mulligan, George Wein, Jack Lesberg, and Buddy Rich) offered some fine, unstudied lyricism, particularly in "Rose Room" and "I Never Knew." Braff played as if he might never play again; each solo had a thousand good notes, a dozen leaping intervals, run upon graceful run, and a beseeching passion.

I wonder if anything this weekend will match the climax of the evening—two numbers by the Archie Shepp quintet, which had Roswell Rudd on trombone, Charlie Haden on bass, Howard Johnson on tuba, and Beaver Harris on drums. Shepp is a complete avant-gardist and a merciless parodist—attributes perfectly accented by his clothes, which consisted of a First World War officer's jacket, tan Glen-plaid pants, a knitted cap, and tinted Ben Franklin spectacles. His best number was that great rarity, a genuinely funny piece of music. It began with slow, mournful, organlike chords, changed to a wild, rocking Sousa-like march, drifted into a mocking treatment of Duke Ellington's "Prelude to a Kiss," in which Rudd gave Lawrence Brown his lumps and Shepp gave Johnny Hodges his, returned to more hair-raising Sousa, more simpering Ellington, and so forth. The tempo went up and down and around, and there were brilliant ensemble clashes and some superb solos. Johnson is an *eloquent* tuba player, and Rudd proved again that he is an extraordinary trombonist who, like any consummate rebel, has one foot planted in the past and the other in the future.

At a party given after the concert for the musicians, Rudd and Shepp and Johnson went at it again. Gerry Mulligan, who would sit in with a treeful of cicadas, joined them, got caught in the maelstrom, and went peacefully under.

July 2nd: Newport generally enjoys hustling fogs and cool, keen winds, but the windless sun this afternoon in Festival Field made it inadvisable to sit down on the folding metal chairs without blowing on them first. The "new thing" was again on deck. Bill Dixon, a trumpeter, presented a dull five-part dirge that was danced to by Judith Dunn, who resembled a melting ice-cream cone. Charles Lloyd, a tenor saxophonist who admires both John Coltrane and Sonny Rollins, was sturdier, and during a quasi-gospel number his pianist, Keith Jarrett, put together a solo full of loose, fresh chords and held-breath rhythms that was a masterpiece. Horace Silver, who seemed Edwardian in contrast, was followed by Coltrane, whose group included the tenor saxophonist Farrell Saunders, another "new-thing" adherent. Saunders' solo in the first number soon turned into a series of thunderous elephant shrieks, which went on and on and on. When I mentioned to a friend that Saunders' solo appeared to have little in common with music, he replied, "Exactly. It's not music and it isn't meant to be. It's simply *sound*, and has to be judged as such. It's like which crosstown street in New York sounds best at noon on a weekday."

Thelonious Monk was perfunctory at tonight's concert, Stan Getz was bad, and the Mel Lewis—Thad Jones big band sounded loud and unleavened. But Nina Simone was also on hand, and she was hypnotic.

She sang a couple of social-protest songs, "I Loves You, Porgy," and some blues made of grits and greens.

July 3rd: We have been in the fiery furnace again all day, and to-night even the moon looked beat. The evening was taken up mainly by Duke Ellington and Ella Fitzgerald. The Ellington band coursed through a dozen numbers, most notably a "Take the 'A' Train" done partly in waltz tempo; a lullaby medley of "Black and Tan Fantasy," "Creole Love Call," and "The Mooche"; Harry Carney's long medita-tion on "La Plus Belle Africaine"; and "Rockin' in Rhythm," which over the years has become a perfect orchestral display piece. Miss Fitzgerald, towing her own drummer (Ed Thigpen) and pianist (Jimmy Jones), joined the band, and they exulted their way through a dozen more numbers, among them a swashbuckling "Sweet Georgia Brown"; a scat-sung version of "How High the Moon," in which snatches of "Mop Mop," "A Hard Day's Night," and "Smoke Gets in Your Eyes" blew by; and a fast "Cottontail" topped by some exhilarat-ing four-bar breaks between Miss Fitzgerald and Paul Gonsalves.

The Teddy Wilson trio, which had Gene Taylor on bass and Buddy Rich on drums, opened the concert, and in a medium-fast "Somebody Loves Me" Buddy Rich got off an unbelievable solo. He began with rolls nailed down by rimshots, which gradually fell into a staccato pattern, and then he broke into double time, spreading his rolls-and-rimshots over his tomtoms; inserted some offbeat undertow figures; exploded all over his set again; sank back to the original tempo while slipping in double-time accents with his foot pedal; fired a fusillade of rimshots; and built up to a super crescendo.

Woody Herman rambled down Memory Lane this afternoon. His band, fifteen or sixteen strong, broke out such old steam engines as "Apple Honey" and "The Woodchopper's Ball," played some of its current book, and then welcomed back three alumni and a ringer—Stan Getz, Zoot Sims, Al Cohn, and Gerry Mulligan. The emotion generated by the reunion overpowered their music, which suggested old Yale bucks warbling "The Whiffenpoof Song." Herman's regular band, which is full of young, clean-cut types, plays with precision and might, and its chief tenor saxophonist, Sal Nistico, should be heard in less combative surroundings.

July 4th: It's Louis Armstrong's sixty-sixth birthday, and the event was duly commemorated this afternoon by Bobby Hackett in "Struttin' with Some Barbecue." Hackett, one of the most graceful jazz musicians alive, also played matchless versions of "I Got It Bad and That Ain't Good" and "Green Dolphin Street," and a marvellous duet with

Dizzy Gillespie in " 'S Wonderful." Before that, Red Allen, hobbled by a hand-me-down rhythm section, worked his way through three remarkable numbers, and, before that, Kenny Dorham, Thad Jones, and Howard McGhee celebrated bebop, with McGhee taking the honors.

The wind finally swung into the north tonight, provoking Miles Davis into playing four surprisingly intense numbers. His tenor saxophonist, Wayne Shorter, demonstrated that he is a commendable Ornette Coleman admirer, while his drummer, Tony Williams, kept up a steady swamping rush of cymbals. Dizzy Gillespie fashioned six fine numbers, but he didn't dance, mug, sing, or joke. He seemed to have left four-fifths of himself at home. The festival was brought to a muscle-bound close by Count Basie and his band, which includes Jimmy Rushing, who was in rough voice, and Roy Eldridge, who, having recently joined Basie, sounded like the new boy in school.

Archie Shepp is the winner and champion.

Monterey 1966

September 16th: I came to the Monterey Jazz Festival, which began tonight, by way of Los Angeles, where I poked around in the ruins of West Coast Jazz, a movement that flourished in that city in the fifties. Los Angeles is not the sort of place you'd expect a night creature like jazz to flourish in. The sky is immense and blinding, and the city is immense and blinding. As a result West Coast Jazz, which got going in the early fifties, was almost diaphanous. Sired largely by the 1949 Gil Evans–Miles Davis–Gerry Mulligan Capitol recordings, it was cool, manicured, and fey. It was a blond music, which had, as Bud Shank, one of its founders and survivors, told me, a "soft, intellectual" quality. Its founders, who also included Shorty Rogers, Jimmy Giuffre, Art Pepper, Carson Smith, and Shelly Manne, were graduates of the finishing schools of Stan Kenton and/or Woody Herman as well as assiduous music students who admired Bartók and Stravinsky. They were supported by several jazz clubs and, more important, by recordings, which seemed at the time to be released at the rate of two or three a week. "It got so any new bass player or drummer who came on the scene was signed up for his own L.P.," Shank said. The movement even fostered its own unofficial recording firms—Contemporary and Pacific Jazz. It reached an apogee in some recordings by Manne and Giuffre and Rogers in which free improvisation and free rhythms were toyed with, and then, according to Shank, two things happened. "New York struck back with hard bop, and so damned many recordings were made the market flooded." West Coast Jazz expired in 1958, and its members drifted into the movie and television studios, where most of them continue as staff musicians, contentedly amassing Porsches, horses, swimming pools, and thirty-foot ketches. The principal jazz clubs in Los Angeles—Shelly's Manne-Hole in Hollywood, and the Lighthouse in Hermosa Beach—now house either out-of-town musicians or such non-studio West Coast performers as John Handy, Charles Lloyd, and Bola Sete. The rest of the jazz in the city is limited to the Neophonic Orchestra, a large Stan Kenton Third Stream group which gives half a dozen concerts a year, and an experimental big band organized by the trumpeter Don Ellis which has been holding forth on Monday nights during the past year in a bar called Bonesville. Los Angeles, like New York, has its share of starving jazz musicians, but they appear to be mostly Negroes who, Shank says, are not proficient enough to work in the studios. "The Negro saxophonists just play saxophone," he told me, "and the trumpeters trumpet. In the studios, saxophonists have to double on everything from flute to oboe, and the trumpeters have to play in three or four styles. So, in spite of all the screaming and crying, it's not racial. Benny Carter has grown rich in the studios, and so have other Negroes."

The concert tonight was taken up by desultory performances by three of the movers and founders of West Coast Jazz—Evans, Mulligan, and Dave Brubeck, the last of whom presided over a miniature West Coast movement in San Francisco in the late forties. Evans appeared with a twelve-piece band, recruited on both coasts and including Mulligan, Elvin Jones, Johnny Coles (trumpet), and Howard Johnson (tuba). It had reportedly been rehearsing for a week, but nothing went right. The solos were weak, the brass and reed sections faltered, and the rhythm section communed with itself. Even the amplification system was awry. Evans' music, with its butterfly sonorities and tricky rhythmic turns, demands perfection. Brubeck's quartet seemed to be visibly coming apart. Joe Morello and Gene Wright, at stage left, literally huddled together throughout the performance, Brubeck pumped aimlessly away at stage center, and Paul Desmond, usually an articulate and flourishing improviser, shaped manicured sounds at stage right. It is disheartening that Brubeck, as safe as I.B.M. for over a decade, hasn't seen fit to experiment by adding new instruments and new blood.

The evening freshened considerably when Vi Redd, a blunt, funny singer and alto saxophonist, came onstage. Miss Redd, who worked with the exotic organ-and-vocal-trio group Earl Hines brought to New York a couple of years ago, sings in the hard, glancing fashion of the early Dinah Washington and plays like a backwoods Charlie Parker. Count Basie, minus Roy Eldridge, who once mysteriously said he *never* goes to California, marched through a dozen numbers, most of which suggested that he should strip down, as he did in 1950, to a first-rate small band built chiefly around his piano—one of the hidden glories of the age.

September 17th: Bola Sete, the Brazilian guitarist, appeared midway tonight with Sebastian Neto on bass and Paulinho on drums, and it was a classic event. Sete plays unamplified guitar, achieving a richness and clarity of tone that shame all amplified guitarists. He uses a great many chords, connecting them with short single-note passages, and he invariably plays softly. His style is free of the histrionics of the flamencan guitarists and of the neon drone of most contemporary jazz guitarists. Sete's bassist and drummer work beautifully with him, and in the last of half a dozen numbers, all done in South American rhythms, the group became indivisible. It turned into a delicate, rippling rhythmic machine that moved gradually over tambourines, tuned bells, and gourds, to a marvellous drum solo by Paulinho. He used a *cuica* (a drumlike instrument with variable pitch) and sticks, which flickered quietly and effortlessly back and forth between his tuned bells, his tomtoms, the domes of his cymbals, and the rims of his drums, and he brought to mind—so gentle and fresh were his movements—the offhand displays Sid Catlett warmed himself and his audiences up with.

The rest of the concert was passable. The tenor saxophonist Booker Ervin preceded Sete. Ervin invariably plays with considerable fervor, but somewhere between his imagination and the sounds that emerge from his horn a peculiar transformation takes place. Everything turns to wood. Wooden notes follow wooden smears that follow wooden runs, and one soon falls into a bamboo dream. Evans was on hand again and sounded brighter in his mother-of-pearl way, and there were rundowns by an arch singer named Carol Sloane, by Cannonball Adderley and his brother Nat, and by a quasi-"new-thing" tenor saxophonist named Joe Henderson. By this time it was midnight, and I wondered if Newportitis had begun to afflict Monterey, a festival long celebrated for its tidiness and economy.

The notion that jazz needs to be buttressed by m.c.s, narrators, and other such apologists dies hard. In fact, this afternoon it almost stifled what turned out to be a magnificent performance. When the curtain opened Jon Hendricks, the singer and people's poet, was seated before a dozen small children. He proceeded to read them a poem, written in couplets by himself, that was a loose history of the Negro in America, and every now and then he paused to allow the performers stationed behind him to sing and/or play. These included Big Mama Willie Mae Thornton, Muddy Waters, Shaky Horton (a harmonica player), Memphis Slim, the Paul Butterfield Blues Band,

and a rock-'n'-roll group called Jefferson Airplane. Hendricks spoke repeatedly of the "children," by which he meant the Negro people and the squirming semicircle before him, and of the "un-Civil War," and then gave a facetious imitation of a slave auctioneer. But the performers finally broke into the clear. Muddy Waters and Memphis Slim were in excellent voice (Memphis Slim sang one of his aching, tempoless blues), and Big Mama Thornton, an unheralded blues singer who rarely wanders from Oakland, where she lives, was empyrean. She is a giant woman who affects short hair and ankle-length skirts, and she moves with the inimitable grace that only certain outsized people seem to possess. She has a fine contralto voice, and her sense of dynamics is striking. She can move from a whisper to a shout in one bar, and she knows Billie Holiday's trick of wandering along behind the beat and then pouncing on it by jamming five or six words together in one sustained note. She sang a dozen numbers, most of them blues, and their power and invention and grace stayed with the listener well into the evening. Jefferson Airplane and the Paul Butterfield Band were surprises. Jefferson Airplane consists of two singers, two guitarists, a bassist, and a drummer. They sang and played two good blues, but it was too bad that their solo female member, Signe Anderson, wasn't given a number to herself. She has a strong, affecting voice which was rarely audible. The Butterfield group includes two Negroes and four whites (electric harmonica, two electric guitars, electric organ, electric bass, and drums) who worked their way through three numbers, the last of which was a ten-minute collective free-for-all blues that had much in common with some of the "new-thing" scrambles. The electronic din was terrific, but the music it amplified stayed afloat.

September 18th: It has been made plain this weekend that electronic instruments are, for better or worse, here to stay (an electric saxophone is now on the market, and John Coltrane and Benny Carter have each bought one), and it has been proved that popular music is again moving toward jazz for sustenance and direction. More news was offered this afternoon: The four-four beat is practically dead. More than half the groups we have heard have used odd time signatures, and this afternoon Don Ellis and his twenty-piece band played five crowning numbers that were in five-eight, five-four, twenty-seven-sixteen, seven-eight, and nine-four. The countdown alone on the twenty-seven-sixteen number took about a minute, and all through the number lips moved and heads nodded. The results here and elsewhere were mixed; melodic content was often sacrificed for rhythmic complexity. Nonetheless, the band plays with fire and precision, thanks to Ellis, who is a demoniac conductor. One could *see* him pulling difficult chords out of the brass and reed sections. Equally startling was Steve Bohannon, a nineteen-year-old drummer who plays with exceptional invention and authority. Ellis himself plays a special four-valve trumpet, which enables him to reach quarter tones more easily. He tends, accordingly, to quarter-tone it all over the scale, and at times he resembled an avant-garde Al Hirt. One observer summed up the band this way: "Man, it's just the Stan Kenton band of today. You remember, everybody thought what Kenton was doing in the forties was so strange? Well, they got used to it. And the same thing will happen with Ellis. People will be dancing to him in twenty-seven-sixteen, and with their eyes closed, too."

Tonight was, with one exception, anticlimactic. Randy Weston, a blurred post-bop pianist, played for an hour and twenty-five minutes, in company with Ray Copeland, an earnest bebop trumpeter, Cecil Payne, another bebop holdover, and Booker Ervin. Denny Zeitlin, the bearded San Francisco psychiatrist and pianist, was fast and empty, and Carmen McRae demonstrated again that she is probably the most skilled—albeit mannered and brittle—popular singer alive. The Ellington band, in satisfactory form, closed the weekend and accompanied Bunny Briggs in "David Danced Before the Lord with All His Might" and "Honeysuckle Rose." Briggs was, as usual, a delight. He executed spinning, stomping offbeat steps; he raced from one side of the stage to the other, his feet clicking a thousand to the yard; he slid through huge, funny half-time strides and sudden running tiptoe steps; and, for good measure, he did the Frug and the Watusi. Even Johnny Hodges, who had spent an hour stonily contemplating the middle distance, watched.

Newport 1967

June 30th: Tonight was touted as a history of jazz and the "Schlitz Salute to Jazz in 1967" (the beer people plunked down a twenty-five-thousand-dollar subsidy for the evening), but it turned out to be an astonishing parade of pianists made up of Willie the Lion Smith, Earl Hines, Count Basie, Thelonious Monk, and John Lewis. (The concert also turned out to be in the classic horn-of-plenty Newport Jazz Festival tradition; there were no fewer than ten groups, and the concert lasted over five hours. The departing crowd, bent and shuffling, resembled a mass of Stepin Fetchits.) Hines was the guidon. After a good solo rendition of "You Can Depend on Me," he was joined by Ruby Braff for a couple of surprisingly successful duets. The two men, both self-preoccupied ornamentalists, had never player together before, but they got off a graceful "These Foolish Things" and a fast, intent "Rosetta." Hines' solos were full of his arhythmic whirlpools and upper-register, single-note jubilations, and Braff managed to move in apposite parallels. Willie the Lion, got up in his summer uniform (straw skimmer, white jacket, and cigar), played a vigorous if brief "Carolina Shout" and then teamed up for three numbers with Don Ewell, a disciple of Jelly Roll Morton and Fats Waller. Smith, who gives the deceptive impression when he plays that he is stretched out on a chaise longue, is almost always unpredictable, and tonight was no exception. He produced booming, irregular chord patterns and rifle-shot single notes, while Ewell, a correct but swinging pianist, was an admirable foil. Basie backed Buddy Tate and Buck Clayton in two sensuous numbers and then headed up his own cartel, but he was, lamentably, visible only in short solos and behind soloists. (When will someone get Basie into a recording studio with a first-rate rhythm section and let him loose—an event that hasn't taken place for over twenty years?) An all-star reunion of former bebop kings—Dizzy Gillespie, James Moody, Milt Jackson, Thelonious Monk, Percy Heath, and Max Roach—was disappointing, save for Monk. Gillespie seemed inhibited, Moody was uncertain, Jackson was mechanical, and Roach, as is his custom, was on Cloud 9. But Monk, stewing enjoyably in his own inexhaustible juices, was imperturbable, particularly in "How High the Moon," in which he took an excellent solo and supplied Gillespie with a stream of jarring chords that suggested a sheriff peppering the ground around an outlaw's feet. John Lewis brought up the rear with the Modern Jazz Quartet, demonstrating again that there are few pianists—tonight's diamonds included—who put as much grace and thought and intensity into each chorus.

The evening had other pleasures. The Newport Jazz Festival All-Stars (Ruby Braff, Pee Wee Russell, Bud Freeman, George Wein, Jack Lesberg, and Don Lamond) offered, among other numbers, a slow "Sugar" in which Russell, more sotto-voce than usual, fashioned —or perhaps was fashioned by—a four-bar phrase made up of incredibly juggled notes, and a slow "Summertime" in which Budd Johnson, sitting in on soprano saxophone, wailed and pirouetted à la Sidney Bechet. The concert was closed by the Albert Ayler quintet, a "new-thing" group that includes Ayler (a saxophonist), his brother (a trumpeter), and the drummer Milford Graves. Most of their efforts were expended on an occasionally funny parody of what sounded like a Salvation Army hymn and of fragments of "There's No Place Like Home" and "Eeny-Meeny-Miney-Mo."

July 1st: The weather is getting restless. It is still cool, but fog has been doing the mazurka up and down Narragansett Bay all afternoon, and tonight it circled once about the town and fell asleep. So did much of tonight's concert. The John Handy Quintet (vibraphone, guitar, bass, drums, and the leader's alto saxophone) punched and plodded through two endless numbers, one a musical attempt at "what it took to get James Meredith into the University of Mississippi" and the other a Spanish-tinged "new-thing" number called "Señor Nancy." Nina Simone, a Juilliard-trained pianist and singer who relishes a mean country blues, got hung up in a couple of interminable laments about loose men and fast women, and Dizzy Gillespie, appearing with his quintet, did four by-rote numbers. But the oddest disappointment was the new and revolutionary Gary Burton Quartet, which has Larry Coryell on guitar, Steve Swallow on bass, Stu Martin on drums, and the leader on vibraphone. Burton's group is working toward a distillate compounded of rock and roll and jazz, but these important explorations were only fitfully apparent. Coryell and Burton played an intricate duet using a variety of rhythms, and in a slow blues Coryell, who is the first great hope on his instrument since Charlie Christian and Django Reinhardt, hit on one of those seemingly stumbling but perfectly executed phrases—several barely audible be-hind-the-beat single notes followed by silence and a leaping, brilliant run—that Charlie Parker coined. At twelve o'clock Buddy Rich ap-peared with his big band, and the pumpkin turned into a golden coach. Rich started with a medium blues, soared through Bill Hol-man's ingenious arrangement of the McCartney-Lennon "Norwegian Wood," and went on to a display number, the "Bugle Call Rag." His solo was a wonder. It incorporated a section in which his left hand moved at a thousand r.p.m.s on his snare while his right hand floated casually back and forth between his tomtoms, a long, diminuendo roll that sank to barely audible knitting-needle clicking on his snare rims, and a Big Bertha climax. No sooner was the number over than Rich, bowing and sweating, launched into what appeared to be an introduc-tory twelve-bar solo in medium tempo, reared back and said, "What'll we play?" It was a throwaway gag, but it was also an incredible little solo, a perfect solo. Gillespie ambled onstage and blew a dozen choruses of blues with the band, and for the final number, an eleven-minute version of "West Side Story," he climbed into the trumpet sec-tion, whispered to the other trumpeters, yawned, peered elaborately at the sheet music, and ogled and shouted at Rich, who, his hands windmills in a high wind, never batted an eye.

The afternoon concert was labelled "The Five Faces of Jazz," and it was devoted to Middle Eastern music, pseudo-ragas, Afro-Cuban funk, the bossa nova, and "Norwegian Wood." The participants in-cluded Herbie Mann, the Hungarian guitarist Gabor Szabo, Luis En-rique of Brazil, and such ringers as Gillespie and the German trombonist Albert Mangelsdorff. A ho-hum day at the U.N.

July 2nd: More fog, accompanied by snappy winds and low, pressing clouds. The afternoon concert began with half a dozen selections by Nobuo Hara and his Sharps and Flats, an eighteen-piece Japanese band. Swathed in smiles, the group was a formidable cross between late Jimmie Lunceford and early Stan Kenton, and its soloists suggested J. J. Johnson, Art Farmer, and Clifford Brown, plus Gene Krupa laced with Louis Bellson. In three numbers the band accompanied Housan Yamamoto, who played a large wooden flute called the shakuhachi. He gets a husky, pleasing tone on his instrument and a direct, lyrical quality not unlike that of Joe Marsala. The main event was a vibra-phone workshop—Bobby Hutcherson, Gary Burton, Red Norvo, Milt

Jackson, and Lionel Hampton. Burton sent up a ghostly unaccompanied ballad that was all willows and Debussy and moonshafts; Norvo produced a creditable "I Love You" (Cole Porter's) and then went into his old anthem, "I Surrender, Dear." He ended with a funny "Ida," for which he turned off his resonator and, using heavy mallets, clumped around the keyboard like a slow-motion tap-dancer. At odd intervals he shot out his right elbow—clearly a prearranged signal for Roy Haynes, his drummer, to play a rimshot. Haynes misfired as often as not, and it was good hamming. The rest was predictable. Hampton unloaded his customary two-by-fours, Hutcherson jammed a hundred notes into each measure, and Jackson kept his lyric cool. All five vibraphonists got together for a closing blues; then the rain, floating around the rafters for the past twenty-four hours, came, blending its sound perfectly with the heavy work onstage.

The rain was still needling in low and hard and cold at eight, when the evening began. As it turned out, we could have all stayed home. Bill Evans, along with Eddie Gomez (bass) and Philly Joe Jones, swam steadily toward his own surface but never reached it; Max Roach and his quintet struck off hard-bop clichés; Woody Herman's big band dipped into the gospel bag, the blues bag, and the flag-waver bag; Miles Davis, wearing a dinner jacket and an untied bow tie, spent more time offstage than on; and the Blues Project, a heavily amplified five-piece group that has been moving from rock and roll toward jazz, was allowed just two numbers before being unplugged.

July 3rd: With a couple of exceptions, tonight was a continuation of last night. (The rain, coming in tropical explosions, continued all morning and then subsided into fog.) The Dave Brubeck Quartet showed more candlepower than has been its wont in recent years, and Sarah Vaughan wandered through eight follow-me-if-you-can numbers. The evening and the festival were closed by Lionel Hampton and a big band made up largely of Hampton alumni, among them Milt Buckner, Joe Newman, Frank Foster, Benny Powell, Jerome Richardson, and Snooky Young. The alumni, however, spent most of the dozen numbers sitting on their instruments while Hampton labored at the vibraphone, the drums, and the piano. In "Flying Home," though, Illinois Jacquet, who had played well earlier in the evening, went through his celebrated calisthenics, and it was like hearing Francis Scott Key sing "The Star-Spangled Banner." The other successful numbers in the concert were done by Red Norvo, Ruby Braff, and the Wein-Lesberg-Lamond rhythm section. Norvo floated earnestly over his vibraphone, playing excellent tag in his exchanges with Braff and Lamond, and looked—with his bearded, benign, expectant way of continually lifting his head from his instrument and searching the audience—like God watching out for the Devil.

The afternoon was given over almost wholly to big bands. Don Ellis's nineteen-piece group, outfitted with an eight-man rhythm section (three bassists, four drummers, and a pianist) and a mass of electronic equipment, played five absorbing numbers. There were fugues and passacaglias, raga-like passages, time signatures of five/four, three-and-a-half/four, and seven/four, a sterling parody of "Bill Bailey, Won't You Please Come Home?" and electronic effects that sounded like echoing caves. The concert ended with an extravaganza called the Milford (Massachusetts) Youth Band. It is, as far as I know, the largest jazz band in history, for it boasts sixteen saxophones, eleven clarinets, five trombones, twelve trumpets, a bass, four woodwinds, a French horn, drums, and three percussion. The band ranges in age from eleven to eighteen and includes nine girls. It played a recent Basie number, Benny Goodman and Artie Shaw, a blues, a Kentonish avant-garde number, a ballad, and a Near Eastern number, and played them almost as well as any current big band. The soloists were nearly as good. Best of all were the glorious passages in which the brass section, eighteen strong, opened up.

Newport 1968

July 4th: It is Louis Armstrong's sixty-eighth birthday and the country's hundred-and-ninety-second, which means that Armstrong has been around over a third as long as his country, and so is running neck and neck with General Motors, A. T. & T. and Con Edison. It is also the festival's fourteenth birthday, and not its announced fifteenth, since the 1961 concerts were a popular-music replacement erected on the ruins of the 1960 festival, which was sundered by the Newport riot—a bellwether uprising if ever there was one. All that happened tonight, though, was a wild, crazy-legs cadenza by the pianist Joe Zawinul near the end of Cannonball Adderley's "Maria." It sounded like Bartók on a tear, and it was delivered with just the right touch of ham. For the rest of its time the Adderley group rummaged in its blues-gospel-funk-rock bag—"soul soap" music, as a friend appositely christened it—and later Nina Simone rummaged in hers. We also heard Mongo Santamaria, a conga drummer who leads a proficient Latin blues band; the guitarists Jim Hall and Barney Kessel, who played separately and together, the first declaiming for the introverts of the world and the second for the extroverts; and Gary Burton's group (Larry Coryell, Steve Swallow, Roy Haynes), which, disavowing its earlier revolutionary tendencies, shimmered like moonlight on the Ganges.

July 5th: The afternoon was sunny and limned by haze, and the evening fog made the trees look like low, gray-green clouds. The fog was also onstage and in the eyes of the beholders, for tonight we rambled down Memory Lane. The Basie band played itself for a couple of numbers and then offered Jimmy Lunceford's arrangements of "Cheatin' on Me" and "For Dancers Only." Joe Thomas, Lunceford's tenor saxophonist and singer (not to be confused with the trumpeter of that name), was ferried in from Kansas City for the two numbers, and he was wonderful. He is a genuine jazz singer and he remains— though he is now an undertaker—one of the best graduates of Coleman Hawkins great academy. Basie was replaced by Woody Herman, who graciously played two Goodman arrangements, backed Jack Leonard singing Tommy Dorsey's "Marie" (the brass section swooped through Bunny Berigan's solo), did Glenn Miller's "In the Mood," accompanied Erskine Hawkins in "Tuxedo Junction" and "Tippin' In" (Hawkins had a swinging, interesting band, but his banshee trumpet playing is no better now than it was twenty-five years ago), accompanied Bob Eberle in Jimmy Dorsey's "Amapola," "Tangerine," and "Green Eyes," and closed with Artie Shaw's "Nightmare" and "Summit Ridge Drive." In many ways Sumerian history seemed fresher, but more was to come. Charlie Barnet led the Ellington band (with Nat Pierce on piano) in seven Barnet numbers ("Skyliner," "Pompton Turnpike," "East Side, West Side," and so forth). Since Barnet's main inspiration was the Ellington band, it was two mirrors staring at one another. Then Ellington himself appeared and played "Take the 'A' Train," "Passion Flower," "Sophisticated Lady," "Things Ain't What They Used to Be," and four slightly less shopworn numbers. Nostalgia Promenade was capped by a reconstituted Dizzy Gillespie big band using Gil Fuller arrangements which were so inoperable that I left midway in the third one, learning later that I had missed Benny Carter, who sat in for several numbers, one of them a statuesque "I Can't Get Started."

The afternoon concert was notable only for Rufus Harley's playing a bagpipe in a pleasant tune called "Windy" (he somehow supplied all the notes that have been missing from the instrument since it was invented); a great Dizzy Gillespie open-horn solo in "Swing Low, Sweet Cadillac" (he had his quintet with him), which began with soft, bouffant phrases and ended with shouts linked by Mad Hatter runs; and four numbers by the Elvin Jones trio (Joe Farrell, flute and tenor saxophone, and Jimmy Garrison, bass), including a standing-ovation bass solo in "Risa" and a long, pagoda-structured drum solo in "Kayiko's Birthday March."

My master-of-ceremonies scorecard is filling up. It already lists George Wein, Father Norman O'Connor, John Hammond, George Simon, Alan Grant, Billy Taylor, and André Baruch. A choral number arranged for them by Gil Fuller would be suitable before the weekend is out.

July 6th: By and large, this afternoon was, as they say at *Down Beat,* a gas. Montego Joe, another conga drummer, brought on another

Latin blues band, and it played with a rocking precision epitomized by the solos of its tenor saxophonist, Bobby Brown, who magically combined the late John Coltrane's adventurousness with a loafing, old-fashioned lyricism. Tal Farlow, who has only recently emerged from a long semi-retirement, demonstrated—along with Johnny Knapp, Junie Booth, and Mousie Alexander—that inactivity is a two-edged sword. His ideas were fresh and sure and flowing, but his execution seemed stiff and calculated. Knapp, a many-handed pianist who recalls the basso-profundo ebullience of the late Eddie Costa, offset Farlow's perfectionism, and so did Booth, a good, limber Charlie Mingus bassist. Then Sonny Criss, a forty-year-old alto saxophonist and Charlie Parker offshoot, played four numbers with Billy Taylor, Booth, and Alexander. "Willow Weep for Me" was a masterpiece. It included declamatory Parker-like phrases, long rests, and whispering runs. Its dynamics were extraordinary and its structure was flawless. It was the sort of performance that crystallizes everything, that makes time stop and wait. The remainder of the afternoon was a jumble. Benny Carter came on with Duke Ellington, Johnny Hodges, Jeff Castleman (bass), and Rufus Jones (drums), and the set got off on the left foot when Ellington facetiously introduced Carter as the man a symphony musician would consult about jazz and a jazzman would consult about the symphony. During the six tunes, Carter was allowed just three solos, and, although Carter is one of our most esteemed composer-arrangers, the tunes were all by Ellington or Billy Strayhorn. Backstage observers reported that after the performance Carter, a man of remarkably even humor, was shaken. The eighteen-piece University of Illinois Jazz Band, finishing up the afternoon, played with an aplomb and conviction which ironically suggested that when a form of jazz can be executed so well by the very young it has been exhausted. (*Vide* New Orleans jazz, Dixieland, stride piano, and bebop.)

The evening began well and ended irrelevantly. Alex Welsh, a cornettist and the leader of a fine seven-piece English swing band, backed Bud Freeman, Pee Wee Russell (whose "Pee Wee's Blues" and "Love Is Just Around the Corner" were subtle and fresh and affecting), Ruby Braff, and Joe Venuti, who, at sixty-eight, managed "Body and Soul" and "Sweet Georgia Brown" much as he might have forty years ago. Then Joan Crawford, appearing on behalf of Pepsi-Cola for not altogether clear reasons, introduced Duke Ellington. "Hi, I'm Joan Crawford, and I can't tell you how wonderful it is to be with all my friends on this magnificent evening." She continued with a fruity eulogy to Ellington. When a genial heckler shouted something, she stopped, yelled "Shut up! You just shut up," and finished her script in a shaking voice. Ellington, possibly feeling a little maladroit after the afternoon, kissed Miss Crawford, played nine hand-me-downs and refused to end his set. (He finally left the stage, after Woody Herman, appearing from the wings, attempted to dance with him, whereupon George Wein announced the intermission, leaving the band sitting there with its mouth open.) The evening was rung down by Hugh Masekela, a South African Harry James, and by Dionne Warwick, a homogenized gospel singer.

July 7th: The afternoon was given over to Ray Charles, and—stirringly beautiful, a little miraculous—it ranked with those celebrated Newport afternoon concerts of gospel singing (1957) and tap-dancing (1962). The evening was unavoidably anticlimactic. (Wouldn't it be better, since Sunday night is a gray and tapering time anyway, to simply have one Sunday concert, starting around three and ending at eight?) Ramsey Lewis, a tall, heavy-handed pianist, passed out three or four helpings of soul soap, and was followed by an odd, ethereal vocal trio from California called the Sound of Feeling and made up of a singer-pianist, Gary David, and the twins Alyce and Rhae Andrece. The group concentrates on impossible harmonies, the notes that exist in the cracks of the piano keyboard, and such metres as seven-four. There were Bergian sounds and spook sounds and Paul Verlaine set to music, but few sounds of feeling. It was chilly, expert music, and it prompted a man sitting nearby to observe that it was "not very conducive to audience participation." Roland Kirk, a one-man reed section who seems to carry huge bags of sound around with him, sweated and swung and stomped through six numbers, sometimes playing his instruments separately and sometimes all at once. His clowning has yet to conceal the fact that he is a consummate musician. Don Ellis' infallible nineteen-piece Los Angeles band agreeably closed the festival with a number in thirteen-four, a country-and-Western in seven-four, an ingenious reworking of Charlie Parker's "K.C. Blues," and an electrophonic number that summoned up other planets, other galaxies.

The Charles concert began, as is now customary, with a dozen numbers by his fine big band, his vocal quartet (the Raelets), and a singer and dancer named Billy Preston. The Master, dressed in an olive velvet jacket, came on after the intermission, and before his first number was over his presence—Billie Holiday had the same thing and Mahalia Jackson has it—seized Festival Field; he could have done "The Beer Barrel Polka" and "Moon of Manakoora" without losing an ounce of attention. In the course of seventeen numbers, he sang his incredible anthem, "Georgia on My Mind," getting off a "Now I said, Georgia" in a high soft moan that shook the timbers, and backing himself all the while on piano with marvellous, digging blues figures.

He sang "Marie" in a bright, funny way, recalling his "Alexander's Ragtime Band," and the Beatles' "Yesterday" and "Eleanor Rigby," turning them into altogether new numbers. He sang a slow, swaying "Let's Go Get Stoned," he swung "You Are My Sunshine," and he ended with a long, layer-upon-layer version of "What'd I Say" that swung so hard it made the audience leap to its feet.

New York   1969

February 16th: Word has come through that Pee Wee Russell died yesterday in Alexandria, Virginia, at the age of sixty-two. Most lives are uphill, but Russell's was almost perpendicular. He was a shy man trapped in a sausage body and a clown's face. He sidled rather than walked, and his deep voice seemed to back out of him, producing long, subterranean utterances that were either unintelligible or very funny. And when he tried to escape into alcohol he became mortally trapped. His style—the chalumeau phrases, the leaps over the abyss, the unique *why?* tone, the use of notes that less imaginative musicians had discarded as untoward—was, paradoxically, his final snare and his glory. People laughed at it. It was considered eccentric, and because eccentricity, the kindest form of defiance, baffles people, they laugh. But those who didn't laugh understood that Russell, behind his Surrealistic front (his magnificent face resembled C. Aubrey Smith's minus the Empire), had discovered some of the secrets of life and that his improvisations were generally successful attempts to tell those secrets in a new, funny, gentle way. To be sure, he never revealed anything *out*right, probably because he enjoyed making his listeners work as hard as he did. (His late and devoted wife, Mary, once opened an interview with a journalist by saying, affably, "Pee Wee can be an s.o.b., you know.") And when, late in life and at Mary's goading, he took up painting, the results were an astonishing visual extension of his aural circumlocutions. Russell embossed his sound on the world, and his wife knew it when she told me, to his delight, that his playing embarrassed her.

February 18th: Russell's homemade sublimity had a lot in common with the machine-tooled sublimity of the Modern Jazz Quartet which appeared tonight at the Metropolitan Museum. Russell's musical life was an endless experiment, and so, in its ethereal way, is the M.J.Q.'s. More than that, both Russell and the M.J.Q. were and are dedicated to the humaneness of the blues, which, from breath to breath, can embrace or blister the listener. The most remarkable thing about the Quartet in recent years—aside from the fact that the long association of its members has bred not indifference but steady musical growth—has been the gradual coming to the fore of John Lewis' piano playing. (Like Russell, Lewis is classically shy.) His longer and more frequent solos now have a ringing, engraved assurance that matches Milt Jackson's much praised inventiveness and that, in turn, moves Percy Heath and Connie Kay to impassioned efforts. Lewis attractively championed himself tonight, particularly in "Three Little Feelings," in which he constructed a solo full of his customary blue-pearl, upper-register single notes and of brand-new dissonant chords that obliquely reached climax after climax.

February 19th: Genuine jazz singers tend to have jerry-built voices, an intuitive rhythmic intelligence, a scary sense of intonation, and a freedom with melismatics that blows two-syllable words up into five and deflates three-syllable ones to a vowel. These characteristics are kept in balance by the one gift they all share—honest-John emotion and the ability to transmit it. Anita O'Day, who opened at the Half Note last night, is the uncommon reverse. She is a jazz singer by calculation and design. Each husky, sandblown note is placed exactly behind, on, or in front of the beat, the syllables are expanded or contracted with millimetric care, she wavers her pitch for effect. She steers the listener's ear every inch of the way and she also transfixes his eye. Each inflection, beat, and tone is underlined with a movement: ankles delicately crossed and uncrossed, a rotating left shoulder, a punctuating akimbo elbow, a slow turn, ending with her head jutted forward and her hands horizontal at her sides, or her head in sudden profile and her legs planted jauntily apart. But the total effect can be unsettling. Again and again her perfections bring her to the edge of self-parody, and one longs for the slight slip, the disguised faltering that would make the human being inside the mannerisms and motions and invariably beautiful clothes real. Roy Eldridge and his quintet shared the bill with Miss O'Day, and in "Let Me Off Uptown," their old grandstanding duet from the Gene Krupa days, they got together to see if they could raise some goosepimples. They did.

February 27th: George Wein's Newport Jazz Festival All-Stars—Ruby Braff, Red Norvo, Wein, Barney Kessel and/or Tal Farlow, Larry Ridley, and Don Lamond—is winding up its current stint at

Plaza 9. It is a sleek swing band that uses good materials outfitted in handsome head arrangements. It is also a crazy quilt whose dissimilarities are in steady, jostling harmony. Braff's bravura eloquence is lightened by Norvo's pinpoint embroidery (his notes seem to ascend in visible crystalline clusters when he plays); Farlow's silver lines are blown about by Kessel's southwest winds; Wein, in his good Stacy-Hines-Waller manner, showers emotion everywhere; and Ridley and Lamond provide reliable central heating. Russell, who often played with Wein, would have relished such fast company.

March 1st: One of the least necessary misfortunes of the past twenty years has been the almost unnoticed disappearance of jazz dancing. It was a comic, graceful, ingenious art, but it went out the back door just as television, its potentially perfect medium, was coming in the front. But thanks to the heroic efforts of the late Marshall Stearns, we've had brilliant glimpses in the past decade of such tap dancers as Bunny Briggs and Baby Laurence, Groundhog, Honi Coles and Cholly Atkins, Pete Nugent, and Chuck Green, as well as of the marvellous Savoy Ballroom dancers—Al Minns and Leon James, who appeared this afternoon at Town Hall. It was a genial, dishevelled affair. The wrong accompanying recordings were played, numbers petered out before they got started, Minns' and James' comments backed and filled, and an eight-child "Company," made up of Minns' and James' children, provided brave, cluttered counterpoint. But there were exhilarating moments, when the two men—Minns is heavyset air and James a needle—did a cakewalk full of high knees and akimbo arms and supercilious looks; a dance called "Peckin' " in which they henned and roostered around the stage, their heads darting rapidly back and forth, their knees bent and knocking, their arms drunken wings; a soft-shoe composed of shooting legs and swimming arms; a Lindy Hop in which Minns picked up James and swung him around as though he were a child; and (Minns only) a celebration of Snakehips Tucker, whose slippery undulations suggested spaghetti sliding off a fork. An hour-long Minns-and-James television show, with live music and a brisk, brief commentary, would be consummate.

March 2nd: George Wein has stubbornly offered the proposition in his various festivals—made up of concerts never shorter than three hours and often presenting five, six, and even seven groups—that all audiences are created stoical. Not so. It is not just a matter of ossifying extremities; no listener, however avid, alert, and admiring, can *hear* after three hours. But Wein was at it again tonight, in the first of eight welcome Sunday-evening jazz concerts at Fillmore East. We

heard the Billy Taylor trio; the All-Stars, who were formidable (Farlow and Kessel were irresistible in a duet in "Topsy," and so was Braff
in a medium blues, plunger-muted in the first chorus and tightly muted
and really pedalling in the last); the Herbie Hancock sextet, whose
members believe that if you can't get it out in the first solo chorus
maybe you will in the fourteenth; Thelonious Monk's quartet, uneasily
augmented by Ray Copeland and Benny Green; and Clark Terry's big
rehearsal band, which included Ernie Wilkins, Lou Tabackin, Don
Friedman, and Steve Little. The show lasted well over four hours and
was put on in cavernous darkness, illuminated largely by the Joshua
Light Show, whose "Fantasia" abstractions numbed the eye and dis-
tracted the ear.

April 22nd: Richard Gibson is a hefty, shrewd, funny, well-to-do
forty-three-year-old former investments wizard and a philanthropic
lover of jazz whose chief business now is trying to get the so-called
World's Greatest Jazz Band of Yank Lawson and Bob Haggart on its
artistic and financial feet. He and Lawson and Haggart are the
"owners" of the band, which is set up on a coöperative basis. It included, as of tonight, Lawson and Billy Butterfield, trumpets; Bob
Wilber, soprano saxophone and clarinet; Zoot Sims, subbing for Bud
Freeman on tenor saxophone; Lou McGarity and Carl Fontana, trombones; Ralph Suttton, piano; Haggart, bass; and Gus Johnson, Jr.,
drums. The band is winding up a long stand at the Downbeat, at
Forty-second Street and Lexington Avenue, and late in 1968 it was
formally launched during a five-week stay at the Riverboat. Gibson
has underwritten a significant amount of the band's costs at both
places, and in the next couple of years he is prepared to sink an even
more significant amount into the vision of which the band is only a
part. "It's an absolute necessity that this band succeed," he says. "I
can't build on a loss. But I'm a natural moneymaker. There's no way
for me to succeed and not make money, and there's no way for me
to make money and not succeed. Once the band turns the corner, some
of its profits will spill on me. But first I want these jazz musicians to
make some money. Jazz has failed too many times, for the wrong
reasons." Gibson's vision includes the eventual formation of two totally
different bands, as well as a plan that he refuses to disclose at the
moment. "Look what happened when Walt Disney announced his
'Alice in Wonderland,'" he says. "Somebody else beat him to it, and
his version was, I think, the only movie he ever lost money on." Gibson
is convinced that if his vision crystallizes, the course of jazz will be
changed.
    Not surprisingly, the World's Greatest Jazz Band isn't, but it is,

within its pepped-up Bob Crosby scope, very good. The arrangements are all by Haggart, and they are a fluid mixture of written and improvised ensembles, solos, and—refreshingly—improvised duets. The materials include old-hat numbers ("Come Back, Sweet Papa," "Fidgety Feet"), swing standards ("Avalon," "After You've Gone"), and the up-to-date ("Sunny," "Mrs. Robinson," "Ode to Billie Joe"). The band has the shout and texture of a big band and the agility of a small band. When I first heard it a couple of weeks ago it was having a raggedy night: Butterfield didn't solo at all, Freeman and McGarity chugged, and the ensemble work was *bleu*. Tonight was totally different, and the presence of Sims may have had a lot to do with it. His brimming, long-lined eloquence was everywhere, and he was particularly rewarding in "Mrs. Robinson." Butterfield, who is a trumpeters' trumpeter, was in good, fussy form, and Fontana was superior. But perhaps the most inspirational news about the W. G. J. B. is Bob Wilber, who in the past year has developed an impassioned and original style on the soprano saxophone that comes close to matching the melodic affluence of his old teacher, Sidney Bechet. Most good jazz musicians start faltering at forty; Wilber stopped faltering at forty. The Gibson package at the Downbeat has other surprises. Also on hand are Maxine Sullivan, elfin and gray-haired and beautiful and in perfect, miniature Billie Holiday voice, and Joe Venuti, the wild, irrepressible seventy-year-old violinist whom Gibson tracked down a year or two ago after a long search. (Venuti stories are legion, and one of the best that Gibson tells has to do with a drummer who walked out on Venuti one night years ago. In revenge, Venuti filled the drums left behind with sand and shipped them to the drummer collect. The bass drum alone weighed six hundred pounds.) Most impresarios who have marketed jazz have been businessmen disguised as aficionados. Gibson is both.

May 5th: Tap dancing isn't "the art of walking raised to a baroque magnificence" (the *Times*, April 15th), any more than a cathedral is a glorified rock, but it is jazz music exhilaratingly translated from the abstract into concrete human form. The offspring of the marriage of jazz and the old clog dances, tap dancing has long been hounded by irony. When it was a staple in vaudeville, it was taken for granted as just another example of those picturesque gifts Negroes are born to. It was fun to watch, and taking lessons at the age of eight was the thing to do. Then, twenty years ago, it went underground, and almost automatically it became an art whose proponents were celebrated by being offered jobs as bellhops and elevator men. But this art survives, and every so often it surfaces. For the past four or five Monday nights, ten or so dancers have been gathering at the little Bert Wheeler Theatre in the Hotel Dixie on West Forty-third Street. Present tonight were Chuck Green (around whom the evening is loosely built), Lon Chaney, Big Rhythm Red, Sandman Sims, Raymond Kaalund, Bert and Sandra Gibson, Letitia Jay (who is the show's "coördinator"), and two younger dancers, Jimmy Slyde and Jerry Ames. It was a funny, jumbled evening. Miss Jay and Sandra Gibson lumbered on and off the stage, Derby Wilson (a retired dancer) told vaudeville jokes ("I just saw a cross-eyed woman tell a knock-kneed man to go straight home"), Green reminisced, Gibson was a deafening m.c., and the accompanists—a pianist and drummer, augmented midway by the trombonist Matthew Gee—often operated on their own rhythmic frequency. But there were glistening moments. In the first half of the evening, Kaalund, wearing a rumpled felt hat pulled down over his ears, did a drunken, barely audible soft-shoe. His shoulders, his stomach, and his feet all went in different directions, and he looked as if he were dancing against a high wind. Sandman Sims placed a low, small circular platform on the stage, and, sprinkling sand on it, did the Sand, his body bent and his feet scraping slowly around and around and producing sounds that fell somewhere between wire brushes and a steam engine starting up on wet tracks. The second half of the program was a simulated "cutting" contest in which Chaney, Sims, Rhythm Red, Ames, Green, Slyde, Gibson, and Kaalund each took several solo choruses, some accompanied and some not. Chaney began with the Paddle and Roll, which was full of heavy Baby Laurence steps, terrific kicks, and two-ton slides. He was followed by Kaalund, simultaneously dancing and skipping rope. Ames, who is a Donald O'Connor-Gene Kelly type of dancer, floated back and forth across the stage, throwing in flamencan steps and ballroom-dancing spins. Rhythm Red, an enormous, graceful man, was followed by Gibson, who did complex "wing" steps, and by Sims, whose legs at one point resembled calipers being quickly opened and closed. Jimmy Slyde has learned from Bunny Briggs and Baby Laurence, and he whipped around the stage like lightning, demonstrating great speed but no real style. Then Chuck Green, a tall, Lincoln-like man, pulled the rug deftly and simply out from under his colleagues with two slow, staccato choruses of blues; each step was crystal-clear, his rhythms were locked perfectly in place, and his movements were air-like.

May 18th: At best, music is the most elusive art. It resides only in the ear—you can't touch it or smell it or look at it. Yet most people attending a musical performance unwittingly and perversely try to listen by watching, as if the notes coming from a horn might suddenly appear in comforting schools of half notes and eighth notes. Since the eyes and the ears tend to compete endlessly anyway, visual concentration overrules the ear, and that is what happened to this listener this morning when "Camera Three" offered a twenty-six-minute film about Jeremy Steig, the extraordinary flutist and painter.

The film, called "Jeremy," was produced, directed, and edited by Joel Freedman, who also happens to be a cellist. It was put together over the past year and a half, and it is an attempt, in conservative *cinéma vérité*, to be a fly on the wall in Steig's life. Steig dances and plays by himself on a beach, horses around in the water with David Amram, plays a duet with Amram, plays a duet with Freedman, paints one of his marvellous satyr-choked murals while Freedman plays, and plays with his own group, the Satyrs (Adrian Guillery, Warren Bernhardt, Eddie Gomez, Bob McDonald). In many of the sequences, Steig is bare-chested and in underpants or bathing trunks—an excellent instance of naturalness giving the impression of affectation. There are, when one shuts one's eyes, ghostly patches of music. Steig and Gomez play a little blues, and there are the duets, some of them only bars long, a broken-off free improvisation by the Satyrs, and bits and pieces of Steig playing *a cappella*. How fine it would have been to have one sustained number in which the camera was focussed blindly on a bare wall while Steig, who is an extremely adventurous jazz flutist, was given a chance to stretch out on his instrument and show why the film was made at all.

This afternoon the Duke Ellington Society, an international group of Ellington veneraters, gave its annual concert built around a prominent Ellington alumnus. The celebrant today was the cornettist and violinist Ray Nance, who spent twenty-odd years with the band. Nance resembles many of the musicians who have passed through Ellington's hands, and as such he is a key to the Master's methods. Ellington has perfected a genuinely organic ensemble, and he tends to hire not dominating stars but soloists who possess highly specialized, sometimes freakish talents; to wit, Cootie Williams' plunger-mute work, Rex Stewart's half-valvings, Lawrence Brown's courtly tone, Barney Bigard's fluid attack, Sonny Greer's rattling, ringing sound, and Shorty Baker's evening-meadow tone. These attributes inspire Ellington's compositions, and the compositions flatter and provoke the soloists. Ellington was probably first attracted to Nance because of the feminine-emotion quality in his playing. (Women loom large in Ellington's life and music.) Nance has a soft, pleading tone and a wagging vibrato. He uses short phrases that are apt to jump from a whisper to a shout, and his occasional growls have a sweet rather than a dirty sound. His solos are often illogical, thus compounding their feminine sound, and at the same time they have an affecting querulousness. One still associates Nance with the careful orchestral bouquets that Ellington arranged around him, and hearing him in this afternoon's jam-session surroundings was largely fruitless. On hand in a rag-bag group were Brew Moore (tenor saxophone), Tiny Grimes and Tommy Lucas (guitars), Walter Davis (piano), Carl Pruitt (bass), and Steve Little (drums). There were too many numbers (seventeen), and most of them were taken up by the sidemen while Nance, who is a good clown, hopped around, danced, shouted encouragement, and, almost incidentally, played brief solos. But he did come forward a few times: in a slow, eloquent "Take the 'A' Train," played on violin; in three fine, quiet cornet choruses in "Jack the Bear"; and in a short solo in "In a Mellowtone."

Last spring Mabel Mercer and Bobby Short gave a highly acclaimed recital at Town Hall, and they joined forces there again tonight. Aside from the fact that both singers are dedicated to the notion that song lyrics should have meaning and charm and be intelligible, it is odd that they have been lumped together, for they are wholly dissimilar. Neither is a jazz singer in the strict sense, but Short comes close. He admires Art Tatum (he accompanies himself) and Ivie Anderson. His playing has the jazzy quality of the amateur pianists one heard at parties twenty years ago, and so has his singing, which is hoarse and declamatory and strutting. In the main, though, he is an appealing "personality" singer, a delighted singer. Miss Mercer, who is older, came up through the English musical theatre as a dancer and singer, and she became celebrated at Bricktop's in Paris before coming to this country in 1941. Her voice has slowed to a walk, but she remains a singers' singer. Her phrasing, done in recitative with little flags of melody appended, is exquisite; her diction matches that of Billie Holiday and Mildred Bailey; and, like Miss Holiday, she has an uncanny way of enveloping each tune in its appropriate mood. She rocks her lullabies, her timing invariably gets laughs in her funny songs, she is tender but never sentimental, and her occasional wryness is delivered in a genteel side-of-the-mouth manner. All is stamped by her queenly bearing—open, serene, her pretty face tilted slightly back, her hands coupled loosely in her lap (she performs seated), her back slat-straight.

Short's voice got out of hand dynamically and tonally in the first part of his program (the microphone was no help), but he recaptured it in the second part, which was devoted to Vernon Duke ("Speaking of Love," "I Can't Get Started," "What Is There to Say?"). Miss Mercer was in admirable form. Nothing went wrong, and she was at her regal best in "These Foolish Things," "Love Is Blue" (sung in French), and Bart Howard's "My Love Is a Wanderer." It was a gentle, civilized, skilled evening.

May 20th: The godlike offer too much and they demand too much. They seem cold because they have only themselves to match. They are shameless perfectionists and their light hurts the eyes. Such was Coleman Hawkins, the great tenor saxophonist who died yesterday at the age of sixty-four. Hawkins invented the jazz saxophone, and, more than that, he spent forty years tinkering with his invention—remodelling it, streamlining it, polishing it. Most artists, of whatever kind, find a style that, like the Boston matron's hat, sustains them for life, even when sheer use turns it to self-parody. But Hawkins, instinctively detesting commercialism, changed his style every ten or fifteen years. He began—in the twenties, with Fletcher Henderson—as a nervous, serio-comic performer who spent notes by the thousand. This adolescent choppiness subsided, and he became a classic Romantic with a big-breasted tone and an Echo Mountain vibrato. Then his style lost weight, revealing a fluent, tough, muscled attack—the attack that produced his seminal 1939 recording of "Body and Soul." He passed into his fourth and final phase ten years ago, and it was unsettling. The best of his earlier modes was still there, but there was a new element—a naked, hellfire crying out that suggested he had finally discovered what life is and didn't like what he saw. Hawkins' musical adventurousness—which kept musicians twenty years younger running—was simply a by-product of his unstemmable creativity. He spent most of his life *improvising,* which means that he altruistically gave part of himself away night after night, month after month, year after year. A sculptor can touch his work, a painter can stare at his finished canvas, but improvisation—except in the rare instances when it is recorded—is borne away the second it is uttered. Hawkins' generosity changed jazz, and jazz has changed Western music. One example will do. Harry Carney, the baritone saxophonist, has since 1927 been the rock that Duke Ellington has built his band on, and the Ellington band remains revolutionary and incomparable. Carney idolized Hawkins.

Hawkins' majesty was quietly embodied in his person. He was a handsome, straight-backed, medium-sized man who dressed impeccably and spoke distinctly in a low voice. Even in his later years, eroded by alcohol and the demands of his profession, he was seignorial. He offset his frail, stooped appearance by growing a patriarchal beard. He was always a lesson to watch. Eight years ago he was hired as an accompanist for Ida Cox, the old-time blues singer who had been unearthed and brought to New York to make some recordings. He overslept on the day of the session, but when he came into the studio—his eyes still three-quarters closed, a black felt hat jammed evenly on his head, his suit razor-sharp, and his walk very fast—he was the Chairman arriving, not just a tardy musician. Not long before that he played almost every concert of the fledgling Great South Bay Jazz Festival on Long Island, despite having to work in New York at the same time, and he played with a passion and invention that made the whole enterprise unforgettable. And one evil night several years ago at the Village Vanguard, after the bassist Charlie Mingus had spent an hour berating the audience and his musicians for something or other, Hawkins countered Mingus' rudeness by turning his back on him and playing magnificently into a corner of the bandstand. He courted no one, but he had friends, and Roy Eldridge, the trumpeter, was perhaps the closest. "Coleman was a first-class cat all the way down the line," Eldridge said last night. "He was the old school. He never travelled economy, and, of course, he was like a genius on his horn. I guess I knew him as well as anybody. I got my first job—for twelve dollars a week, in 1927— through him, by copying his solo, note for note, off Fletcher Henderson's record of 'Stampede.' And I was the first person near him after he came back from five years in Europe in 1939. I had a Lincoln and he had a Cadillac, and we followed each other to gigs—double things like that. He was a person people were afraid to talk to. If anything went wrong on a job, they wouldn't go to him, they'd always come to me. He was proud, but he wasn't cold, and he had a sense of humor. He just stayed away from cats he didn't like. People said he didn't like Lester Young, who was supposed to be his great rival. Man, I remember Coleman and I sat up all one night with Lester in the fifties, when we were with Jazz at the Philharmonic, trying to find out why Lester was up so tight. We never did. The last five years, Coleman was sick, and he just about quit eating. All he had eyes for, when he ate at all, was Chinese food, like Lester. But I'd call him in the evening and tell him what I was cooking. I'd tell him such-and-such, and he'd say, 'That sounds pretty good. I'll have to go out and get me some.' The next day I'd call again, and he'd forgotten everything. Coleman always had money, and he always spent it the right way. He'd have a Leica and a Steinway and three-hundred-dollar suits, but before anything else he always laid out six hundred dollars a month to take care of his rent and his wife and children. I often wondered if he had a little income of his own, but I never knew, because money was one thing we didn't discuss. Just a while ago I went out with Coleman when he wanted to look at a Rolls-Royce to buy, and I said to him, 'You'd look ridiculous riding around in that.'

So he bought a Chrysler Imperial. Eight thousand in cash. I don't think he got to put more than a thousand miles on it."

June 17th: Tonight Charles Mingus, the incomparable bassist, composer, bandleader, polemicist, impresario (Mingus products only), and autobiographer (his massive fabled, scurrilous memoirs have finally been accepted by a major publisher), appeared at the Village Vanguard with a quintet and ended a self-imposed two-year retirement. The reports of Mingus that circulated during his retirement were fleeting and characteristic. He had a brush with the police in the Village when he refused to leave the roof of a parked car from which he was photographing a hippie demonstration. He was sometimes seen, in all his Orson Welles bulk, pedalling around the same area on a bicycle. He was evicted from his loft, and the proceedings became the subject of a *cinéma-vérité* documentary. His return has been equally in character, for Mingus, though the most commanding—even domineering—bassist and bandleader in jazz, is a remarkably oblique man. It had been his wont during his retirement to drop into the Vanguard to listen to the music, and several weeks ago Max Gordon, the club's heroic owner, casually asked him when he was going to come out and play again. No definite response. A few days later Mingus left a note for Gordon with his telephone number. Gordon called, and Mingus said he wasn't sure. A week before the opening Mingus said yes and began rehearsing.

Mingus is propelled by his own winds, and they move him at every imaginable speed. He can sit and talk gently of the outrages and stupidities of life; he can verbally lash an audience from the bandstand for half an hour at a time; he can publicly fire and rehire a sideman during an evening; he can play with butterfly delicacy and alarming fury; he can be thin and stunningly good-looking and attractively fat; he can arrive on a bandstand with a satchel containing an axe (Mingus humor: musicians occasionally refer to their instruments as "axes") and then, seated on his customary stool, drink a glass of milk. Tonight he was moving at a still different speed. He looked like a seventy-year-old philosopher summoned to his alma mater for an honorary degree. He spoke to the audience quietly and briefly, he corrected his musicians politely, he smiled a lot, he played like Chopin serenading George Sand, and his expression was placid and benign. (It was also unfailingly alert; Mingus has astonishingly intelligent eyes, and he invariably gives the impression that he *sees* every sound and texture and smell within reach.) The music was equally gracious. Some of his music—in particular his free-for-all ensembles—is demonic, but almost everything tonight was legato and lyrical and loping. There were a lot of ballads and medium-tempo blues, and only with Mingus' "Pithecanthropus Erectus," his marvellous reworking of Cole Porter's "Get Out of Town," did the group manifest some of Mingus' old steam. Mingus, a roll of adhesive tape at the ready, was apparently suffering from Soft Finger, the occupational ailment of out-of-practice bassists, and he took just one complete solo. It was on "In a Sentimental Mood," and it was beautiful. He pulled back on the beat, inserted dazzling runs, slipped in and out of double time, and, with his tone and timbre, gave Ellington's tune a pleased, delighted air. With the exception of the tenor-saxophonist Billie Robinson, the Vanguard group is made up of graduates of the Mingus seminary, and consists of Bill Hardman on trumpet, Charlie McPherson on alto saxophone, and Dannie Richmond on drums. McPherson is a fine Charlie Parker adherent, and Hardman plays with a staccato brilliance that seems in constant defiance of the legato upholstery that his model, Dizzy Gillespie, sometimes rests on. It was a quiet musicale, but an unfailingly absorbing one. Mingus' presence and skill and energy made his sidemen's banalities irresistible and their inspirations godly.

June 18th: Once seen and heard, Mingus hangs around in the mind, so I went back to see him tonight, partly to exorcise him, and partly to test the old legend that jazz soloists spend night after night pouring out fresh improvisations. When I arrived Mingus and his musicians were sitting quietly on a banquette to the right of the bandstand, as if, in a curiously affecting way, they were awaiting an interview with a king—the king, of course, being the audience itself. Mingus still seemed swathed in peace, but he changed abruptly when, as he was seated on his stool and ready for the first number, a well-dressed, half-zonked man said something chummily condescending to him. Mingus pushed his bass at the man and said, "Here, you play, man." Then he turned his back, began playing, and spent the rest of the set looking stonily into the middle distance. The music spoke for him. "So Long, Eric," a tribute to the late Eric Dolphy, was the first number, as it was last night, but it sounded like a different tune. It was relaxed and even sloppy last night. Tonight it was angry and loud and expert. Richmond laid down a wall-to-wall carpet of Elvin Jones sounds, Hardman was quick and brilliant, as were Robinson and McPherson, and Richmond took the sort of head-knocking solo that Max Roach sometimes delivers when he is thinking about white men. "Pithecanthropus Erectus" appeared again as the second number, and it was an exhilarating tumult. Mingus, his fingers heavily taped and obviously hurting him, shifted to the piano, where, with spare dissonant chords and hard offbeat single notes, he pushed the ensembles into savage free-for-alls that were broken by tough solos backed by equally tough riffs and organ chords. The number cleared the air (the drunk, his face floating and blank, looked as if he had been hung by his collar on a coat hook), and it prepared the way for an Ellington medley. Mingus took a solo, but it was cautious and almost inaudible. The set ended and the drunk left, and at the beginning of the next set Mingus the wise and imperturbable returned. Surprisingly, the group played a pair of venerable bebop numbers, "Good Bait" and "Koko." McPherson picked his way handsomely through "Just Friends," and there was a swarming version of Mingus' "Fables of Faubus," his acid memorial to the former governor. The legend of nonstop improvisation *was* true tonight, largely because Mingus demands of his musicians exactly what he boundlessly gives.

Newport 1969

July 3rd: Just after dinner, old Thunder, riding Lightning and leading Rain, careered up Narragansett Bay, and the fifteenth Newport Jazz Festival was off. The storm was the most compelling spectacle of the evening, for the concert resembled one of those saltless concoctions that were tossed together at Town Hall or Carnegie Hall in the fifties and early sixties to lure the college kids who were home on vacation. Anita O'Day, dressed in a spanking, long-jacketed linen suit, evoked her 1958 appearance at Newport, when, with her beautifully honed mannerisms, she had wowed everybody in a performance that lasted only twenty minutes. She evoked it, but—mysteriously—that was all. She sang as well, she looked as well, she moved as well—and nothing happened. The audience was wet stone. Phil Woods and his European Rhythm Machine, made up of the alto saxophonist, a Swiss pianist, a French bassist, and a Swiss drummer, got the same reaction. Perhaps it was Woods. At his best he is an impassioned Charlie Parker adherent, but tonight he sounded unsettled and down. The group's single fine number had little to do with how it was played; it was the tune itself—"Ad Infinitum," a sad, lovely, long-lined melody by the "new-thing" pianist-composer Carla Bley. Young-Holt Unlimited, a soul-soap group whose leaders once worked with Ramsey Lewis, funked around, and there was one of Sun Ra and His Space Arkestra's cosmic Halloween parties. The band, carting hundreds of instruments onstage and dressed in hugoolie robes and tall elf hats, played an enormous number that included punctuating organ shrieks by Sun Ra, a neat parody of a Duke Ellington dreamboat number, some group singing reminiscent of the Modernaires, a passage in which everyone whaled away at a percussion instrument, and a shouting finale paced by Sun Ra striding regally across the stage with a couple of spiky sun symbols. But the evening closed hopefully. Bill Evans, accompanied by the brilliant Eddie Gomez on bass and Marty Morrell on drums, played three delicate ballads and was joined for two more numbers by Jeremy Steig. He developed long, tight, intense solos, with Evans celebrating him every note of the way, and it was a graceful performance.

July 4th: There had been an ominous, stifling atmosphere in Newport on the day of the 1960 riot. The town was choking. Hundreds of cars loaded with boozy teen-agers blocked the narrow streets, and the sidewalks and parks were jammed with even more kids, most of them barefoot and carrying cans of beer. Despite their blurred, rumpled appearance, they didn't look like potential rioters. Their oxford shirts and madras shorts were not inexpensive, and they were quiet. There were just too many of them. But that same night, ten thousand strong and full of beer courage, they stormed the already packed Freebody Park where the Festival was being held, and it took the police, fending off rocks and beer cans and finally resorting to tear gas, a couple of hours to send them packing. The boomerang result, of course, was that the Festival was shut down and didn't reopen for two years.

This afternoon Newport suddenly took on the same teeming, hothouse atmosphere. Even back streets were bumper to bumper, and almost every road was flanked by straggling Indian files of kids carrying packs and blankets and wine bottles. They are startlingly different from their 1960 predecessors, most of whom probably spent today manicuring their lawns and minding their children. Their hair is long and tangled, their clothes are de-rigueur freakish (the boys shirtless or in tank tops and hip-hugging jeans, and the girls in bell-bottoms, with their shirttails knotted together just below their free breasts), and they look dirty. By the time the evening concert began, the situation around the Festival grounds was claustrophobic. The press of cars was unbelievable, and there were kids as far as the eye could see. An army of them was camped on a bluff back of the Festival stage, another army was stretched out on the spacious slope that rings the opposite side of the grounds, and they were ten deep outside the walls and gates of the field. You could have sliced the dust in the air. There were twenty-two thousand people inside the s.r.o. grounds and probably an equal number outside. The reason for this Red Square crush was simple. The concert was to be given over largely to rock groups, and half a dozen or more are scheduled for Saturday and Sunday. The children had come, pilgrims all, to worship their music, their symbol, their weapon. They had come to hear Jeff Beck and Steve Marcus and

Jethro Tull and Ten Years After, and to hear Blood, Sweat, and Tears and the only jazz group of the evening—Roland Kirk, who told them where much of their music had come from, and then, in his clowning, ferocious, multi-instrumented way, demonstrated how that source should sound. They loved it. The savage breast was soothed, and there was no riot.

An odd coincidence: In 1960 there were two jazz festivals in New-port—the doomed Establishment one, and a small, exciting affair that had been hastily organized by Charlie Mingus and Max Roach and that included the likes of Coleman Hawkins and Roy Eldridge, Ornette Coleman, Jo Jones, and Baby Laurence. Today posters appeared on trees and fences announcing that Mingus and the trumpeter Lee Morgan would hold an "underground" jazz festival on Friday and Saturday nights at Cliff Walk Manor, the hotel where the first rump festival had taken place. I stopped in on the way back to my hotel to see if Mingus would pull another champion out of his hat. He didn't. It was a night-club gig, notable only for an irresistible me-ringue played by Morgan (there was no dancing) and for Mingus' work. But ghosts of 1960 were there—Mingus and Roach playing a brilliant fifteen-minute duet, Baby Laurence cannonading all over the the bandstand, Coleman Hawkins and Roy Eldridge in consummate tandem, and a thinner, wilder Mingus passing a derby hat in the audience.

An interesting Canadian rock group, the Lighthouse, beefed up with horns and strings and snatches of improvisation, opened the con-cert this afternoon. It was followed by a disastrous, helter-skelter "jam session" played by fifteen musicians, including Jimmy Owens and Howard McGhee, Benny Green, Buddy Tate and Brew Moore and Cecil Payne, the West Coast pianist Hampton Hawes, Ray Nance (violin), and the impeccable, winning Slam Stewart. A vocalist named Eddie Jefferson sang an embarrassing eulogy of Coleman Hawkins. Sometimes the living are harder on the dead than they are on each other.

July 5th: The kids came down from their rocks and rills this after-noon, and Festival Field, which was frequently almost empty at after-noon concerts in years past, was packed. They heard John Mayall, who was introduced as the thirty-five-year-old father of English rock and who was absorbing chiefly because of his derivations, which include Leadbelly and Muddy Waters and the old Jimmy Giuffre trio. And they heard the Mothers of Invention, whose musical-satirical roots go back to Spike Jones and Borrah Minnevitch and his Harmonica Rascals, and whose put-ons are paralleled by Charlie Mingus and Archie

Shepp. But they also heard the Newport All-Stars and Miles Davis—
an experience meant to explain George Wein's decision to hold what
is turning out to be a jazz-and-rock festival: Take a couple of slices of
rock and spread them with meaty jazz, and the kids are painlessly
educated. But the jazz we have heard so far has been so vapid that
it has turned into the Silvercup bread and the rock has become the
pepperoni. At any rate, Davis was in striving form. Accompanied by
piano, bass, and drums, he played a vast number consisting of short
trumpet statements—some languorous and melancholy, some shrill and
hard, and some unfinished staircases—surrounded by piano and bass
and drum solos. The All-Stars opened the concert, and they were off
stride. On hand were Ruby Braff, Red Norvo, Tal Farlow, Larry
Ridley, Jack Dejohnette, and Wein himself on piano. Farlow and
Norvo were excellent throughout, but the group hung together just
once—in a slow blues memorable for Braff's declamations and for a
one-chorus double-time duet between Norvo and Dejohnette.

The human swarm was almost as dense tonight as it was last night,
but the cars had got where they were going and the atmosphere was
less tense. And there was another difference. Sly and the Family Stone,
a largely Negro rock group, was scheduled, and the audience had
become half black and half white. Gerry Mulligan, with the Dave Brubeck trio, started things off. His humor and eloquence and long, deep
lines were intact, and even Brubeck sounded crisp and authoritative.
Art Blakey and his quintet delivered four motionless numbers, and
then Gary Burton, who has been trudging around for the past couple
of years between jazz and rock, brought on his quartet (Jerry Hahn,
guitar; Larry Ridley, bass; Bill Goodwin, drums), and the two musics
fused. The rhythms were largely rocklike, each number was collective
(jazz and rock), and there were plenty of solos. Hahn was extraordinary. He has a spare, unfashionable style that depends as much on
silence as on sound. His choice of notes is unexpected and his place-
ment of them equally unexpected, and he bends enough of them in
just the right way to bring the goose-pimples out. Burton has given
up his ringing, shushing attack for a Red Norvo clarity, and he played
one number that was a masterpiece. It was unaccompanied, and it
sounded like a many-layered elaboration of "Beyond the Blue Horizon." The whole solo had a staccato, elbows-out effect, but the beat,
though always there, was never directly stated. There was no lagging,
there were no missteps. Nothing was missing and nothing was re-
dundant. It was a perfect piece of music.

Then several astonishing things happened, and they happened so
fast it is difficult to remember their exact order. Sly and the Family
Stone were setting up their twenty or so two-ton speakers and

amplifiers when a heavy, battering-ram thumping began outside the fence to the right of the bandstand. The booming stopped; a huge pole appeared above the fence, waved drunkenly about, and disappeared. Then fireworks, shot from the bluff behind the bandstand, bombarded the audience. It suddenly started raining, and the smell of smoke became unmistakable (the hordes outside, it turns out, had set fire to the grass behind the performers' quarters). George Wein rushed onstage and shouted at Sly Stone, asking him, for God's sake, to start playing. He did, and the dam, bulging for two days, broke. Kids, black and white, came pouring through a huge hole they had made in the fence separating the main area of the field from the box seats and the press section. They came like Visigoths, smashing the box railings and turning over chairs and forcing the occupants to flee. They poured into the press photographers' pit in front of the bandstand, filled it, and climbed up on the stage. Police and security guards ran onstage and there was a five-minute melee, with kids scrambling up, reaching the stage, and being tossed back into the pit. The only thing missing was the boiling oil. Sly and the Family Stone roared away, and then Stone, using lots of "like"s and "man"s and "uptight"s, persuaded the massed kids to sit down. All at once some sort of catharsis was achieved, and everything subsided. There were rumors that Wein would close up shop after Sly and the Family Stone finished, but, wisely, he didn't. The World's Greatest Jazz Band unenviably appeared next, and to its credit it had the kids dancing by the time it was halfway through its third tune, "Harper Valley P.T.A." The band accompanied Maxine Sullivan in four numbers, and she got through, too, and then Stephane Grappelly, the old Hot Club of France fiddler, played three delicate selections. When O. C. Smith, the singer, appeared, the battle was done. The kids had begun filing out singly and in small groups as Grappelly started. Some of them looked turned on, some were unmistakably drunk, but most of them, wet and dirty and scrawny, just looked pooped.

July 6th: Last night's avalanche was not surprising and not new. Children overran the stage at the Paramount when Benny Goodman came to town, Frank Sinatra was attacked by his most ardent admirers, and there was the Beatles frenzy. The trouble with such adoration, aside from bruised bodies and smashed property, is that, paradoxically, it is antimusical. It's hard to listen to Beethoven or Thelonious Monk or Jethro Tull while you are doing the hundred-yard dash to a stage where the crush of people makes listening impossible anyway. To be sure, some rock—with its handmaidens pot and acid, with its vaudeville exterior, with its sternum-shattering volume, and with its unintelligible lyrics—is not meant to be listened to. Beneath its crashing political-social surface (where is the proletarian novel now?), it is designed to provoke a Kubla Khan euphoria. But jazz demands the same quiet attention and openness as poetry, which it resembles. So George Wein is unwittingly staging a war between the rock non-listeners and the jazz listeners. And nobody listens in wartime.

This afternoon an entirely different phenomenon appeared—James Brown, the meteoric singer and dancer. Brown is venerated by Negro teen-agers, and they figuratively took over the field. He danced and sang at *them,* and, massed twenty-deep behind the press-section fence, they relished every word and gesture and step. The whites present seemed transparent. He has a heavy, attractive voice and he is a good, fluid dancer. His voice and dancing are indivisible. In slow ballads his voice is flicked by continual serpentine motions, and when he tears into a fast blues his dancing propels his singing, which may be compressed into one slamming word a chorus—a guttural "baybeee" or drawn-out "ymmyeh." He brandishes the microphone like a rapier, he does the split, he falls down on his knees in mock exhaustion. He screeches into the microphone, whips around to one of his three drummers, chops his hand for a thundering rimshot, goes stock-still, and is abruptly off again. His ten-piece band never stops, and now and then four comely girls dance and sway about the stage—waterlilies on a blowing pond.

Brown's locomotive show cleared the air, and tonight was, by and large, a pleasure. B. B. King, the fine Chicago blues singer and guitarist—if he had Muddy Waters' or Joe Turner's voice, he would be nonpareil—sang half a dozen numbers and gave way to his white counterpart, the newcomer Johnny Winter. King, dressed in a plain suit, sang quietly and affectingly, while Winter, a tall, spidery man in long white hair and pipestem pants and a leather jacket, storked up and down in front of a battleship-sized bank of electronic equipment, shouting unintelligible blues and playing bad blues guitar. King and Winter were followed by routine displays by the Herbie Hancock sextet (polished hard-bop) and the Willie Bobo sextet (polished Latin funk), and then Buddy Rich came onstage with his big band and played four numbers, the last of them his bravura "West Side Story." It was closed with a long tidal-wave, three-ring, twenty-one-gun, now-damn-it, you-listen drum solo. The Festival, which had just ended, finally began.

New York 1970

February 15th: The mystical calendrical succession of Ash Wednesday, Lincoln's birthday, Friday the thirteenth, and Valentine's Day has just passed, so it's a good time to reflect on the strange non-state that jazz has drifted into in the past year or so. (The music, as always, is beloved in England and Europe.) Jazz has never been a popular music, nor has it been the darling of the intellectuals. For fifty years it has gone its iconoclastic, organic, backroom way, piling beauty on beauty and unwittingly providing most of the inspiration for American popular music—the music of the Whitemans and Crosbys and Goodmans and Presleys and Joplins. A multifarious, workaday music, it has found its footing where it could. It has been relished in ghettos and in the East Room of the White House. It has been patted by Leonard Bernstein and by red-necked Mississippians. But even its most steadfast appreciators appear to have stepped back, leaving the music in a recessive condition it has not known since the early years of the Depression. It is not out of fashion, because it has never been in fashion, but it is in a void, a limbo, a no-place. The number and variety of outlets where it can be heard have dwindled steadily, and so has the flow of its recordings. (A subsidized hall of jazz at Lincoln Center would certainly seem logical and essential.) Jazz itself is partly to blame for its plight. In the past decade the younger musicians, driven by racial anger and/or a mistaken aesthetic loftiness, have taken to treating audiences like doormats. At the same time, the music has backed itself into a private, narcissistic cul-de-sac generally known as "the new thing." Few listeners, including friendly musicians, relish half-hour laboratory solos played by performers standing with their backs to the audience. But there are other reasons people aren't flocking to hear the music. The young, mesmerized by rock, surely the most monolithic, pervasive music ever devised, know little of jazz, and older people, besides being pinched in the pocket, are simply afraid of big-city streets at night. Most important, *listening* is becoming obsolescent. Movies and television are visual mediums which tend to leave the ear sitting uselessly by, for it is physically impossible to absorb the visual and the aural at once. The result is the increasing habit of "listening" with the eyes. Reading aloud kept the Victorian ear and mind sharp, but now it is unfashionable, and so is its mechanical successor, radio, which in its best days provided a high-grade mass reading aloud. For all that, jazz—a mercurial, improvisational music that demands Victorian ears—is alive and available and, its recent artistic aberrations aside, in good health.

February 17th: Late last fall Richard Gibson, the Denver business-man and inventor of the World's Greatest Jazzband, leased the Roose-velt Grill for a year, with the laudable, messianic idea of making it an internationally known temple of jazz. To date it has largely been a backwater of old white jazz. Of the thirty-odd performers who have worked there (and for good money), only a few have been under forty, only four have been black, and in the course of half a dozen visits I have not seen a single black customer, let alone one of any color under the age of twenty-five. Gibson, when confronted with these oddities, says that he has not had time to find and hire good young musicians, admits that his musical tastes are limited (consultants with more flexible ears are plentiful in jazz), and denies that he is racially biased. Anyway, the Roosevelt Grill is a square place in which to try to revivify jazz. The music has always flourished in residential neighborhoods—the West Fifties, the Village, Harlem—and the Grill, despite its adjacent convention hotels, is in an area that is empty and forlorn at night. When I stopped in this evening, I heard the World's Greatest Jazzband (Yank Lawson, Billy Butterfield, Bud Freeman, Bob Wilber, Lou McGarity, Kai Winding, Ralph Sutton, Bob Haggart, Gus Johnson, Jr.), a loud, professional, college-prom group that is, like all jazz bands, only as good as its soloists, and they are, with just two exceptions, mediocre. The alternating group, made up of Toots Thielemans (harmonica, guitar), Dick Hyman (piano, organ), Jack Lesberg, and Sol Gubin, was more interesting. It fooled around with bossa novas, folk-rock, and chestnuts like "Stormy Weather" and "Jazz Me Blues," doing them in easy, unusual tempos and filling them with odd tongue-in-cheek notes and chords.

Then I went up to that other temple of jazz, Plaza-9, to hear Oscar Peterson. Jazz is a self-sufficient music that needs few trappings, and Plaza-9, all done up in Edwardian red plush, seems to blot it up. Beyond that, Peterson is difficult to listen to without automatically hearing in the mind his model and master, Art Tatum. He is a massive man with a massive technique, but he lacks Tatum's touch, his inspired harmonic madness, and his subtle, infallible rhythmic sense. Tatum was an original painted American Queen Anne chair with fine Spanish feet; Peterson is an Altman reproduction. The middle-aged white audience included the customary drunk, who throughout Peterson's last early-morning set kept telling his silent companion to be quiet, that it was only ten minutes to ten.

February 19th: Thelonious Monk started a three-day stint with a new quartet at the Village Vanguard, which for thirty years has been one of the best places in the world to hear jazz. Monk carries his own universe within him, and this evening it was apparently in whirling sync, for he was brilliant. He was wearing a new tall black fur hat recently given him in Toronto, but he didn't dance, cavort, or fidget; he simply played, and with a freshness and intensity he hasn't always shown in the past few years. Monk's new group—the old one revolved for eight years around the tenor saxophonist Charlie Rouse—includes Pat Patrick on tenor saxophone, Wilbur Ware on bass, and Beaver Harris on drums. Ware was a member of the memorable group Monk had for a while in 1957 (John Coltrane and Shadow Wilson were also in it), and he probably has a good deal to do with Monk's rejuvenation. Unlike most contemporary bassists, who use an arpeggioed approach, Ware is a "walking" bassist whose solos are full of surprising, measured on-the-beat notes, leaping intervals, quick triplets, and double-stops. And he has a huge tone. He was extraordinary on a fast, funny "Ballin' the Jack," in which, with mock drama, he slipped into half time, then into a sort of free time, then back into tempo. Monk replied with a baroque solo that involved a surrealistic stride bass and rhythms suggesting the meringue. Patrick, who plays somewhat in the manner of Lucky Thompson, seems awed by Monk. Harris is the opposite; instead of underlining Monk's Gothic traceries, he attempts to decorate them.

It was a consummate evening, and I finished it at the Half Note, which, down among the warehouses near the Holland Tunnel, makes the Roosevelt Grill's location seem like Klein's on Washington's birthday. Zoot Sims, who is playing better than he ever has done, was on hand with piano (Lou Ferastino), bass (Vic Sproles), and drums (Mousie Alexander). According to Sims, the piano was approximately a tone and three-eighths out of tune, and as a result his solos had a Balinese quality that reached eerie proportions in "On the Trail" and

"I Hear a Rhapsody." Sims, who is forty-four, is rapidly approaching the pantheon occupied by Ben Webster and Coleman Hawkins and Lester Young. One of the Canterino brothers, who run the Half Note, says that is it not unusual now to take in just forty dollars an evening. Hat-check girls used to beat that.

February 24th: Back to the Vanguard to hear the début, as a leader, of Leon Thomas, a forty-two-year-old singer whose unique scatting has caused fervor recently in the jazz press. (The audiences at the Vanguard are nominal, but they are young, multicolored, and bell-bottomed.) Thomas' materials are conventional, and he often starts his numbers straight, singing in a pleasant baritone reminiscent of Billy Eckstine. Then he will abruptly shift into complex, agile scat singing interspersed with affecting yodels and soft, climbing-and-falling tremolo effects that suggest mourning doves in full song. His innovations are minor but highly appealing. It won't be surprising to hear him yodelling away in due time on the Ed Sullivan show.

It was announced today that Duke Ellington has been elected to the National Institute of Arts and Letters. I wonder which of his myriad beautiful dress shirts he will wear at the induction ceremonies —one with vertical or with horizontal pleats.

April 6th: A paradox: the big-band era, now so lamented for the wrong reasons, is irrevocably gone, but there are more good big jazz bands around than ever before. These include, in addition to the Ellington, Basie, and Herman Institutes, the newer Don Ellis and Buddy Rich bands, Ray Charles's generally overlooked big group, the so-called "rehearsal" bands of Thad Jones-Mel Lewis, Clark Terry, Duke Pearson, Frank Foster, and Bill Berry, the television-network studio bands (most of whose members moonlight in the rehearsal bands), and some of the college "stage" bands (the awesome University of Illinois band, for one). Ellington and Basie have largely maintained their standards; the rest are in every way superior to their nostalgia-ridden progenitors. They are more schooled, they are freer and sounder rhythmically, their arrangements are more imaginative, and their soloists are rarely less than excellent. They are what first-rate big jazz bands should be: exciting, delicate continuums of fine soloists and inspired ensembles. The big jazz-oriented bands of the thirties and forties (Ellington and Basie excepted) formed a conservative, closed-circuit operation (a lot of the pioneering jazz musicians of the time, such as Art Tatum and Coleman Hawkins and Roy Eldridge, made up a parallel movement, and the two rarely converged), while the present big jazz bands are open, adventurous aggregations that use the best available soloists, the best of what the jazz revolutionaries are up to, the best arrangers, and the best of variants like rock, the *bossa nova,* and country-and-Western. That many of these bands do not work steadily is (except economically, of course) a blessing: as non-profit, self-pleasing groups, they are free of one-nighters, fads, and commercialism—the three bugbears of the old big bands.

A visit to the Village Vanguard tonight to hear the Thad Jones-Mel Lewis band confirmed all this. But it was a surprise, too, for the Vanguard, where the band has been appearing on Monday nights since its formation over four years ago, was packed to the cornices—the sort of alert, with-it people one found there when Mort Sahl and Nichols and May first came to town. The Thad Jones-Mel Lewis group is expert and roistering. Its arrangements, replete with handsome voicings and harmonies, are pretty much overrun by the soloists. Pepper Adams, the baritone saxophonist, went on for chorus after chorus in a nervous, I've-got-to-get-this-out fashion in an up-tempo number, "Once Around," and so did Roland Hanna, who constructed a brilliant piano solo made up of difficult simultaneously ascending and descending chords. Richard Davis, the bassist, took over Bob Brookmeyer's arrangement of Fats Waller's "Willow Tree" and, as is his way, was both sensational and stone-cold. Unfortunately, Jones was heard but briefly, and Mickey Roker, Mel Lewis' replacement for the evening, foundered in the sheer mass of the band's sound.

April 9th: Sy Oliver, the principal arranger for Jimmy Lunceford and Tommy Dorsey between 1933 and the late forties, is holding a retrospective of his work at the Downbeat with the help of a nine-piece group that includes two trumpets, two trombones, two reeds, and three rhythm. The Lunceford band, which flourished between 1930 and 1947, the year Lunceford died, has long been regarded as one of the four or five great big bands. As such, it resembles certain works of the imagination that, raised precipitately to false eminence, eventually appear invulnerable, like ivy-covered houses. To be sure, the Lunceford band was remarkably precise (its personnel changed very little during its best days, and its saxophone section often rehearsed, voluntarily, for hours at a time), some of its arrangements were ingenious (Oliver's "Organ Grinder's Swing"), it had humor and flavor, it was danceable, and it was a good show band. But it was not a great jazz band. (Compare it to Ellington and Basie, or even to Cab Calloway, Andy Kirk, and Benny Carter.) It used static two-beat rhythms, or a four-four beat that tended to sag or stampede. It was an arranger's band, an ensemble band, which favored florid saxophone writing (contrast Ellington's, Carter's, and Mary Lou Williams'), brass-bound trombone and trumpet figures, and section work that resembled thunderheads shouldering through the sky. Its novelty numbers, often built around a vocal trio, moved between parody and the maudlin, suggesting that the Lunceford band was the first and only all-black Mickey Mouse band. Its up-tempo instrumentals were windy and unswinging. And the band's soloists, in the cramped spaces granted them, were rarely better than mediocre. (Compare their astonishing counterparts in the Ellington and Basie bands.) Sy Oliver had a lot to do with all this, and later he had a lot to do with the metallic, Germanic quality of the Tommy Dorsey band, which became the white counterpart of the Lunceford band.

The band Oliver has at the Downbeat is a remarkable replica of the Lunceford band. It is precise, funny, maudlin, clever, and unswinging. The arrangements are stripped-down versions of the originals, and such numbers as "Margie," "Four or Five Times," "Yes Indeed!" "Cheatin' on Me," and "Ain't She Sweet" are full of soupy saxophones, bruiting trombones, and sticky rhythm. But there is an interloper in the band—a young tenor saxophonist, Bobby Jones, who, every time he soloed tonight, converted the group into a jazz band. He is a close student of Zoot Sims. He was particularly memorable in a long two-beat version of "Stardust"; using high notes, tumbling arpeggios, and big-bellied melodic bursts, he managed the old Chaplin trick of being very funny and very moving. The inscrutable expression on Oliver's face during all Jones's solos was absorbing.

Late in the evening, my head full of cute muted trumpets (another Oliver trademark) and toy-soldier rhythms, I went over to the Roosevelt Grill for the final moments of Bobby Hackett's quintet (Vic Dickenson, Dave McKenna, Jack Lesberg, Cliff Leeman), which will soon be dissolved when Dickenson replaces Kai Winding in the World's Greatest Jazz Band (which will give the group *three* worthy soloists) and the rare Benny Morton replaces Dickenson in Hackett's group. I heard just four numbers, and they were perfect. Hackett and Dickenson together are the Jack Sprats of jazz. Hackett is cool, golden, and mathematical, and Dickenson is hot, shaggy, and funny, and between them they encompass most of what is worth knowing about jazz.

April 12th: Early in the afternoon I stopped in again at the Grill, where Bill Berry's new rehearsal band will be appearing for a few more Sunday afternoons. Roughly half the band is made up out of the Merv Griffin studio band, and present this afternoon, along with Berry, a brilliant trumpeter, were the equally brilliant trombonist Bill Watrous, Richie Kamuca on tenor saxophone, George Dorsey on alto saxophone (he is also in Sy Oliver's Downbeat band), Dave Frishberg on piano, and Jake Hanna, who was subbing for the drummer, Sol Gubin. The band's arrangements, which generally reflect Ellington or latter-day Basie, are by Al Cohn, John Bunch, Berry, Billy Byers, and Roger Pemberton. It is a light, precise, aggressive band, and its soloists are often stunning. Watrous is spectacular. He is a multi-noted performer in the manner of J. J. Johnson, but there is nothing predictable or glacéed in his work. He uses high notes, wild smears, intense, jumbling Dickie Wells phrases, and he can juggle the beat in any way he chooses. Frishberg, an eclectic pianist whose daffy style is nonetheless completely his own, has been lurking superbly around New York for years, and he was exceptional this afternoon. And so was Berry, whose long, long solo in "Stella by Starlight" was a marvel of construction, lyricism, and invention. But most commanding of all was Hanna, who drove the Woody Herman band in the early sixties. His time is impeccable, as are his taste and sense of dynamics, and he has the airborne, propelling beat that only drummers like Dave Tough and Sid Catlett had. (Part of this is due to his having refreshingly resurrected the Chinese cymbal.) I doubt that Berry's band would be the same without him.

At the end of Berry's second set I went over to Philharmonic Hall to catch the last half hour of a concert by the Preservation Hall Jazz Band from New Orleans. It was made up of DeDe Pierce (cornet), his wife, Billie (piano), Willie Humphrey (clarinet), Jim Robinson (trombone), Cié Frazier (drums), and the operator of Preservation Hall, Allan Jaffe (tuba). Excluding Jaffe, a spring chicken, the average age was sixty-eight. The music was sweet, primitive, out-of-tune, honest, wandering, and winsome. After Berry, it was like starting to weed your lettuce and coming on a brontosaurus bone. The hall was full, and the audience ranged from an interesting sprinkling of young blacks to Senator Javits, who sprinted out just before the last number— a sedate and angelic reading of "Just a Closer Walk with Thee."

After dinner I went to Uncle John's Straw Hat, a spacious former banjo parlor on West Forty-ninth Street. For the past several months, Frank Driggs, an A. & R. man and jazz scholar, has been holding Sunday-night sessions there, built around the best of the surviving swing musicians. The group tonight consisted of Taft Jordan (who played with Chick Webb and Duke Ellington), Boe McCain, a tenor saxophonist from the Southwest, and Nat Pierce, Gene Ramey, and Jo Jones. It was, all in all, an uneventful evening. Jordan is not one of Louis Armstrong's ablest admirers, and McCain is one of those tenor saxophonists who use a big tone and lots of notes to disguise an almost total lack of invention. Pierce struggled with a grievously out-of-tune piano, Ramey was dependable, and Jones was all by himself on the mountaintop.

April 26th: Back to the Straw Hat for a happy occasion—the first appearance in New York in almost a year of Buck Clayton, who has been recuperating from a lip operation. (Louis Armstrong has undergone a similar reconstruction in recent years, but Clayton's difficulties were complicated because the *inside* of his lips was split.) Clayton was supported by two old compeers—Buddy Tate and Jo Jones—and by Ramey and the pianist Ray Tunia. Jones, as is not always his wont these days, was subdued and thoughtful, frequently providing the ocean-motion high-hat that was one of the buoying glories of the old Basie band. Tate *always* works. He played a long, anguished clarinet solo in his own slow "Blue Creek," displaying the spare, lemony tone that is the sole property of Southwestern reed men, and all his tenor-saxophone solos were arranged in big pillows of emotion—hard, on-the-beat runs, scaling cries, slow-motion bent notes, and the earnest, almost trembling tone that is nearly unique to Herschel Evans and Tate. Clayton improved steadily during the evening, and by the time he got to the last set he had stopped missing notes and was playing with fervency and courage. There aren't many Buck Claytons left in jazz—performers who play with an introverted, inventive, sweet lyricism—and it is a delight to have him back.

April 29th: A phone call today from a friend tells me that Jim Hall, the guitarist, and Eddie Gomez, the bassist, are opening tonight in a new place at Tenth Avenue and Fifty-first Street called the Guitar. It turns out to be a small neighborhood bar that has been attractively refurbished by a black lawyer named Fred Hayes. The bar seats about twenty, and there are a dozen tables in an adjacent area near a tiny bandstand. There are no microphones, but you can hear, as well as see, from anywhere in the house. One of the wonders of jazz is how musicians of sympathetic bent who may never have played together can, without rehearsals and with little verbal communication, sit down and play rich and indivisible music, which is exactly what happened tonight. In most of the numbers Hall started with an a-cappella chorus, soft and out-of-rhythm, and shifted into four-four time. Gomez entered from below, playing a countermelody and gradually increasing his volume. The two instruments, sounding like half a dozen, then wove intricately around one another for a couple of choruses, building considerable rhythmic tension. Then Hall soloed, while Gomez "walked" behind him. Hall backed a Gomez solo with quiet, on-the-beat chords or with pushing off-beat puffs. In the final ensemble the two men sank into the marrow of the melody, turning around and around inside it, and then surfaced easily and brightly in the last four bars. Hall has always been a light, clean guitarist who has shied away from the multi-noted garrulity of most of his colleagues, but for a long time there was a studied, almost static quality to his playing. His phrases tended to come out in lumps, and he did not always swing. Now he flows continually. His phrases are still short and lucid, but they are full of intense, sudden figures that catch one unawares, they swing evenly and confidently, and they are invariably affecting. And there are few bassists to match Gomez, who is just twenty-six. He is a virtuoso who often plays his notes a fraction below pitch, with a sliding, dizzy sound, and he plays with a steady passion that in at least one number, "Body and Soul," became almost frenzied. The two men fashioned a rarity—a *totally* improvised music, grounded in easy, impeccable musicianship.

May 12th: Johnny Hodges died yesterday at the age of sixty-three. (Ironically, he was stricken not on the road, where he spent most of his life, but in a dentist's chair in New York.) For thirty-eight years he sat stone-faced in the front row of the Ellington band, his eyes hooded, his parrot nose pointed straight ahead, or, if he was tired, which he was most of the time, with his eyes closed and his head resting on his right hand. Then, when Ellington called on him to solo, he would get up slowly (it seemed to take forever, though he was only about five and a half feet tall), roll like a sailor to the front of the stage, give Ellington a quick, ferocious look for having disturbed him, and start to play. And out would come one of the most lyrical and eloquent sounds of this century. His style, buffeted by several musical revolutions and by the brief ascendancy of Charlie Parker, never changed. His slow ballads, often written by the late Billy Strayhorn, were unbelievably sensuous. They were full of feline soto-voce phrases, silken pauses, and those celebrated and astonishing glissandos, which fell dangerously but perfectly through a couple of octaves like a driver sailing off a hundred-foot cliff. When he played the blues, which he loved, he suddenly stepped out of this finery and became a rocking, down-home performer who swung as hard as any jazz musician who ever lived. He was one of the pillars as well as one of the pinnacles of the Ellington band, which will never sound quite the same again, and no one knew where his genius came from. Hodges, who, when he talked at all, talked about baseball and Westerns, never let on, even to his oldest friend, Harry Carney, who once said, "Johnny and I grew up on the same street in Dorchester, Mass., and we saw each other just about every day. We exchanged records and we'd copy choruses from Fletcher Henderson and Sidney Bechet and the Hot Five. Then he left home, and when he came back, a year or so later, he was a big-timer. He had a Mexican bankroll—that's a big bill on the outside that covers a roll of ones—and Bechet had given him one of his soprano saxophones. But he picked up his playing on his own. He could always play; I guess it was a natural gift."

Newport 1970

July 10th: Newport, as Henry James discovered, can make a philosopher of anyone. Its contrasts do it: airborne eighteenth-century houses within calling distance of bloated eighteen-nineties mansions; Cinema-Scope skies, capable of simultaneously displaying a line squall and a clear three-quarter moon; a rocky, blowing coast and acres of asphalt parking lots; oceanic meadows and jumbled back streets; and those venerable opposites—Trinity Church and Touro Synagogue. All of which led me back this evening to the philosophical speculation about every fat man's containing a thin man struggling to get out, which immediately suggested the Newport Festival and its resident thin man, jazz. For sixteen years the Festival has continued to put on pounds, with its increasing number of acts (many musicians bitterly resent this assembly-line programming and, economics willing, have long since forsworn the Festival), its longer and longer concerts, its growing gaggle of m.c.s, and its many do-nothing groups. And yet every once in a while the thin man escapes. He certainly did tonight. The evening was designed as a celebration of Louis Armstrong's seventieth birthday on July 4th, but it was a lot more than that. (The only eulogistic clams came from Senator Claiborne Pell, who appeared to forget Armstrong's name at the climax of his encomium, and from Armstrong himself, who, in the middle of singing "Just a Closer Walk with Thee" with Mahalia Jackson, suddenly switched to "Hello, Dolly!" to Miss Jackson's consternation.) The ten-strong Eureka Brass Band from New Orleans opened the evening. Its members had room to roam around the stage as if they were marching, and the acoustics suggested the group's glorious reverberations when it parades through one of the narrow streets in the French Quarter. Cap'n John Handy, the irrepressible seventy-year-old alto saxophonist who seems to have absorbed everyone from Sidney Bechet to Charlie Parker, was on hand, and there were a snare drummer (Cié Frazier) and a bass drummer (Booker T. Glass) who between them managed sliding boomlay-boom patterns that any bebop drummer would admire. Bobby Hackett brought on a faultless quintet (Benny Morton, Dave McKenna, Jack Lesberg, Oliver Jackson), and it was a delight to hear Hackett's Armstrong-Beiderbecke bells alongside Morton's climbing, worrying melodies. Then a beguiling group called the New Orleans Ragtime Orchestra appeared. It was put together earlier this year by Lars Edegran, a Swedish pianist who has been working in New Orleans for the past four or five years, and it consists of trumpet, clarinet, trombone, violin (William Russell, the great New Orleans jazz scholar), and the leader's piano, bass, and drums. It is a facsimile, right down to the arrangements, of the ragtime band led by John Robichaux in New Orleans before the First World War. (Ragtime, an elegant, complex, non-improvised music that flourished, mostly in the form of piano music, from 1900 to 1920, was one of the mainsprings of jazz.) It is a warm, gentle ensemble music (there are no solos) that moves along in waltz time or two-four time and accomplishes that spooky trick of making one feel nostalgic for an era and place and way of life one has never known. Particularly memorable among the numbers played were "St. Louis Tickle" (1904) and "Creole Belles" (1900). The Ragtime Orchestra was followed by six sterling trumpeters who in various ways were brought into being by Armstrong—Joe Newman, Hackett, Jimmy Owens, Wild Bill Davison, Ray Nance, and Dizzy Gillespie. ("Louis Armstrong's station in the history of jazz is unimpeachable," Gillespie announced before playing, "and I would like to thank him for my livelihood.") Each, in top form, played two numbers, backed by McKenna, Larry Ridley, and Jackson, and the finest moments were offered by Gillespie in a slow, languorous "Ain't Misbehavin'" and in "I'm Confessin'," in which he sang an affectionate mock-parody of Armstrong; by Hackett's "Thanks a Million"; by both of Davison's numbers (he is, I suppose, wholly out of fashion, but, in his rampaging bent-note way, he is admirable); and by Owens' superb "Nobody Knows the Trouble I've Seen," in which he played the tune in the low register, unobstrusively changing a note here and an accent there, which resulted in a first-rate piece of improvisation that sounded like straight melody. After Nance's second number Armstrong himself appeared and sang three numbers, accompanied by the rhythm section and Hackett's glancing obbligatos. Armstrong is still recuperating from a nearly fatal illness and he is not allowed to play his trumpet for more than an hour a day. But he looks fit and composed, and he was in excellent voice. The ovation was tumultuous, as was fitting for the man who made jazz a majestic music.

After the intermission the Preservation Hall Jazz Band, made up of the nucleus of the Eureka Brass Band, played five stirring numbers, then gave way to Mahalia Jackson, who sang magnificently, thereby raising a curious point of musical physiology. Small singers are apt to sound delicate and even remote, while larger ones are almost always formidable. The last time I heard Miss Jackson, three years ago, she had lost a great deal of weight and her enormous voice had dwindled to a magisterial whisper. Now she has regained most of that weight, and with it her voice. Her first six numbers were stunning, and when she got to "Just a Closer Walk with Thee" she became almost savage. Her statuesque stage presence is celebrated, but in "A Closer Walk" she charged back and forth, growled, danced, shouted, and clapped her hands, and when Armstrong joined her she almost swallowed him. And after the "Hello, Dolly!" aberration had been swept aside and the two of them began "When the Saints Come Marching In," the results were empyrean.

July 11th: This afternoon's concert started at noon and ended, about fifteen hours later, around six. The first three sets were in "workshop" form, and they involved two violinists, four trumpeters, and four drummers who played and then answered questions, most of which went like "Are you planning any more albums?" or "Did you go to music school?" Of the violinists, Jean-Luc Ponty and Mike White, Ponty was by far the more impressive. A classically trained player, he has the tone and technique that most jazz violinists lack, and his reading of the old "Yesterdays" was, with its John Coltrane colorings, rich and assured. The trumpeters (Owens, Gillespie, Newman, and Nance) played onstage while the drummers (Philly Joe Jones, Elvin Jones, Jo Jones, and Chico Hamilton) played at the back of the field, and after the trumpeters' first number, a good "Sunny," I went over to hear the drummers. They were, with the exception of Philly Joe Jones, who was neat and forceful, in a desultory, self-absorbed mood. Jo Jones appeared baffled, Chico Hamilton was stiff, and Elvin Jones was inconclusive. The trumpeters were followed onstage by a Rocklike Japanese quartet led by Sadao Watanabe, who was introduced as the Charlie Parker of Japan. Elvin Jones' quartet and Chico Hamilton's quartet went by, and so did a quintet led by Gary Burton. Keith Jarrett was on piano with Burton, and in the first number he played a fascinating, out-of-tempo solo that touched on Debussy and Schubert and Bill Evans. By this time it was five o'clock and my battery was dead. Still another group was scheduled, but I went back to my hotel to recharge and watch the swallows relish the evening.

The thin man got out for a while tonight, and it was exhilarating. Kenny Burrell, accompanied by Ridley and Lenny McBrowne, opened the proceedings, and then acted as a rhythm section for Dexter Gordon, the forty-seven-year-old tenor saxophonist who has spent most of the past decade in Europe. Absence sometimes jams the memory, and I had forgotten how persuasive Gordon was in the early fifties, when, combining elements from the styles of Coleman Hawkins and Lester Young and Charlie Parker, he constructed the model later followed by Sonny Rollins and John Coltrane, who in turn brought along almost every tenor saxophonist who has appeared in the last fifteen years. Gordon has the ironwood tone that is now commonplace among tenor saxophonists, and an equally familiar amelodic way of phrasing that is made up of pitching runs, espaliered blocks of notes, and chameleon rhythms. There are few open places in his solos, which, with their cathedral-like intricacy and weight, are difficult to absorb at one hearing. He is a musician's musician who goes after the mind and not the emotions. He was, according to the hair-raising logic that governs most of the programming at the Newport Festivals, allowed only two numbers, but they were just about perfect. The second one, "Darn That Dream," was closed with a winding coda that recalled some of the weighty proclamations Coleman Hawkins liked to end his slow ballads with. The violinists, augmented by Ray Nance, reappeared, and Nance played an unabashedly soaring blues and a "Summertime" that was so intense it leaned on the listener. Dizzy Gillespie's new group played five predigested numbers, and then accompanied Don Byas, the fifty-seven-year-old master tenor saxophonist, who, like Gordon, has long been based in Europe. Byas, who is one of the most proficient admirers of Hawkins' operatic side (Hawkins was myriad; mere facets of his style often provided entire foundations for other players), was also allowed just two numbers, but they were spacious enough to reveal his curving melodic lines, his Southwestern tone (a yearning, big-bellied quality shared by Herschel Evans and Buddy Tate), and his ability to swing very hard. He also demonstrated that innate, dowagerlike assurance and poise that seem unique to the best of the musicians who came up in the thirties. Next, Nina Simone, who has become more interested in the message in her songs than in the singing of them, posed here and there about the stage for a half hour, and then made way for a blessedly short set by Herbie Mann, a flutist who is also good at posturing, and his group. The evening was closed by the Ike and Tina Turner Revue, a funny, churning ensemble that consists of a nine-piece band led by Ike

Turner, who plays guitar; the Ikettes, a female trio that dances and sings; and Mrs. Turner, who is beautiful and a fine shouter. The materials were gospel-soul-funk-blues, and I lost track of them when I got to watching one of the Ikettes, a tall, angular girl who liked to turn left when her compatriots turned right and who kept her mouth in a steady O, either because she was out of breath or because of sheer astonishment at finding herself where she was.

July 12th: There are always one or two please-the-people-and-make-a-buck concerts at the Newport Festival, and tonight was one of them. Eddie Harris, a fashionably hard tenor saxophonist, started things, and then backed a young and extremely talented composer named Gene McDaniels who sang a couple of his own songs. He is a sharp, eloquent lyricist, and the best of his songs, "The Silent Majority" (pronounced "majoaratee"), had, among other necessary things, a couplet about the silent majoaratee "gathering around the hanging tree." Les McCann, the pasha of soul-soap music, came on. He was followed by Leon Thomas, the singer and yodeller. Thomas should attempt "The Star-Spangled Banner"; the results might be definitive. More soul soap, this time from the Adderley Brothers, and then Buddy Rich appeared. He looked gray and tired and his band sounded the same. He did, though, get off a series of stunning four-bar breaks on a medium blues. Ella Fitzgerald finished the program, and she provided further proof that a singer's weight is to the voice what yeast is to bread. She has slimmed down considerably and so has her voice. It has the high, bobby-sox quality of her "Tisket-a-Tasket" days, and it made all her songs, which ranged from "Satin Doll" to "Raindrops Keep Falling," sound piping and pale.

Most of this afternoon belonged to the thin man, but not until the appearance of Roberta Flack, a singer-pianist in her late twenties. She is a handsome, poised performer, she has a rich, steady contralto, her phrasing runs in the gospel tradition, and she has an electrifying sense of dynamics. Her first five numbers were roomy and subdued, and then she let loose on "Reverend Lee," a funny affecting song by Gene McDaniels about God's sorely tempting a preacher. Her handling of the words "Reverend Lee," repeated a dozen times during the song, was magic. Each time they came out differently, but in the best version she made the two words into ten, jamming some syllables together, separating others, and all the while granting almost each letter a different note. Then Bill Cosby, one of the champion people, brought on his twelve-piece Badfoot Brown and the Bunions Bradford Marching and Funeral Band. It is made up largely of Los Angeles musicians and includes a tenor saxophonist, a trombonist, two fender bassists, three guitarists, two pianists, an organist, and two drummers. In the first two numbers the band accompanied Shuggie Otis, a sixteen-year-old blues guitarist and the son of Johnny Otis. He played a slow blues and a medium blues, and they were spectacular. The first was full of yearning and misery and pain (he is a motionless performer who smiles steadily, and the contrast between his coolness and the passion pouring out of his guitar was hilarious), and the second was a glistening celebration of cheerfulness and good feeling. Then the Bunions Bradford came on and for forty-five minutes played one number, apparently arranged by Cosby, that was, though too long, comic and ingenious and unique. It also swung as hard as anything I've ever heard. Most of the instruments were electronic, and the piece, which was blues-based, included samplings of just about everything good that has been invented in the past decade and a half by the "new thing" school, by Charlie Mingus, by the Modern Jazz Quartet, by John Coltrane, by Miles Davis, and by the best rock groups. The tempo went up and down, there were dozens of slamming breaks, there were improvised duets, mountainous organ-chord climaxes, snatches of wild blues shouting (by the organist, Stu Gardner), a walking-bass passage, and a section in which the organist sang and played a rheumy, a-cappella "White Christmas," which was startlingly interrupted several times by drum duets. Cosby conducted the piece with such intensity and precision and humor that one had the impression that he was *playing* the band.

July 13th: Over forty thousand people attended the Festival, despite uncertain weather and despite its being one day shorter than usual. Even better news is that the audience was made up largely of kids who had come not to be sociological but to listen. Maybe the end of the tunnel is in sight.

Newport 1971

July 1st: I came up to the Festival a day early to indulge an incurable addiction to Newport. I am staying in a sort of hotel—a boarding house wearing a dickey, really—at the mouth of Narragansett Bay. Its small, shiplike, glass-enclosed dining room seems to hang above the bay, and during dinner we were given a spectacular Newport show. In minutes, the rocks and water slid from gray to blue to black. Rain exploded, and the bay, which had been moving at a sagacious roll, was spun into a seething chop. A small sailboat, its jib draped crazily across its bow, limped past like a three-legged dog. Lightning danced on the rocks, the water, and the towers of the Newport bridge three miles away, and the thunder applauded again and again. The storm lasted the length of a set, and it was a fine preamble to the weekend, which looks enlightened and even stirring. Ray Charles and Duke Ellington and Aretha Franklin will be on hand, but so will such rarities as T-Bone Walker, Gene Ammons, Harry Edison, Joe Turner, Eubie Blake, and Illinois Jacquet.

July 2nd: Tonight's concert was old-fashioned and mostly trudging. The newest Stan Kenton band, minus its ill leader, appeared, and it resembled every other Stan Kenton band. The arrangements by Ken Hanna and Bill Holman and Johnny Richards were rigid and cumbersome. The trumpets, five strong, screamed or played pastel muted figures; the trombones, also five strong, hummed heavy hymns; the saxophones frolicked in between. A new young drummer, John Von Ohlen, carried on with tremendous verve and precision, but to little avail. The music suggested the Chrysler Building translated into sound. The Buddy Rich band, which often seems like a diminutive Kenton group, moved through six made-in-Hong Kong numbers that were lighted by a tantalizing interlude played by Rich's new pianist, Bob Petersen—gospel chords and easy runs and good off-notes, all done with an immaculate touch. It was the only time I have seen Rich, a preoccupied man, nodding and smiling at one of his sidemen. But his admiration ended there, for that was the last we heard from Petersen. Rich's final number was given over to one of his unique and miraculous drum solos. It was played at double time, the original tempo, and half time, and it included a blinding single-stroke roll, a left-hand figure that few drummers could play with both hands, figure-eight patterns all over the set, breathless tickings on his snare rims, and a cymbal-roaring finale. Because of Rich's ubiquity in recent years, it is all too easy to take him for granted.

Last winter, Duke Ellington gave an odd and addled concert in New York. The band played unevenly and without appetite, the selection of numbers was lackluster, and the evening was closed by two surprising spectacles. In the first, Paul Gonsalves came down off the stage and soloed in the audience—a ham routine that was considered hot stuff at Jimmy Ryan's thirty years ago. And in the finale, a pseudo-rock piece called "One More Time," the whole band lined up stage front and played an endless series of riffs while Ellington's vocalists bounced around and sang. And Ellington did it again tonight. Two of his numbers, "Afro-Eurasian Eclipse" and selections from the new "Brava Toga Suite," were played out of tune and out of cadence; Cootie Williams lumbered through "Take the A Train" (Ray Nance, whom the number was originally built around, remained in the trumpet section); there was a number from the "New Orleans Suite," and then the band went into "One More Time." The audience, made up of the hip and the faithful, looked on in disbelief, and Ellington looked at the disbelief with disbelief; when the number was over, he uncharacteristically turned on his heel and walked off the stage without a word.

Roberta Flack closed the evening. She is a marvellous singer, with a rich and beautifully controlled contralto, but she is weighed down by much of her present material. She sings too many message songs and too many dirgelike ballads. But it is another matter when the tempo goes up and she tackles numbers like "Reverend Lee" and "To Love Somebody." In the latter, she gave an extraordinary demonstration of improvisation by repeating the theme words, strung to a gently descending pattern of notes, at least a dozen times, singing them differently each time: "you don't know what it's like—to love somebody," "you don't *know* what it's like to love somebody," "you don't know—what it's like—to *love* somebody." It was a brilliant performance.

The kids, who came in armies two years ago to hear the rock groups at the Festival, are, mysteriously, back. They are camped by the thousand on the hillside above Festival Field and on the bluff behind the bandstand, and the air smells of pot. But the mood is not claustrophobic and ominous, as it was from the start that other weekend.

July 3rd: Eubie Blake, the eighty-eight-year-old composer and pianist, started things off this afternoon, and he was a delight. He played a ragtime piece, his fingers Jack-be-nimble, and he jazzed up "The Merry Widow Waltz." He played a Cole Porter number and he did his own "Memories of You" and "I'm Just Wild About Harry." He did them all as he would have done them seventy years ago, and they had a cheerful, innocent, take-me-out-to-the-ballgame air. Willie the Lion Smith, a crackling seventy-three, followed with four supreme numbers, including a novelty piece called "Hot Ginger and Dynamite," which he sang very well. Both Blake's and Smith's styles cry out for drum accompaniment (wire brushes and no foot pedal), and it was too bad somebody didn't sit in. Charlie Mingus's sextet (Lonnie Hillyer, Charlie McPherson, John Foster, Bobby Jones, and Virgil Day) got off four striving numbers, among them "Pithecanthropus Erectus" and his funny, rinky-dink parody of "Cocktails for Two." Hillyer's Mickey Mouse trumpet was faultless, and so was Jones' spaghetti-leg Ted Lewis clarinet. The only member of the group who was not with it was the drummer, Day, but he was attempting a music that expired long before he was born. Freddie Hubbard, exploring that curious and lifeless extension of bebop known as hard bop, was interminable, and so was the New York Bass Violin Choir. Formed a year or so ago, the group consists of seven bassists (Milt Hinton, Ron Carter, Richard Davis, Sam Jones, Michael Fleming, Lisle Atkinson, and the leader, Bill Lee), a vocalist (A. Grace Lee Mims), a pianist, and a drummer. They played a fifty-minute folk operetta that had to do with life in Snow Hills, Alabama. Lee, who wrote the piece, narrated, sang, and pantomimed, Mrs. Mims sang, and the fiddles provided accompaniment and contrapuntal sections, most of them bowed. Some of Lee's talking was funny and even affecting, but he and Mrs. Mims are dreary singers and the music lacked melodic spine. It was the sort of effort that avant-garde high school seniors sometimes get off as a graduation-day special.

Tonight the kids had bonfires going on the hill, and the roads around Festival Field were choked with bluejeans and bare feet. It's clear now why they are here: no other big festivals are scheduled anywhere this weekend, and they want to hear Aretha Franklin, who's on tomorrow afternoon.

Chase, a new group made up of four trumpets, guitar, organ, bass, drums, and a singer and led by Bill Chase, who once played lead trumpet for Woody Herman, turned out to be four blasting trumpets glued to a rock-rhythm section. The trumpet solos were mostly high-note and largely inaudible, and the singing was mediocre. Dave Brubeck and Gerry Mulligan, accompanied by Jack Six on bass and Alan Dawson on drums, took over, and in a medium blues Mulligan fashioned three superb, husky, down-home stop-time choruses. (There is no need to worry about Brubeck anymore. He is what he is—a jovial amateur pianist who happened along at the right time with the right music and made a million.) Dionne Warwicke, who is the test pilot of the Burt Bacharach-Hal David combine, and who has added an "e" to her last name on the advice of her astrologist, sang a dozen Bacharach numbers. Either Bacharach, who has great style, has just one song, which he writes endless variations of, or Miss Warwicke sings all songs exactly alike, for every number sounded the same.

Then, just after Miss Warwicke's last number, the trouble started. Ten minutes before, I had noticed kids dropping over the wooden wall at the back of the Field, but everything was still calm. When Miss Warwicke finished, George Wein walked rapidly to the front of the stage and made an emotional and frightening and ill-worded announcement to the effect that the audience was in danger (of what he didn't say), that we should file immediately and calmly from the Field, and that the concert had been shut down by order of the chief of police. Suddenly, three loutish kids appeared in the aisle back of where I was sitting and shouted obscenities at Wein, and then I understood what Wein was trying to say: We were in for the same disruptive rumpus that took place two years ago when the kids smashed down fences and poured into the Field. The front of the Field, where the box seats and press section are, was cleared in jigtime, but the crowd to the rear stayed put and roared its displeasure at having the concert stopped (Mary Lou Williams and a jam session led by the organist Jimmy Smith were still to come). Then the avalanche hit. Hundreds of kids poured through the boxes and the press section, smashing chairs and railings, and up onto the stage. (They had got only to the foot of the stage two years ago.) The lights onstage went out, but for more than an hour the kids sat there chanting, stamping thunderously in rhythm, shaking their fists, and yelling more obscenities. Gerry Mulligan's voice was heard briefly over the loudspeakers, telling the kids to cool it, and then Father Norman O'Connor, who had been the m.c., made an impassioned plea, which seemed to have some result. The noise died slowly down, and by midnight, all passion spent, the brouhaha was over.

July 4th: It was announced this morning that the authorities had decided to close the Festival down. The kids had, with classic effect, cut off their noses to spite their faces. They had also, as professed non-

Establishment people, aborted one of the great non-Establishment musics. After breakfast I went out to the Field. The front section was all splintered wood and garbage. The stage is constructed of immense steel girders and it was intact, but a grand piano had lost its keyboard cover and some of the ivory on the low-register keys. I played a chorus of blues and the piano still worked, though. I noticed a young, blond-haired, bearded man picking up garbage at the back of the stage, and I asked him what had happened last night. "The vibes were bad," he said affably. "On Friday night, they were beautiful. You couldn't walk twenty-five feet up on the hill without someone smiling at you. But things began going bad yesterday afternoon. The kids were calling the cops pigs and the cops got tired of it and started poking the kids with their nightsticks. I came down from the hill last evening and a cop yelled at me and stuck his stick in my gut, and it started then for me. Anyway, most of the kids on the hill were not really into jazz. They were here because of Aretha and because other people were here, and they were here because they've learned you can get a lot of nice things free, that you don't have to pay for everything, which is still a fad, not a philosophy. The kids who broke down the fence were malcontents and they were stoned, but you don't get stoned unless something is wrong in the first place." He pulled a couple of mimeo-graphed sheets from his pocket and handed them to me. "Unlike two years ago, the kids were prepared this time," he said. The sheets were titled "Festival Street Sheet," and they had been issued by the Potemkin Bookshop in Newport. They told the kids where they could crash, not to hitchhike in front of cops, where there were bathrooms, when sun-rise and sunset were, where to go for help on bad trips, where to swim and rent bikes, what to watch out for in the way of bad dope, and how to behave toward the natives:

> It's obvious that some people are making a lot of bread from your being here this weekend, and they could be treating you a lot better. But most of the people who live in this town aren't making money off this festival—they're just trying to survive a pretty confusing weekend. These people shouldn't be ripped-off or hassled—this means small stores, people's lawns, and people's feelings. Be cool to the people.

I walked to the back of the Field, and the word "malcontent" seemed mild. Five sizable sections of the ten-foot-high chain-link fence that encircles the Field had been flattened, and the inner wooden fence was full of jagged holes that looked as if they had been gnawed by huge rats. It was a prime instance of nature abhorring a vacuum.

The kids camped on the hill, which was now covered with a snow of garbage, had looked down on the big empty spaces at the back of the Field and, souped up by apple wine and drugs, decided they should be filled.

It was the seventeenth Newport Jazz Festival, and, things being the way they are, it may well be the last major festival of any kind anywhere. About the only invulnerable place you could hold another one would be Radio City Music Hall.

New York   1971

July 6th: Louis Armstrong was the first great American musician. He all but invented jazz, which remains the wellspring of American music. He was an old-fashioned, even medieval clown who nonetheless never seemed dated. And he was the first famous black man who from the point of view of both races seemed to transcend color. He was absolutely true to himself throughout his fifty-year career. (His birth date, July 4, 1900, was both ironic and apt.) Fame and money never separated him from reality. He finally wore out physically, but he suffered no moral or spiritual decline. His living habits—a small house in Queens, red beans and rice, decent whiskey and decent clothes—never changed. He could have retired many years ago, but he worked harder when he was sixty-five than when he was twenty-five. As he grew older, he simply became a heavier, more astute version of the tough, rough, smart kid who grew up in New Orleans with pimps and thieves and killers. His gleaming teeth and pop-eyes were often regarded as an Uncle Tom mask, but that isn't what they were. John Barrymore's crutch on the stage was booze; Armstrong's was his mugging.

His career has been justly, if incompletely, celebrated. It included his year and a half in the Colored Waifs' Home in New Orleans, where he was taught the bugle and the cornet (the cornet he played there is on display at the New Orleans Jazz Museum, and it is a moving, dinosauric sight, gray and battered, with a heavily notched mouthpiece); his being brought to Chicago in 1922, as second horn, by Joe (King) Oliver, who was nonpareil on his instrument; his conversion, as a twenty-four-year-old sideman, of the Fletcher Henderson band from an imitation of a white dance band into the first big jazz band—a conversion that changed another Henderson sideman, Coleman Hawkins, from a musical dervish into the founder of the tenor saxophone; his revolutionary Hot Five and Hot Seven recordings, made between 1925 and 1928; his leadership of makeshift big bands during the thirties and early forties, and of makeshift small bands during the fifties and sixties (Armstrong had his share of ego, for he rarely hired his peers, an exception being the short-lived band that included Jack Teagarden, Earl Hines, Barney Bigard, and Sidney Catlett); his emergence as a best-selling vocalist in numbers like "Blueberry Hill," "Mack the Knife," "Hello, Dolly!" and "Mame" (his voice, though it eventually thickened and slowed, was a marvellous extension of his playing); and his worldwide travels, on his own and for the State Department. But almost forgotten in his career are the astonishing recordings he made between 1929 and 1933. They were, and are, startling, unique, and beautiful. His style, though it had an assist from Joe Oliver and perhaps Bessie Smith, was his own. Yet it was more than a style; it was a way of playing music, of improvising, that had never existed before. He had an abundant, even tone, a spare vibrato, a command of every register of his instrument, and a dazzling, uninhibited rhythmic sense. (Armstrong was not, despite what his obituaries say, a virtuoso; his skills, instead of existing for themselves, were exactly meet to what he had to say.) His style was outwardly a simple one. He used few notes, he played in a highly melodic fashion, and his solos—except for the grandstanding strings of high C's that capped his public appearances in the thirties—were brief and to the point. He was imitated by every horn player in the twenties and thirties, but none managed to reproduce him. Instead, his best followers—Red Allen and Roy Eldridge and Buck Clayton and Joe Thomas and Bobby Hackett—absorbed his lyrical essence and formed singular styles of their own. (Armstrong's musical influence was immeasurable, and it can be argued, without too much musicology, that the Beatles themselves could not have existed without him.) The solos that Armstrong recorded in the early thirties in such numbers as "That's My Home," "Basin Street Blues," "I Gotta Right to Sing the Blues," and "Laughin' Louis" are unearthly. They are full of open spaces; stately, climbing swoops; dark, harrowing low-register blue notes; and stunning leaps and rhythmic turns. They have a majesty and grace and poetry that are unlike anything else in music. Armstrong never lost his magisterial quality. (The only time his career took a dip was in the mid-forties, when the big bands disappeared and bebop arrived; there is a Gjon Mili photograph of him seated beside a confident Roy Eldridge, and he looks beat and dejected.) This magisterial quality appeared in the fifties in a couple of Columbia

L.P.s and in a collaboration with Duke Ellington. It appeared late one night at the 1958 Newport Jazz Festival when he sat in with a high school band and played "On the Sunny Side of the Street." It was there in the split-second way he spaced the words "This is—Louis, Dolly," in the famous recording. And it was still there, in a hesitant, wounded fashion, the last time we heard him play—on Dick Cavett's show, a year or so ago.

We should all go back to his recordings of the early thirties. They are what the country was once all about.

II
The Duke 1967–1970

Small Band

Duke Ellington's unique five-week stand at the Rainbow Grill is a sorrowing one. Not long before the engagement Billy Strayhorn, Ellington's indivisible alter ego since 1939, died, and certainly part of Ellington went with him. (Ellington continues to speak of Strayhorn in the present tense; his not being at bandside seems simply to mean that he is at home for the evening.) But for every sorrow there's a boffola. In mid-June Ellington was made an honorary Doctor of Music by Yale University—a too late and too little award that was accompanied by the kind of feather-boa citation one might hear at a Midwestern clubwomen's luncheon honoring a retiring president. It was the sort of well-meaning insult that has dogged Ellington for much of his forty-four-year career and that he has long parried with gracious irony. Despite all this, the Rainbow Grill stint is immensely heartening, for it proves that the older Ellington gets (he is now a buoyant sixty-eight) the more adventuresome and creative he becomes. During the past several years he has fashioned a program of collar-buttons-to-the-front "religious" music, which he has played successfully in churches all over the Western world. He has finished and recorded (with Strayhorn's great help) his notable "Far East Suite." He has charmingly reconditioned various popular songs of the moment, and he has done a series of subtle and ingenious parodies of such as Paul Whiteman, Stan Kenton, Woody Herman, and Wayne King that suggest that parody is simply imperfection perfected. And now he has settled down at the Rainbow Grill in a workshop jam-session way with an eight-piece group taken from the big band for what may be the longest engagement for dancing he has played in New York or anywhere else since the thirties. Old numbers are being streamlined and regalvanized before one's eyes, and new numbers are being poked, shaped, lobbed, and weighed.

The cream of the big band is on hand, and it includes Cat Anderson, Johnny Hodges, Paul Gonsalves, Lawrence Brown, Harry Carney, John Lamb (bass), and a new drummer, Steve Little. It is without question the equal of any small jazz band ever assembled, and in some ways it surpasses its big brother. It has the depth and timbre and revolving colors of the bigger group, but it is also looser and more intense, and the soloists, through simple thinning, have more space and time to roam in. Hodges and Carney are playing with exceptional beauty. (Carney frequently uses his bass clarinet, on which he sounds like wind moaning across the mouth of a volcano.) Anderson, who is generally restricted to high-note grandstanding, is revealing a subtlety and skill that challenge the great days of Cootie Williams and Rex Stewart. Brown is less industrial than usual, and Gonsalves, who sometimes breaks his mainspring, is ticking perfectly. At least a dozen of the numbers I heard were classic Ellington. These included a "C Jam Blues" that was better than the celebrated 1942 recording (Anderson shivered and shook his way out of his solo and Carney began his with a great, sashaying break); a "Sunny Side of the Street" in which Hodges left fat, dying notes all over the bandstand while the band played organ chords and a double-time figure that explained his intensity; an easy, rocking "Rosetta"; and a "Happy Go Lucky Local" that came to a climax in a roaring-unison stop-time passage by the whole band. Most of the new numbers were handsome medium-tempo blues, one of which, "Sky Blue Suit," ended with Anderson composing muted poems to himself while the band slid gently through the final chorus. And of course there was Ellington, playing first-rate piano, smiling, signing autographs, hugging old friends, playing requests ranging from "I Can't Get Started" to "Something to Live For," and doing his funny monologue about finger-popping on the afterbeat while the band delicately hummed "Things Ain't What They Used to Be." It was the essence of Ellington—a silly, funning exterior designed to disguise a man whose music continues unmatched. To miss Ellington at the Rainbow Grill would be like turning off one's radio just as Lindbergh was about to land.

1967

Which Ellington
Are You?

Protean figures like Picasso and Bertrand Russell and Duke Ellington are frightening because they engulf us, because their infinite variety mocks our single-track ways. But such giants are vulnerable, too, for their helter-skelter natures force them to continually split up and run off in all directions at once. Thus, the diffuse Duke Ellington who gave a concert of "sacred" music recently at the Cathedral of St. John the Divine seemed to have little in common with the straight-ahead Duke Ellington who led an exhilarating contingent from his big band last summer at the Rainbow Grill. It was even hard to believe that this new Ellington was related to the Ellington who gave his first church concert in Grace Cathedral in San Francisco in September of 1965. That Ellington appeared to be on to something. The concert had its overblown, quasi-holy sides (chanting choirs, solemn vocalists, a Formica piety), but it was exciting to hear the band in full stride in a *cathedral*—not so much because of the building's sacredness but because the band matched its architectural and acoustical grandeur. Moreover, the band, surely the most original and beautiful musical aggregation in the world, was kept in the fore, and in at least one number, "David Danced Before the Lord with All His Might," it achieved a grandstanding majesty—Bunny Briggs dancing, Louis Bellson soloing, and the band shouting, all at once. But Ellington's new program of sacred music, which was given its première at St. John's, is altogether different. Every once in a while Ellington, who tends to view life with a pastoral, prismatic cheer, allows himself to be pressured into taking himself seriously, and that's apparently what happened the other night.

At first, the concert—perhaps because of wishful thinking—seemed like a put-on, as Alice Babs, a flawless soprano from Sweden, sang this Ellington lyric:

Heaven, my dream,
Heaven, divine,
Heaven, supreme,
Heaven combines
Every sweet and pretty thing
Life would love to bring.
Heavenly Heaven to be
Is just the ultimate degree.

But after half the fourteen or fifteen numbers had been got through, it became clear that Ellington was in Sunday earnest. These numbers sported just about every "serious" church-music device. Two sizable choirs sang and chanted together and separately or backed a singer named Jimmy McPhail; the cathedral's organist offered a "dialogue" that was all crescendo and no diminuendo; Ellington played a syrupy hymn, accompanied only by bowed bass; and the lyrics, all by Ellington, went on and on in a confectionary way about God and the Golden Rule and Salvation. The final number, "Praise God and Dance," was pure Radio City. The band and the vocalists and the choirs, blending hosannas, were surrounded by two batteries of dancers who, after crashing imaginary cymbals together and jitterbugging around, leaped down the main aisle and out of sight. It wouldn't have been surprising at this point if the Ark in life-size Styrofoam had floated out of the shadows, its complement in full bray.

The band, reduced most of the evening to accompaniment, kept its stately cool. Harry Carney had the opening number to himself, offering a gentle solo with one of those marvellous bent phrases that seem to force melodic beauty to its limits. Johnny Hodges and Paul Gonsalves and Russell Procope (on clarinet) were given brief bits, and the two drummers on hand, Steve Little and Sam Woodyard, traded solos that at least had some godlike thunder in them. But best of all was "The Shepherd," a blues built around Cootie Williams' muted and open horn. Williams' once tricky, curving agility with a mute has slowed to a lumber, which is just what a Grand Canyon like St. John's calls for, and when he let loose a couple of burning growls and a heavy-winged open-horn passage it suddenly seemed that the seventy-five hundred people in the cathedral were in the right place at the right moment.

1968

Return Engagement

Where, for a few blessed hours, can one shake the hellhound Chaos, which seems to be after every last one of us, by simply hearing such celestial cleansing art as "Mood Indigo," "It Don't Mean a Thing," "Solitude," "Black and Tan Fantasy," "Sophisticated Lady," and "Rockin' in Rhythm" played by their composer and seven members of his brilliant atelier? At the Rainbow Grill, a handsome, Captain Nemo ship floating some nine hundred feet above the city, where Duke Ellington, in company with Cat Anderson, Johnny Hodges, Harry Carney, Paul Gonsalves, Lawrence Brown, the bassist Jeff Castleman, and the drummer Rufus Jones, is proving that he remains, in his seventieth year, the unacknowledged but undeniable Master of all Western music. When Ellington appeared with his choicest grapes last summer at the Rainbow Grill for the first time (anywhere, outside of a recording studio), it was a triumphant time. The band seemed the best small one ever assembled, new materials were broken out nightly, and Ellington himself, despite the death a short while before of Billy Strayhorn, was ebullient and gracious. (He has long been taken for granted without, as it were, ever really having been accepted in the first place. So no one recorded the stint last year—an incredible sin of omission in a time when it is difficult to open one's mouth without being taped.) But on the first night I went up to the Rainbow Grill last week, Strayhorn's passing seemed to have caught up with Ellington. For the first time he looked his age. "When I got a copy the other day of the new album we did of Billy's tunes," he said, "I couldn't even look at it, let alone listen to it. I just threw it on the bed." When the dog feels down, the tail stops wagging, and that night Ellington and the band were quiescent. New materials were not in evidence, a lot of medleys were trundled out, and there were half a dozen perfunctory vocals by Trish Turner and Tony Watkins. But, as in every Ellington performance, there were corrective moments: Ellington's crystal chime notes behind Harry Carney's bass clarinet on "Creole Love Call"; the classic Hodges' "On the Sunny Side of the Street"; Cat Anderson's loving parody of Louis Armstrong on "Me and You"; Paul Gonsalves' two choruses on "Body and Soul," one very slow and full of his labyrinthine Charlie Parker-Ben Webster rushes, and one in triple time, where he managed to stay just *ahead* of the beat; and Strayhorn's last blues, "The Intimacy of the Blues," which had two singing choruses apiece from Hodges and Anderson and Gonsalves.

One of the extraordinary things about Ellington and his men is their ability, in the face of a non-stop, year-in-and-year-out schedule, to continually pull surprises out of their hats. When I went back to the Rainbow Grill the next night Ellington looked his customary forty, and from the beginning—Cat Anderson's plaintive, barely audible muted solo, backed only by the bassist, on "Black and Tan Fantasy"—the band shone and jumped and worked. It rocked behind Hodges on "I Got It Bad," with Carney providing mother-earth, basso-profundo hums. It rocked behind Trish Turner on "Sonny" and "Look at Me," and it shouted on "Happy-Go-Lucky Local," while Gonsalves, his shoulders hunched and his face screwed prune-tight, played perhaps a dozen freighted, impassioned choruses. (Gonsalves is one of the few great cumulative improvisers.) A loose, careering "C-Jam Blues" had startling breaks by Anderson and Gonsalves and Carney, and there was a rough but right "Main Stem," one of Ellington's most ardent and complex and beautiful blues. Hodges smoothed the deep suède of Billy Strayhorn's "Passion Flower," and at the beginning of the second set Ellington, seated in semi-darkness by himself, played Strayhorn's "Lotus Blossom." (He has said it is the tune Strayhorn most liked to hear him play.) He played it to himself, and of course he played it for Strayhorn, who surely heard.

1968

The Duke's Party

Last week, on April 29th, the incomparable Duke Ellington was finally given his due by his country. The White House threw a black-tie seventieth-birthday party for him, and President Nixon presented him with the government's highest civilian award, the Presidential Medal of Freedom.

I arrived at the White House with my wife via the southwest gate at a quarter to ten. There was a chill in the air, and it was drizzling. We were ushered swiftly through a handsome oval reception room into a small room full of cabinets displaying the china used by various Presidents. (I learned during the evening that the White House, with its myriad military aides and attendants, ushers its guests about with classic grace; one has the sensation of being constantly and gently propelled over velvet.) Earl Hines, sipping champagne as he stood with his back to the Canton china used by George Washington, was watching a Navy Band trio made up of a drummer, a saxophonist, and an accordionist. "That's the damnedest accordion I ever heard," he said. "It sounds like a *guitar*. It's just luck I'm here, and I'm very happy about it. Duke and I have been *very* close friends for a *long* time. I just finished an engagement at Blues Alley here, and tomorrow I'm off for South America." Willie the Lion Smith, in his traditional garb of derby, horn-rimmed glasses, and cigar, drifted by looking like a well-slept owl, and Gerry Mulligan and Clark Terry, who were carrying their horns, began to play with the trio. Gunther Schuller, the classical composer who is head of the New England Conservatory of Music and who is one of Ellington's most fervent admirers, came in, followed by George Wein. Marian McPartland was talking with Leonard Feather, the jazz critic, in a corner. The music was booming, and the guests had overflowed into an enormous arched hallway. Soon the aides wafted us upstairs and into the Great Hall, where a receiving line had formed. The President, the Duke, Mrs. Nixon, and Ruth Ellington, the Duke's sister, were receiving the guests near the door of the Blue Room, and across from them a contingent from the Marine Band was playing. I hadn't seen Ellington since last fall, when I spent three days on the road with him and the band in the Deep South, and the contrast between the two situations was startling. The three days were typical of the non-stop, no-vacations life that Ellington has led for forty-six years. On a Monday night he played a sacred-music concert at South Carolina State College in Orangeburg. On Tuesday Harry Carney, his great baritone saxophonist and sometime chauffeur, drove him (and me) two hundred and twenty-five miles to Fort Valley, Georgia, where, ten minutes after our arrival, at eight o'clock, he started giving a concert at Fort Valley State College. Immediately after it was over, we piled back into the car and drove four hundred miles to Vicksburg, where he was scheduled to give a Wednesday-night concert. The Fort Valley-Vicksburg jaunt is unforgettable. Carney drove very fast over mile after mile of two-lane concrete roads. It was pitch-black, and the headlights seemed to bounce off the darkness. Ellington dozed a little and then said "Lights." Carney, maintaining his speed, switched on the overhead light, and the road all but disappeared from view. Ellington, dressed in his usual long-haul costume of an old sweater, rumpled pants, and a black bandanna tied around his head, pulled a thick sheaf of papers out of a small bag he takes everywhere and began to write. (The bag is shaped like a doctor's bag and was given him by Billy Strayhorn as a double gag, since Ellington holds an honorary degree from Yale and the bag was meant to hold the pills and other medicines he is never without.) Ten minutes later, Ellington said "O.K.," and Carney turned the light off. A similar work period took place every twenty minutes or so for the next three hours, and then we stopped for scrambled eggs and grits in a little town in Alabama. We were treated courteously, but nobody recognized Ellington. An hour or so later we stopped for gas, and Ellington called New York and talked with his doctor and longtime friend Arthur Logan about some ailment that was bothering him. It was four o'clock. I fell asleep, and woke up in another gas station, near Jackson, Mississippi. The sun was coming up. Carney had got out of the car to pay for the gas, and the attendant, a white man in his fifties, asked him, "Hey, is that Duke Ellington?" Carney nodded, and the man came up to Ellington's window. Ellington rolled it down and shook hands and said, "How's it going?" The attendant said, "*Are* you Duke Ellington?" Ellington nodded.

"Wow! I've been listening to your records all my life. This is a great honor." Ellington rolled up the window and we drove off. "And I almost made it safely to the border," he said.

And here he was in the White House, in a tuxedo and a white ruffled shirt, standing next to the President and still nodding and smiling and shaking hands. When I reached the President in the receiving line, I told him he was doing a noble thing giving such a party, and he uttered a perfect "Pshaw!" Ellington looked at me blankly, and I told him my name. He gave his Mona Lisa smile and said, "And I was afraid *you* wouldn't remember *my* name." After being greeted by Mrs. Nixon, who looked frail and bemused, and by Miss Ellington, who was almost invisible under a huge wig, my wife and I were ushered into the East Room, where several hundred chairs had been set up. Television and newsreel cameramen were packed into a screened-off area in the back of the room. (The *Times* reported that this was the first time the White House had ever allowed such an event to be covered by television cameras.) A ten-piece band was waiting on a dais in the front of the room, and it was a sterling group, made up of Hank Jones, Jim Hall, Milt Hinton, Louis Bellson, Bill Berry, Clark Terry, Urbie Green, J. J. Johnson, Gerry Mulligan, and Paul Desmond. Vice-President Agnew was standing between the band and the audience, beaming and looking like a maître d. When the room was full, the President and Mrs. Nixon, followed by Ellington and his sister, entered, and everyone stood. I can't resist such fillets of melodrama, and I got a lump in my throat. The President, moving in a quick, wooden way, jumped up on a platform in front of the bandstand and, in his deepest rain-barrel voice, said something to this effect: "Sit down, please, ladies and gentlemen. This is a very unusual and special evening in this great room. Before the entertainment begins, we have a presentation to make. I was looking at this name on here and it says 'Edward Kennedy'"—he paused—"'Ellington.'" Laughter. "For the first time during this Administration I have the honor of presenting the Presidential Medal of Freedom." Ellington, standing pensively beside Mr. Nixon, was reading the citation over his right shoulder. "In the royalty of American music, no man swings more or stands higher than the Duke." The President handed Ellington the medal. Everyone stood, and the applause was thunderous. "Thank you, Mr. President," Ellington said, and, taking Mr. Nixon by both arms, he conferred *his* celebrated award—the classic French greeting of left cheek against left cheek, right against right, left against left, and right against right. The President blushed and took a seat in the front row. Ellington said thank you again and listed the four freedoms that Billy Strayhorn had lived his life by—freedom from hate, freedom from self-pity, freedom from fear of possibly doing something that might help someone else more than it would him, and freedom from "the kind of pride that could make a man feel that he is better than his brother." Ellington sat down between Mrs. Agnew and his sister, and the President jumped back up on the platform and said, laughing, "One thing has been left out of the program—'Happy Birthday.' Please don't go away while I try and play it, and everybody sing, please, in the key of G."

Everybody sang, and then the band went to work. The music, which lasted an hour and a half, was exceptional. Some two dozen numbers were played, and almost all were by Ellington and/or Billy Strayhorn. The high points included Gerry Mulligan's "Sophisticated Lady"; a duet by Terry and Berry in "Just Squeeze Me"; a gorgeous Urbie Green solo in "I Got It Bad and That Ain't Good"; a long, stamping "In a Mellow Tone"; an ingenious medium-tempo version of Ellington's ordinarily dreamy "Prelude to a Kiss," arranged by Mulligan; three exhilarating choruses of "Perdido," by Earl Hines; and a caroming Louis Bellson drum solo in "Caravan." Then Willis Conover, who had arranged the musical festivities, introduced the musicians. Ellington stood up, bowed, and sat down after each name. The President darted back to the platform and said, "I think we all ought to hear from one more pianist." He pulled Ellington from his chair, and the Duke took the microphone. "It's the greatest compliment to be asked to follow this orchestra. I shall pick a name—gentle, graceful, something like Pat." He sat down at the piano and improvised a slow, Debussy-like melody that brought the room to dead silence. Shouts of applause followed, and Mr. Nixon announced that if everyone would move into the Great Hall for refreshments, the East Room would be cleared for a jam session and dancing.

I went out into the lobby looking for celebrities, and found them— Mr. and Mrs. Richard Rodgers, Mr. and Mrs. Otto Preminger, Geoffrey Holder and his wife, Carmen de Lavallade, Mr. and Mrs. Harold Arlen, Daniel Patrick Moynihan, Mahalia Jackson, the Reverend and Mrs. John Yaryan (he was one of the sponsors of Ellington's first sacred-music concert, in Grace Cathedral in San Francisco in 1965), Dr. and Mrs. Logan, Mr. and Mrs. Cab Calloway, and Mr. and Mrs. Billy Eckstine.

Ellington himself moved easily from cluster to cluster, and when he got near us my wife said to him, "I was so glad you kissed President Nixon." "I think he liked that," Ellington replied. "I always kiss all my friends. So now he belongs." I asked him why he was wearing such a conservative shirt, and he said, "The man who was supposed to bring my pleated blue satin shirt lost it or forgot it, or something, and I had to go out and buy this *and* these studs and cufflinks."

A roar of music burst out of the East Room. Lou Rawls was shouting the blues, and he was followed by Eckstine and Joe Williams. Half the accompanying band was made up of the all-stars, complemented by Dizzy Gillespie, and half by members of the Marine Band who looked as if they were in Valhalla. The chairs had been pushed back and dancing began. Geoffrey Holder, an enormous man in a black velvet outfit with satin trim, leaped around with Miss de Lavallade, and Ellington danced in turn with Mrs. Logan, his sister, and Mrs. Yaryan. He did a peppy foxtrot. George Wein sat in on piano and was followed by Ellington. Then Ellington and Willie the Lion Smith (Smith taught Ellington forty-five years ago) played a duet, and so did the Lion and Marian McPartland. Harold Taylor, the former president of Sarah Lawrence College, sat in on clarinet. Ellington danced some more, looking fresh and happy and very young (he was due to fly to Oklahoma City for a gig the next morning at eight), and then he went over to Dr. Logan, who was sitting in the front row. The Doctor took his pulse and pushed Ellington back on the dance floor. The Nixons had gone to bed shortly after midnight, but the East Room rocked on until well after two.

I said goodnight to Ellington near the front door of the White House. He embraced me and my wife, and then, as if it had been her party, paid her the kind of compliment women take with them to their graves: "I'm so glad you could come. You looked so beautiful, and you brought such dignity to my party." He waved, and we went out.

So, as such evenings go, it was pretty fine. In fact only one thing was really wrong: the band, excepting Harry Carney, wasn't there. That magnificent assemblage is Ellington's voice, his right hand, his palette, his instrument, and not to have it present left an irremediable hole in the evening. But the next time I see the Duke I'll ask him about it, and he'll have the right answer. He always does.

1969

A Day with the Duke

Not long ago, I suggested that Duke Ellington be given a grant of, say, a hundred thousand dollars, so that he could take six months off from his wearying round of worldwide one-night stands to record or re-record the cream of the compositions he has written in the past forty years. The results, on about twelve LPs, would constitute a kind of Ellington collected works, and would stand as one of the pillars of Western music. The response to the suggestion has not been surprising. The foundations, busy handing money out to retreads and the moribund, have been silent, and the letters I got ranged from the ineffectually enthusiastic to one from a New Jersey woman who said, in effect, why bother Ellington with such a project when she and her husband had every Ellington record and I was welcome to stop by any time and hear their collection. So it has been business as usual for Ellington, with one rending exception—the death, early in May, of his great alto saxophonist Johnny Hodges. Ellington spent last fall on a backbreaking European tour, and in January he went to Australia, New Zealand, Japan, Thailand, and Laos. This spring he celebrated his seventy-first birthday and attended the New Orleans Jazz Festival, where he introduced his "New Orleans Suite," which is reported to include superb musical portraits of Louis Armstrong, Sidney Bechet, and Mahalia Jackson. At the end of June he goes to Europe again for a month, and in August he will take up his celebrated annual stand at the Rainbow Grill. In the meantime, the honors and awards continue to flow in. He was recently given a Doctor of Humanities degree by the Christian Theological Seminary in Indianapolis and a Doctor of Music degree by Assumption College in Worcester, and in late May he was inducted into the National Institute of Arts and Letters—a first, as far as I know, for anyone connected with jazz. A friend of mine who was at the Institute ceremonies told me that Ellington was given a standing ovation. But the main reason I bring all this up now is that I was recently lucky enough to spend a good part of a day following the Duke around the city. New York *is* Ellington's home (he keeps an apartment on West End Avenue), but he is here only a couple of times a year, and when he is, his schedule tends to be even heavier than it is on the road.

I met him around three-thirty in the afternoon at the National Recording Studios at Fifty-sixth and Fifth, where he was to record part of the music for a ballet commissioned by the American Ballet Theatre. The ballet is called "The River," and will be given its première at the New York State Theatre at Lincoln Center on the twenty-fifth of June. He greeted me with his French two-kisses-on-each-cheek and said, "What time did I call you last night?"

"Around twelve-thirty," I replied.

"I didn't get to bed until ten this morning, what with working on the ballet. I'm tired, babe, tired."

But he looked extremely well, and even his working clothes—an old blue sweater, rumpled gray slacks, and blue suède shoes—looked good. He went immediately into the recording booth, which, like most of the places Ellington goes, was crowded with relatives, friends, and hangers-on. Present were Stanley Dance, the critic and one of Ellington's right-hand men; Michael James, Ellington's nephew and an aide; Joe Morgen, his press agent; an admirer of thirty-five years' standing named Edmund Anderson; and a couple of admiring women. Ellington examined some sheet music and went out into the studio. He spoke to several members of the band and got loud laughs in response and, standing in the center of the studio, said, just before the first take, "We're going to get lucky on this one. Derum, derum, derum! One, two, three, four!" Rufus Jones started a rapid machine-gun beat on his snare drum, which was echoed on a glockenspiel and on timpani. The band came in, and the piece, called "The Falls," turned out to be unlike anything I had heard Ellington do. But then nothing new of his is quite like anything he has done before. The section passages of "The Falls" are brief but dense and booting, there are solo parts by Paul Gonsalves, and there are extraordinary dissonant full-band chords. And all this is done against the furious *rat-tat-tat-tat* of the snare, the glockenspiel, and the timpani. It is exciting, tight crescendo music, and it reminded me of some of Stravinsky's early stuff, except that it was unmistakably a jazz composition. Ellington conducted (Wild Bill Davis sat in on piano), using the traditional upside-down-T-square motions in a slow, wooden way, as if he were swimming through molasses. All the while he chewed on something and rocked his head from side to side.

While the piece was played back, he sat in the recording booth with his head bowed, his eyes closed, and a hand on each knee. He looked up when it was over. "A waterfall—you can always *see* the top and you can always *hear* the bottom," he said. "So you've got the top and the bottom, and you can put anything you want in between."

He returned to the studio, and Anderson said, "Last November, I shot some film of the band in Paris. Afterward I told Johnny Hodges, who in all the thirty-five years I knew him never said more than two words, 'I got some great footage of you tonight.' He shouted at me, 'Not tonight! Not tonight! My eyes looked so bad!' Which was all the more amazing when you consider that on the stand Hodges kept his eyes closed most of the time."

Ellington led the band through six or seven more takes until he got the right one, and after a break he went to work on a part of the ballet called "The Mother." It is slow and ruminative, and includes a lovely flute solo by Norris Turney. Again, there were several takes, and the session ended at six-thirty. Ellington made some phone calls, kissed several women hello and goodbye, and, surrounded by Morgen, Dance, and a friend who was driving for Ellington, a broad-shouldered Greek named Chris Stamatiou, left the studios for the City Center to talk with Alvin Ailey, who is choreographing "The River."

Down on Fifth Avenue, Ellington asked Stamatiou where his car was, and Stamatiou said in a garage around the corner. Ellington asked him how far it was to the City Center, and he said a block or so—an easy walk. "You mean you want me to *walk* a block? Well, I might as well, but it'll be the longest walk I've had in years," Ellington said. He started west on Fifty-sixth Street, moving in the determined, stiff way of older men with tired feet. He got a lot of double takes, and whenever he passed a garage or a restaurant with its complement of New York early-evening sidewalk loungers, he was greeted with, "Hey Duke!" or "Mr. *Ellington!*" Each time, he looked interested and said "How you been?" or "How's everything?" and shook hands as if he were greeting friends he hadn't seen in twenty-five years. He went in at the back door of the City Center and up to the sixth floor, where he sat down abruptly with Ailey at a small table by the elevator door. They talked for twenty minutes, and then went down to wait for Stamatiou and the car. They continued talking, but the car didn't come, and after fifteen minutes Dance called the garage and found out that the car had broken down. Ellington kissed Ailey goodbye, and we got into a cab and headed downtown. It was about seven-thirty.

"We're going to the Half Note," Dance said. "Hugues Panassié's son Louis is in the country making some sort of film on jazz, and he asked Duke if he would mind coming down to the Half Note to be in a short sequence."

Ellington, who sat next to the taxi-driver, a young, bearded man, pulled a bright scarf out of his pocket and knotted it around his head turban-fashion. The driver, peering at Ellington out of the corner of his eye, missed a crucial right-hand turn at Dominick Street, and the Holland Tunnel appeared. Ellington asked Morgen if he knew where the hell we were going, and Morgen said he had seen the Dominick Street turn just after we passed it. The driver made a hundred-and-eighty-degree swing in front of the Tunnel and stopped a moment later at the Half Note. Ellington took off his scarf and got out.

Inside, Ellington gave Panassié, an engaging man in his thirties, the de-rigueur greeting and asked him what to do. Panassié said he would like him to sit at the bar for a few minutes and answer a couple of questions. Mike Canterino, one of the owners of the Half Note, gave Ellington a Coke, and, bathed in blinding light, he sat down on a bar stool. "You know, I'm not really dressed for this sort of thing, but let me light a cigarette, so I'll look sophisticated," he said. He knocked over the Coke and said, "Oh, my! I'm the only nuisance I know who *knows* he's a nuisance!" The cameras rolled, and Ellington, looking as if he were in his living room with a few friends, spoke intimately about Panassié's father ("He serves the same muse I do"), and went on, "I don't think any music should be called jazz. I don't believe in categories. Years ago, uptown, I tried to get the cats to call it American Negro music or Afro-American music, because jazz just isn't right. Louis Armstrong plays Louis Armstrong music, Art Tatum plays Art Tatum music, Dizzy Gillespie plays Dizzy Gillespie music, and if it sounds good, that's all you need."

At about eight o'clock the klieg lights went off, and Panassié thanked Ellington fervently. Our party of four walked to Sixth Avenue to find a cab, and on the way Ellington kept hitching up his trousers, which were secured by an old belt buckled at one side. "When I got that degree in Indianapolis last week, I had this same problem," he told Dance. "I was wearing a gown and all, and when I went out on the stage my pants started slipping, and I had to pull them up right through the gown. I don't know whether it's this stomach I've got that's causing the trouble or whether it's just that my bottom is getting smaller."

At Sixth Avenue a young black policeman greeted Ellington: "Hey, Duke. You waiting for the A train?" Ellington said he was waiting for a cab, but asked if there *was* an A train somewhere around to get back uptown in. A cab arrived, and Ellington gave a Central Park South address.

"His sister Ruth's apartment," Dance said.

Miss Ellington's apartment, which looks out over the Park, is mostly off-white, and the windows are hung with heavy glass-bead curtains. There are a couple of big glass-topped tables, and in the corner is a small bar. She greeted her brother warmly, and he slumped into a chair, stretched his legs out straight, and threw his head back on a cushion. He closed his eyes. Miss Ellington, who wore a big blond wig, a yellow blouse, and purple slacks, asked him if he wanted some Chinese food. He said no, he was just going home to bed. Stamatiou appeared and, leaning over Ellington, apologized about the car. Ellington grunted and waved one hand. A man in a white coat brought him a Coke, putting it down carefully on a paper coaster that showed a bass drum with a caricature of Ellington's head on it and the word "Duke" beneath. I asked Ellington about the ballet.

He opened his eyes halfway, took a sip of Coke, and lit a cigarette. His eyes closed again. "I'd been thinking about it for a while, and a year or so ago I was lying on a hotel bed in Vancouver and Alvin Ailey was with me and the story just came out," he said. "The river starts out like a spring and he's like a newborn baby, tumbling and spitting, and one day, attracted by a puddle, he starts to run. He scurries and scampers and wants to get to the marsh, and, after being followed by a big bubble, he does, and at the end of the run he goes into the meander. Then he skips and dances and runs until he's exhausted, and he lies down by the lake—all horizontal lines, ripples, reflections, God-made and untouched. Then he goes over the falls and down into the whirlpool, the vortex of violence, and out of the whirlpool into the main track of the river. He widens, becomes broader, loses his adolescence, and, down at the delta, passes between two cities. Like all cities on the opposite sides of deltas, you can find certain things in one and not in the other, and vice versa, so we call the cities the Neo-Hip-Hot-Cool Kiddies' Community and the Village of the Virgins. The river passes between them and romps into the mother—Her Majesty the Sea—and, of course, is no longer a river. But this is the climax, the heavenly anticipation of rebirth, for the sea will be drawn up into the sky for rain and down into wells and into springs and become the river again. So we call the river an optimist. We'll be able to play the ballet in any church or temple, because the optimist is a believer."

He took another drink of Coke, and after a while I asked him about Johnny Hodges.

"All I have to say is in the eulogy I wrote. Pastor John Gensel read it at the graveside. Hey, Stanley, have you got a copy of the Johnny Hodges eulogy?"

Dance rummaged around in his briefcase and handed me a double-spaced typewritten sheet. The eulogy began, "Never the world's greatest, most highly animated showman or stage personality . . . but a tone so beautiful it sometimes brought tears to the eyes. This was Johnny Hodges. This *is* Johnny Hodges. Because of this great loss, our band will never sound the same." It ended, "I am glad and thankful that I had the privilege of presenting Johnny Hodges for forty years, night after night. I imagine that I have been much envied, but thanks to God, and may God bless this beautiful giant in his own identity. God bless Johnny Hodges."

Dance said, "Hey, Duke, you're on television now, with Orson Welles on the David Frost show."

Ellington opened his eyes, heaved himself to his feet, and moved rapidly out of the room, saying, "Oh, he's one of my favorite people—Orson Welles. I've got to see him."

1970

III
Reviews 1967–1971

The Burning Bush

John Hammond's "Spirituals to Swing—1967," given at Carnegie Hall, was a marvellous, multivoiced celebration. The living celebrated themselves. (Only seven of the forty-odd performers had appeared in the first "Spirituals to Swing" concerts in the late thirties, but in the main they provided the best music.) The living celebrated the dead. (Among the large and attentive crowd of ghosts from the earlier concerts were Sidney Bechet, James P. Johnson, Charlie Christian, Lester Young, Herschel Evans, Hot Lips Page, Albert Ammons, and Fletcher Henderson.) Hammond quite rightly celebrated himself. (Without his daring ministrations we probably would not have been blessed by Billie Holiday and Count Basie and Teddy Wilson and Christian.) And it was a fine celebration of the blues; aside from several standards and a couple of gospel numbers, the entire program was blues.

George Benson, a young guitarist and Hammond's newest protégé, got the festivities off to a predictable start. He has a brilliantine tone, and he is apt to use ten notes where one or none would do, but he plays with a conviction and an occasional wildness that have been missing from the guitar since the days of Jimmy Shirley. Marion Williams, long the ballast of the Clara Ward Singers, came on next, accompanied by Marion Franklin on piano, Milt Hinton, and Jo Jones. In recent years gospel singing has become brittle and showy, and Miss Williams is a resounding example. She can growl, trill, shout, and drop, between eighth notes, from the top of her range to the bottom. And she can writhe and sashay and wink. It's a good show, and once in a while—as at the end of "Nobody Knows the Trouble I've Seen," when she rocketed in mid-syllable from an electric trill to a booming growl— it's a great one.

Then a small band made up of Buck Clayton, Buddy Tate, Edmond Hall, Count Basie, Hinton, and Jones ambled through—with Tate in the lead—a medium blues that discussed swinging, emotion, honesty, and beauty. Basie floated off the stage on a wreath of smiles and was replaced by Ray Bryant, and Joe Turner appeared. Turner's voice is big and flattish and hard and almost vibratoless, and he applies it to his words as if it were a trowel. His lyrics have no wrinkles and no edges. And he has a matchless sense of rhythm and cadence, sometimes moseying along behind the beat and sometimes squeezing ten or so words into a single quick phrase. He opened with a medium blues, and it was immediately clear that he was in perfect voice. (Despite his size and seeming nonchalance, Turner can be nervous and erratic.) His next number was unbelievable. He began, a cappella, with a ringing, iron rush ("Iliveacrossthestreetfromajukejoint"), then suddenly slipped into a slow, slow walk ("and all night we play the blues"). The verses went by, Clayton took two superlative choruses, and then Turner thundered the words—with the band in full, mounting voice behind—"I want the sun to rise, the wind to blow . . ." Well, it was the Voice coming from the burning bush, and Turner, allowing the audience to get its face on straight again, next rolled through an easy blues, one whole rocking chorus of which was taken up simply by the word "Yes," uttered offbeat every couple of bars. Only masters can simultaneously proffer sentimentality and emotion, and that's exactly what Turner and his old friend Pete Johnson did in "Roll 'Em Pete." Johnson, who has been ill and in seclusion for the past decade, was propped up in a chair at the keyboard, and, energized by Turner and the soloists, he took three choruses in the treble while Bryant handled the bass. Clayton and Tate and Hall were admirable accompanists throughout, and Clayton demonstrated in each number that his obbligatos, which he has lent to everyone from Billie Holiday to Paul Robeson, are among the graces of the age—muted, they call from behind far hills; open-horn, they insist like warm sunlight.

John Handy unluckily got caught with his sextet (violin, cello, guitar, bass, and drums) between Turner and Big Mama Willie Mae Thornton. Accompanied by Clayton et al., she sang five blues that had all the mountainous intensity of Turner's blues. She reached some sort of celestial point in her third number, which was done in a nearly motionless tempo, by starting, "I got a sweet little angel, and I love the way he spreads his wings." The words were softly walked out, as if they were newborn, and by the time she had repeated the line, raising her voice and her volume slightly, an absolute spell had fallen.

The end of the evening had every right to be anticlimactic. Count Basie and his big band, augmented once again by Harry Edison, played three numbers, including a funny nonsense blues sung by Richard Boone, and were joined by Clayton, Hall, Tate, Turner, and Jo Jones, all of them backed by Basie on the organ, which he causes to tremble and sigh and whisper.

1967

All Work and No Play

The antediluvian practice of calling on entertainers to perform six nights a week has had mixed effects on jazz musicians, who, of all performing artists, most need replenishment. It has provided young musicians with essential on-the-job training, and it has, through sheer exposure, put the music in front of what has almost always been a tin-eared public. But in the main it has caused deviltry. The weak have collapsed by the wayside or have turned to drugs or alcohol, and the strong, with rare exceptions, have become self-parodists or by-rote performers. A fair-labor-practices reform has clearly been needed, and the reform began to take drastic do-it-yourself shape four or five years ago when Sonny Rollins, dissatisfied with the effect of the treadmill on his playing, went into temporary retirement. Ornette Coleman followed not long after, and others have done it since. (Needless to say, some of these furloughs are brought about by a lack of work, but all of them depend on generous friends and/or breadwinning wives.) Coleman, in particular, appears now only in occasional concerts, and the results have been beneficial. He has had the time to take up new instruments (trumpet, violin, and musette), and he has had the time to compose. More important, his playing, freed of the old tyranny, has grown steadily.

This was apparent when Coleman, in company with a quartet (David Izenzon and Charlie Haden on bass and Charles Moffett on drums) and the Philadelphia Woodwind Quintet, gave a concert at the Village Theatre. The sum of the evening was more impressive than its parts. Coleman demonstrated that he has continued to compress his alto-saxophone style without sacrificing its fire and fluency. (When he first came to New York, seven or so years ago, he was cornucopic; he had a million notes in his head, and he must have purged himself of most of them the first year. It was a bewildering experience for his listeners, but in the process he learned the great secret of selectivity.) Time and again at the concert he slipped into almost inaudible passages ("The Little Symphony," "Love and Sex"), and throughout he revealed complete control. He delved comfortably into the middle and low registers of the trumpet for the first time ("Just for You"), and on the violin ("A Capella for Four Wise Men") he curbed the histrionic tendencies he often shows. He got a tone on the musette that moved pleasantly back and forth between a conch and a bagpipe ("Buddha Blues"). Coleman's group is a model of collective interplay. Haden, playing pizzicato, and Izenzon, playing arco (they swapped roles in "Atavism"), worked simultaneously, while Moffett issued a steady persiflage of melodic counter-rhythms. New Orleans jazz has withered, but its greatest gift to music—the improvised ensemble—haunts everything from rock 'n' roll to the "new thing."

The Philadelphia Woodwind Quintet played a Villa-Lobos piece and a short, tentative exercise by S. A. Chambers. Then, at the end of the concert, Coleman joined it in a new composition of his own, "Forms and Sounds." The form, straight from the church, was call and response; Coleman played a dozen or so brief cadenzas on the trumpet, each of which was answered by the quintet. And the sounds consisted of Coleman's squirting, high-note phrases and the wood-and-leaf textures of the quintet. The piece, though, suggested a series of parentheses strung out side by side, and it was disappointing that Coleman played *with* the quintet only in its final passage.

Perhaps Coleman will find his way toward appearing more often. His feet remain firmly in the old blues and his head is full of celestial things—a balanced presence that could offset a great deal of the malarkey that afflicts the rest of the "new thing."

1967

Maestro

I eat frequently at a small Italian restaurant in Oyster Bay because its surprising jukebox has offered, for several years, Glenn Miller's original, 1942 recording of "A String of Pearls." Near the end of the record there is a twelve-bar cornet solo by Bobby Hackett that remains in its design (scalar), tone (moonlike), and lyricism (Bach) one of the recorded improvisational wonders. Like Bix Beiderbecke's solos with Paul Whiteman, it suggests a nugget in a fleshy palm. Then one evening "A String of Pearls" was gone. Hackett, who has spent most of his career locked up in second-rate bands or in the studios or as a distant-meadow soloist in mood recordings, had vanished again. But not long after, a new recording appeared—"Creole Cookin': Bobby Hackett" (Verve), in which he plays eleven refurbished New Orleans and Dixieland standards in company with a thirteen-piece band. It is the first jazz record he has made in a decade and it reveals him, waste spaces notwithstanding, in all his beauty.

Hackett was born in Providence in 1915. His father was a blacksmith and his mother produced nine children. The family was poor and Hackett quit school at the age of fourteen to go to work in a Chinese restaurant called the Port Arthur, where he played guitar and violin. Then Louis Armstrong came through town and Hackett, awed, took up the trumpet. ("I've never been the same since," he has said. "That man was and is the greatest hot-trumpet player in jazz. All you have to hear is four bars. Dizzy Gillespie told me once that he never heard Armstrong until he came up to New York and I said to him, 'Boy, you were lucky!' ") In the late thirties, after a long stint at the Theatrical Club in Boston, where he played with Brad Gowans and Pee Wee Russell, Hackett landed at Nick's in Greenwich Village and became

a part of the round robin that included Russell, Gowans, Zutty Singleton, Billy Butterfield, Dave Tough, Joe Sullivan, and Eddie Condon.
But he didn't belong in it, any more than Tough or Russell did. After
a short, sour turn with his own big band, he joined Horace Heidt, the
Lawrence Welk of his day, and His Musical Knights. ("I was the only
musician in the band that Heidt would allow to wear a mustache. It
was a mark of respect, I guess.") He was with Glenn Miller as a
guitarist and occasional cornet soloist in 1941 and 1942, and in the
mid-forties he spent two years with Glen Gray. Since then, his light
has flickered even more fitfully. He was a studio musician with A.B.C.
for fifteen years, and in the middle fifties he made a highly successful
series of mood-music recordings with Jackie Gleason—"Music for
Lovers Only," "Music, Martinis, and Memories," "Music to Remember
Her." In the late fifties he assembled a remarkable sextet, which
played for a year or so at the Henry Hudson Hotel. It was a doubling
wonder. Tom Gwaltney played the clarinet and the vibraphone, Dick
Cary arranged and played the piano and the alto horn, Tom Dengler
played tuba and cornet, and Ernie Caceres doubled on clarinet and
baritone saxophone. (Buzzy Drootin was on drums.) The group
achieved a remarkable variety of textures and sounds, poked fun at
the sacred cows of jazz, and was, all in all, a delight. It made one
middling recording and, for a lack of bookings, went under. Hackett
has recently travelled and recorded with Tony Bennett as an accompanist, and a year ago he formed a neat quartet which surfaces now
and then.

Hackett is short and thin and trim. He has a worn, cheerful face
and receding patent-leather hair, and he speaks in a low, soft drawl.
He invariably looks in focus, and this precision is the basis of his
style. For many years he has been identified, like Jimmy McPartland
and the late Red Nichols, as an admirer of Bix Beiderbecke, and with
good reason. His tone, which is quiet and shining, resembles Beiderbecke's, and so does his three-steps-up, two-steps-down method of improvising. But his sustained notes and way of playing just behind the
beat and of occasionally slipping into double time are straight out of
Louis Armstrong. Hackett is a unique and successful alloy of Beiderbecke and Armstrong. His style, which was well set when he first appeared in New York, has changed only in being steadily and micro-
scopically refined. At medium or fast tempos he gives the impression
of floating just above the melody and harmonies of the tune he is
improvising on. He will start a solo with six or seven building-block
notes, cemented with round, glancing grace notes. These will be
placed in an ascending cluster of three notes, followed by a large
interval with the fourth note at its bottom, and a second ascending

cluster. Without pausing, Hackett will dodge between registers with a singsong Beiderbecke effect, then hold the last note of the phrase briefly, adding to it the politest vibrato in the business. Then he will move through an ascending-descending passage somewhat similar to the opening one and move through a juggling, double-time phrase, complete with gentle slurs and more intervals and capped with another vibrato, and then tuck in a line of backward-leaning notes before the solo ends. His solos are almost always short and wasteless and perfect. They suggest a careful statement-with-solution of a mathematical problem, each figure clean and spare, each with a singing, exultant lyricism. Hackett keeps his arts and sciences under one roof. The surface of his solos is so smooth and precise that they would appear as faultless under a microscope as they do to the naked eye. Hackett is an ambling marvel in slow blues and ballads. He makes the melody move easily, curving it gracefully, lengthening it here or telescoping it there, and all the while filtering it through a pastel spectrum. The result is a high lyricism that bells and flies and that has nothing to do with sentimentality (Johnny Hodges) or the downhome (Emmett Berry). Like Buck Clayton, Hackett is an ingenious obbligato player. Put end to end, his soft fills and lolling under notes would form remarkable sotto-voce solos. At a celebrated Carnegie Hall concert in 1947, Hackett's background figures made Louis Armstrong sound like a nightingale.

On hand with Hackett in his new album are, among others, Zoot Sims, Bobby Brookmeyer, Pepper Adams, and Bob Wilber. The arrangements, done by Wilber, fall between pleasant spoofing ("When the Saints Go Marching In" slips into rock-and-roll rhythm in its middle section, with Hackett loafing in the air above it) and the quaint lumber used by the old Bob Crosby band. Sims has two very brief solos, Brookmeyer is not heard enough, and Adams is not heard at all. But Hackett, like Armstrong in the early thirties, is often moved to heroics by the banal. In "High Society" he plays a fascinating set of geometric variations on the celebrated clarinet solo, and in "Basin Street Blues" he constructs a solo that is all hills and hollows and rises viewed from a low, slow plane. He takes two equally good choruses in "Muskrat Ramble," and in "New Orleans," "Lazy Mood," and "Do You Know What It Means to Miss New Orleans" he pedals easily up and down the melodies. ("New Orleans" closes with a fine duet between Wilber, on soprano saxophone, and Hackett, but it is unaccountably faded out before it is finished.) Miles Davis once admiringly said of Hackett, who is a musicians' musician, "Man, he don't *ever* miss a note!" That is correct.

1967

Coltrane

The late John Coltrane had become a messiah by the time of his death (he was just forty), in part because of the extraordinary adulation he received. He won all the awards, popular and critical; he was even elected to the *Down Beat* Hall of Fame, an often posthumous gallery containing both small peanuts and prophets. He recorded frequently and with apparent complete freedom, and he worked steadily. He was placed in the forefront of the avant-garde, and he was the cause of unbelievable amounts of disastrous eulogistic prose. He was copied slavishly by younger saxophonists. Yet his messiahship was partly his own doing, for in his last years his music became increasingly "religious." One album was called "A Love Supreme," the love being for God, and among the titles in another album, "Meditations," were "The Father and the Son and the Holy Ghost," "Compassion," "Love," "Consequences," and "Serenity." And he talked increasingly to his liner-note writers of uplifting people through his music, of inspiring them "to realize more and more of their capacities for living meaningful lives." But attempts to write program music succeed only in the mind of the composer or performer. One man's requiem is another man's polka.

Getting through the reverential cities of Troy that Coltrane vanished under is only the beginning of getting at Coltrane himself. He wasn't even easy to *listen* to. He had a blank, aggressive tone, and in his moments of frenzy, which were frequent, he repeated series of manic shrieks, wails, and screams that hurt the ear and stopped the mind. (His apologists were fond of pointing out that none of us really know what *music* should or should not sound like, but instinct, which can instantly isolate ugliness or beauty, knows better.) And he never stood still long enough to be heard properly. More and more, newness for the sake of itself became his very art. In the late fifties he ran the chords, playing endless thirty-second notes. (Until then, he had been a hard-bop saxophonist who had come up through rhythm-and-blues bands and groups led by Johnny Hodges and Dizzy Gillespie.) In the early sixties he shifted to modal improvising, to the scalar intricacies of Ravi Shankar. Not even his instrument was sufficient, so he took up the soprano saxophone and the bass clarinet and the flute, and he experimented in his groups with odd instrumentations. In addition, he tampered with form and harmony and rhythm. In a recording called "Ascension," he brought together two trumpeters, five saxophonists, two bassists, a pianist, and a drummer, and they played a racking non-stop thirty-eight-minute piece that alternated between jittery solos and demonic free-form ensembles. Moreover, he believed that long-windedness is not the soul of boredom, for sometimes one number lasted an hour and sometimes his solos went on for forty-five minutes. But every once in a while his restlessness passed and he came to a halt, stopped preaching, stopped screeching, and played a straightforward slow ballad or medium-tempo blues, and one suddenly understood what Coltrane was—the essence of good, old-fashioned lyricism. Such statements can be found in his best recording, "Crescent," and they are magnificent, in the way of Louis Armstrong and Sidney Bechet and Charlie Parker at their lyrical best. These solos are, in the singular manner of all great jazz improvisers, more human than musical. His tone deepens and yields, and he uses long, heavy phrases pulled along by a questing vibrato. His rhythmic placements are surprising, and so are his notes. It is magniloquent improvising, and at its most peaceful— the opening and closing statements of "The Drum Thing" in "Crescent" —it is imperishable. But born poets like Coltrane sometimes misjudge the size of their gifts, and in trying to further them, to ennoble them, they fall over into sentimentality or the maniacal. Coltrane did both, and it is ironic that these lapses, which were mistakenly considered to be musical reflections of our inchoate times, drew his heaviest acclaim. People said they heard the dark night of the Negro in Coltrane's wildest music, but what they really heard was a heroic and unique lyrical voice at the mercy of its own power.

1968

Small Print

One of the persistent beliefs in jazz is that the byways of America are peopled with unknown geniuses who, if they were brought out, would astonish us all. But the world of jazz is small, it has an almost telephonic grapevine, and touring musicians who at one time or another play most of the general-store towns have notably curious, open ears. Another belief is that jazz contains a sizable population of excellent but underrated musicians who, because of mischance, the winds of faddism, or retiring personalities, exist in a permanent twilight, and this is true. Their names are legion, and a few of them are John Collins, Buddy Tate, Emmett Berry, Joe Thomas, Jimmy Rowles, Ed Shaughnessy, and Benny Morton. Of these men, Morton, with his delicate, evasive style and self-effacing manner, is in some ways the most underappreciated. He is, indeed, not even listed in Leonard Feather's "Encyclopedia of Jazz in the Sixties," although the rest of the above are.

A handsome, immaculately tailored man with a dreaming, affable face, Morton is sixty-one and was born in New York City. He joined Fletcher Henderson when he was nineteen and fell under the spell of Jimmy Harrison, who, along with Jack Teagarden, converted the trombone from a sidesplitter into a musical instrument. Morton worked with Henderson off and on until the early thirties and, after a five-year stint with Don Redman, went with greatest of the Basie bands. He joined the Café Society Uptown-Downtown troupe in the early forties, and eventually became a member of Teddy Wilson's Uptown band. In the mid-forties he made a lot of imperishable (and now unavailable) recordings, among them a twelve-inch 78-r.p.m. Blue Note, "Conversing in Blue," on which he and Barney Bigard and Ben

Webster fashioned a closing chorus that, in its wandering, whispering lyricism, is one of the glories of jazz. Then he went underground, and he has since subsisted in the studios, in Broadway pit bands, and even in the Radio City Music Hall orchestra. A week or so ago Morton suddenly surfaced at a concert given at the Half Note by a group called the Jazz Giants, and in a recording made in Canada recently by the same group on the Sackville label.

Morton's style remains exactly what is was thirty years ago. It is an inward, private style, as if he and his instrument were in constant, shuttered colloquy. His tone is quiet and even, and he uses none of the glissandi and whoops invented by Dickie Wells and carried on by J. C. Higginbotham and Vic Dickenson. But his solos, instead of sounding restrained, have a deliberate, uphill air, and they rely for their affecting moments not on smears or burred tones but on elegance and logic. He is, in large part, a melodic embellisher who will either shadow the written melody for whole choruses at a time or launch into short-phrased, seemingly inverted improvisations (always capped by a searching vibrato) that tint and heighten the original melody. He is a contradictory legato performer who in a slow tune will lag behind the beat for half a chorus and then slip into an earnest, jogging double time, and who in a fast number will play winding, half-time phrases that alternate with direct, on-the-beat variations. Morton demands close scrutiny. He plays in small print, and it is not until the end of a solo—with its repeated, slightly varied phrases, long-held single notes, and abrupt, almost bouncing on-the-beat notes—that its ordered, mannerly design can be seen completely and clearly. Many jazz improvisers lurch from peak to peak, which tends to obscure the empty valleys, but Morton moves on a wide-open plain.

Morton has found himself in motley bands before, and the Jazz Giants is one of the oddest. Wild Bill Davison is on cornet, the late Edmond Hall's brother Herbie is on clarinet, Claude Hopkins is on piano, Arvell Shaw is on bass, and Buzzy Drootin is on drums. Morton, though he is the only member of the band who does not have his own display number, is the cement between these opposites, both in ensembles, where he plays discreet secondary solos, and in his actual solos. He was indispensable at the Half Note (particularly in "Them There Eyes" and "Bill Bailey"), and also in the Sackville recording ("Them There Eyes" again, and "I Would Do Anything for You," in which he takes a masterly solo).

1968

One-Man Band

By releasing "Art Tatum: Piano Starts Here"—four of the solos on the record constitute Tatum's first recording session, in 1933, and the rest are from a concert given in Los Angeles in 1949—Columbia reminds us how astonishing Tatum was. Blind in one eye and three-quarters blind in the other, he was a short, slow-gaited man with a warm, obscure face and stubby, unpianistic hands. He died in 1956 at the age of forty-six, and he was astonishing from the time of his recording début, when he was just twenty-two, until his death. No one ever knew exactly what he was or what to do with him. He was said to be the greatest jazz pianist who ever lived and he was said to be not a jazz pianist at all. He was admired by classical pianists, by George Gershwin, by jazz musicians, and by dazzled, tin-eared laymen. People poked fun at his ornate style and his interpolations in his solos of "Rhapsody in Blue" and "Stars and Stripes Forever," and then wept at his next brilliance. And the problem hasn't changed. He is still mentioned with awe and he is still put down, he is thought old-fashioned and ahead of his time, and nobody has decided yet what kind of pianist he was. If he he had been a white man, he might have become an exceptional concert pianist or a great straight-ahead jazz pianist. But not much was lower and more disconnected in the Depression than a Negro, so Tatum, his talents bulging, was unwittingly forced to become a new, one-man musical form that had something in it of Beethoven's most complex harmonies, Horowitz's technical brilliance, a funning, almost anti-jazz improvisation, a rhythmic complexity and sureness that was African, and a mammoth self-assurance. All this was superbly stamped by his *sound*, which was immediately identifiable after any two bars of his music.

Tatum, like Duke Ellington and Louis Armstrong and Charlie Parker, sprang from virgin soil. In the manner of all great innovators, he looked carefully around him and behind him before he jumped, learning from Fats Waller his stride techniques and his respect for touch and precision, from Earl Hines his single-note melodic lines and maelstrom arhythmic breaks, and from God knows where a technique that few pianists of any sort have matched in this century. Then he jumped, and his odd, doubly frustrating career began. He put together a desultory small band, and it was soon clear that the context suffocated him. He was already a one-man band who helplessly welled up and swamped his sidemen. So he went out on his own and became a sensation. He converted the Fifty-second Street clubs where he often played into small, jammed temples. When the reverence most audiences accorded him was marred by drunks, he simply dropped his hands from the keyboard in mid-number and waited, his body motionless, until an almost audible quiet fell, then resumed playing. In the early forties Tatum put together a trio with Tiny Grimes on guitar (Everett Barksdale eventually replaced him) and Slam Stewart on bass. It had its moments, particularly in the ensemble interplay between the three musicians, but in the main Tatum sounded hobbled, and he again went out on his own, remaining successful and solitary until he died. (One of the few times Tatum knuckled under and simply became one of the turbines driving the band occurred during an amazing concert in January of 1944 at the Metropolitan Opera House. He had his solo outings that evening, but for most of it he was just a member of possibly the most sensitive and powerful rhythm section ever assembled. Al Casey was on guitar, Oscar Pettiford on bass, and Sidney Catlett on drums, and the four men developed a cyclonic propulsion.)

Tatum's second hurdle—his materials, or lack of them—was always there. With the exception of Duke Ellington and Fats Waller and a few others, it is only in the past fifteen or so years that jazz musicians, weary of the standard popular tunes, have begun writing their own materials. Before that, they generally reworked what was available, often and obviously rising to their best heights with Gershwin and Ellington and Arlen and Youmans and Kern. (Sometimes the reverse was true. One of the best solos Lester Young ever played was in "Flat Foot Floogie.") Tatum was an exception. He apparently had no desire to compose on paper, so he composed when he played. He did this by building baroque castles out of his arpeggios and chords and arhythmic whirlpools, and by using a sly, oblique wit that made listeners know exactly what he thought of the tune. Like most of the other Eastern pianists (Hines, Mary Lou Williams, the stride men), he never took the blues seriously. He loved to parody boogie-woogie and his rare straight blues came through broadly smiling.

Tatum's style was notable for its touch, its speed and accuracy, and its harmonic and rhythmic imagination. No pianist has ever hit notes more beautifully. Each one—no matter how fast the tempo—was light and complete and resonant, like the letters on a finely printed page. Vast lower-register chords were unblurred, and his highest notes were polished silver. (Tatum, needless to say, never muddied anything with the loud pedal.) His speed and precision were almost shocking. Flawless sixteenth-note runs poured up and down the keyboard, each note perfectly accented, and the chords and figures in the left hand sometimes sounded two-handed. Such virtuosity can be an end in itself, and Tatum was delighted to let it be in his up-tempo flag-wavers, when he spectacularly became a high-wire artist, a scaler of Everests. Tatum's bedrock sense of rhythm enabled him to play out-of-tempo interludes or whole choruses that doubled the impact of the implied beat, and his harmonic sense—his strange, multiplied chords, still largely unmatched by his followers, his laying on of two and three and four melodic levels at once—was orchestral and even symphonic.

Tatum would begin a medium-tempo number by playing, or playing with, the melody in ad-lib tempo for the first sixteen bars, rushing at and away from the melody, breaking his phrases with almost coy pauses, and then dancing on again. He would slip into a four-four tempo in the bridge with straight Fats Waller chords, using loose tenths in the left hand, and, near the end of the bridge, he would disappear into an arpeggio that climbed, descended, and reclimbed the keyboard, coming to an end in the middle of the final eight bars, where he would resume his ad-lib ministrations. He would start the second chorus in tempo, drop into sharp, on-the-beat single notes—*this* was Tatum the jazz musician, the no-nonsense improviser—and, for fear of letting such gravity get out of hand, abruptly shy away into another extended run, which would dissolve into a huge, arhythmic passage compounded of circular, bucking chords that lasted for the entire bridge. They would be followed by a snatch of stride-piano oompah bass, which rocked back and forth against chopping offbeat chords in the right hand. The final chorus would be a reprise of the first chorus and would often end in a ha-ha flatted chord that left the tune and the listener hanging in air. The fast numbers—the now-don't-you-forget-*this* numbers—were a dizzying mixture of meteoric runs, seemingly made up of thirty-second notes, stride-piano passages so fast they made one want to shout, spinning, out-of-tempo breaks, and madcap, on-the-beat single-note passages.

All of Tatum is on the Columbia release. The four early numbers reveal him still in the process of putting together his flying machine. The wind-whipped arpeggios are already there, but, though resplendent, they are disconnected and largely meaningless. Fats Waller is much in evidence, and so are Earl Hines and even Bix Beiderbecke. The harmonies are still ahead of their time. But Tatum is a perfect whole in the 1949 Los Angeles concert. Almost every number has passages to ponder and weep over—the runs being poured back and forth between the two hands in "Someone to Watch Over Me"; a "Yesterdays" that is a complete rebuilding of the tune, from the first note to the last; a tidal-wave, up-tempo "I Know That You Know"; a delicate and (so rare for Tatum) fond version of "Willow Weep for Me"; an incredibly light and deft takeoff to boogie-woogie in "Tatum Pole Boogie"; and a "Man I Love" with an arpeggio, lasting some eight bars, that no other pianist would dare because it is impossible.

1968

Miss Bessie

Munificence can be its own reward, but munificence that unexpectedly turns a profit is even better. Such is the case with Columbia's meticulous and unstinting Bessie Smith reissue project, which is now over half finished and which has suddenly become a best-seller. Since last summer, ninety-five of the magisterial singer's recordings have been brought out in three lavish two-LP sets ("Bessie Smith: The World's Greatest Blues Singer"; "Bessie Smith: Any Woman's Blues"; and "Bessie Smith: Empty Bed Blues"), and there are two volumes, of sixty-four recordings, still to come. The five volumes will be her collected works, for they will include almost everything she recorded. The exceptions are twenty unissued sides whose masters Columbia now cannot find, two not wholly certifiable sides made for another label at the outset of her career and mysteriously credited to the singer Rosa Henderson, and the sound track of Dudley Murphy's invaluable 1929 two-reeler, "St. Louis Blues," in which, backed by a choir and a medium-sized band, she sings the Handy blues with empyrean results. (This version of "St. Louis Blues" has long been put down by Bessie Smith admirers, who have grumbled about the choir's getting in the way of her voice and about the film itself, which they consider disrespectful and tacky. But the massed sounds of the choir and band act as a fitting catapult for her voice, which *was* of operatic proportions, and the picture, at once silly and remarkably stark, is the sole record we have of what Bessie Smith looked like in action. Murphy, who went on to do his famous "The Emperor Jones," was, like Carl Van Vechten, part of the Black Renaissance movement. Murphy wrote the scenario, which has to do with a black pimp who takes all Bessie's money and jilts her, and he made the film in three days in the summer of 1928 in a studio on Fourteenth Street.)

To Columbia's great surprise, the albums have taken off like a shot, and what started out as sort of a foundation altruistic project, a musical-archeological dig into the works of a blues singer who died thirty-four years ago, has become a thriving investment. Fifty thousand copies of the first album have been sold, and, of all three, more than a hundred thousand. Also surprising and heartening is that the records are apparently being bought not by jazz buffs (most of them probably have the four-record Bessie Smith reissue set that came out twenty years ago and included just forty-eight numbers) but by middle-class young people. (Last year, the late Janis Joplin shared the cost of a headstone for Bessie Smith's grave, which had been unmarked since her death.) So Bessie Smith is again playing Daddy Warbucks to Columbia. The other time was in 1923, when her first release, "Down Hearted Blues" and "Gulf Coast Blues," sold upward of a million copies and helped pull the company out of bankruptcy, a rescue that is hedgingly acknowledged in a footnote in the second album:

> It has often been said that Bessie Smith's recordings saved Columbia from bankruptcy. People close to the situation agree that the enormous sales of her records certainly were a contributing factor, but point out that such commercially popular artists as Bert Williams, Eddie Cantor, and the Two Black Crows recorded for the label, too.

Her whole life tended to be an irony. She was one of the great figures in what will probably be the last folk-art explosion in this country. (The first, which began around 1700, flourished in a miraculous manner until the Civil War, and it included primitive painters, furniture-makers, housebuilders, glass-makers, tinsmiths, potters, fraktur artists, woodcarvers and ivory-carvers, and quilt-makers.) It was a black folk-art explosion, which gained momentum at the turn of the century and is just now running down, and most of its members escaped into the world from the ghetto. But Bessie Smith, unlike such peers as Bill Robinson and Louis Armstrong and Duke Ellington and Ethel Waters, didn't. She performed almost entirely before black audiences, and the occasions were so utterly black and foreign to whites that when Carl Van Vechten recalled a concert she did in Newark in 1925 he sounded like a fever-ridden nineteenth-century explorer describing a newly discovered Stone Age people:

She was very large, and she wore a crimson satin robe, sweeping up from her trim ankles, and embroidered in multi-colored sequins in designs. Her face was beautiful with the rich ripe beauty of southern darkness, a deep bronze brown, matching the bronze of her bare arms. Walking slowly to the footlights, she began her strange rhythmic rites in a voice full of shouting and moaning and praying and suffering, a wild, rough, Ethiopian voice, harsh and volcanic, but seductive and sensuous, too, released between rouged lips and the whites of teeth, the singer swaying lightly to the beat, as is the Negro custom.

Now, inspired partly by the expressive words, partly by the stumbling strain of the accompaniment, partly by the powerfully magnetic personality of this elemental conjure woman with her plangent African voice, quivering with passion and pain, sounding as if it had been developed at the sources of the Nile, the black and blue-black crowd, notable for the absence of mulattoes, burst into hysterical, semi-religious shrieks of sorrow and lamentation. Amens rent the air.

Her recordings were made exclusively for black people, and in time Columbia even put "race records" on her labels. She worked on black vaudeville circuits (principally the Theatre Owners and Bookers Association, whose initials commonly stood among black performers for Tough on Black Asses), and she travelled in her own railroad car, which amounted to a high-class portable ghetto. Her life and death were chronicled only by the black press. (Even after she was dead, she was, in 1960, inadvertently kept in her place by Edward Albee's "The Death of Bessie Smith," a play built around the supposed racial reasons for her death instead of around her talents as a singer. But Albee has not been the only misguided Bessie Smith apologist. Through the years a compounding miasma of melodramatic half-truths have grown up around her and have converted her into an outsized tragic figure who was eventually toppled by her color and by her boundless appetites. Little of this is true.) Her life was an astonishing feat of magic; she was wealthy, famous, and inordinately gifted, yet she remained almost completely invisible to the white world.

But she was fleetingly visible in the black world, too, where history was mainly oral and frequently embellished. One of five or more children, she was born in poverty in Chattanooga sometime in the nineties. Her father died shortly after her birth and her mother died when she was nine. By the time she was in her teens, she had performed—probably as a dancer and clown and singer—in local amateur shows, and she had worked tent shows with Ma Rainey, the great blues singer. It is not certain how often she appeared with Ma Rainey, but it is clear from the recordings of both of them that Ma Rainey, who was ten years older, taught her a good deal, even though Bessie Smith refused to acknowledge it later on. (A not uncommon instance of artistic perverseness, when one considers how Hemingway eventually turned on Gertrude Stein, who taught him a lot about such technical matters as rhythm and repetition and the *mot juste*.) Bessie Smith continued working tent shows, but in 1923, after a couple of false starts on other labels, she made her first successful record, for Columbia. The next five or so years were meteoric. She divided her time between T.O.B.A. tours and Columbia recording sessions in New York. She made a great deal of money and became a mountainous presence in the black world. But the worms of decline were already at work. She and her husband, a Philadelphia policeman whom she married in 1923 and parted from in 1929, ran through her money (for a time it had been carefully watched over by Frank Walker, a Columbia official, and she had even bought a house in Philadelphia), and she began drinking heavily. And fashions were changing. Radio and movies had created a demand for more sophisticated singing, and by the late twenties her record sales had dropped precipitously. By the early thirties, she had dropped into semi-obscurity. Then she appears to have pulled things together, and in 1937, the year she died, she was planning a recording session, she was back on the road doing tent shows and theatres, and it has been suggested that she was thinking of acting (see the course of Ethel Waters' career).

Her death was nightmarish and stupid, and until the facts were dug up by two enterprising reporters—Sally Grimes, who published a story about Bessie Smith's death two years ago in *Esquire,* and Chris Albertson, who has just completed what should be the first reliable and thorough biography of Bessie Smith—it had been widely believed that she died after being badly injured in an automobile accident near Clarksdale, Mississippi, and after being refused admittance to a white hospital—the pivot, indeed, of Albee's play. Miss Grimes and Albertson reconstruct what happened this way: Bessie Smith was travelling South with her common-law husband and manager, Richard Morgan, from Memphis to Darling, Mississippi, where she was to do a show. It was around four on a Sunday morning in September and there was no moon, but the stars were out. Despite Albee, Morgan was not drunk. Ten miles north of Clarksdale, he ran into the back of a mail truck pulling out onto the road. (Rented mail trucks were used to deliver the Memphis Sunday papers.) The top was ripped off the car and it turned over. Minutes later, Dr. Hugh Smith, a surgeon who now practices in Memphis and who was going fishing with a friend, pulled up. They moved Bessie Smith from the middle of the road onto a grassy shoulder. (Smith didn't learn who she was until later.) Her right arm was almost severed at the elbow, she had been crushed internally, and she was bleeding. Another car, failing to see Smith's, piled into it, and two more people were hurt. A couple of ambulances arrived forty-five minutes later, and Bessie Smith was apparently taken to the G. T. Thomas Hospital, in Clarksdale. (The hospital no longer exists.) The ambulance driver who took her recalls that she died en route, but Albertson has found her death certificate, and it says that she died at the hospital just before noon and that her arm had been amputated: "Bessie Smith didn't have a chance," Smith told Miss Grimes. "I have no way of knowing the course of that ambulance, but I'll still say this, it wouldn't have made any difference if she'd been hurt with her injuries on the front steps of the University Hospital in Memphis. In 1937, with no blood bank and a lot of new techniques that weren't available then, she didn't have a prayer to survive. And it's quite probable that even in this day and time she wouldn't have made it."

To judge by her photographs and the glimpses of her in "St. Louis Blues," Bessie Smith was a stunning woman. She was five foot nine and generally weighed around two hundred, but she looks to have been all muscle and no fat. Both Zutty Singleton and Ethel Waters remember that she was not Bessie but Miss Bessie. She had a broad face, a high forehead, and a brilliant smile. Her fingers were long and graceful. She favored furs and boas and wigs and long, flowing robes. Like most heavy drinkers, she eventually became two people. Around 1933, Red Norvo and Mildred Bailey frequently had dinner with her and Morgan, in Harlem or at the Norvos' house, in Forest Hills (Bessie Smith enormously admired Mildred Bailey's singing—a whale applauding a minnow), and Norvo remembers her being "meek, humble, even-tempered, retiring," and not in the least Uncle Tom. Mezz Mezzrow, the clarinettist, recalls meeting her one night in a Chicago club: "When I told her how long I'd been listening to her records, how wonderful I thought they were . . . she was very modest—she just smiled, showing those great big dimples of hers, and fidgeted around, and I asked her would she do 'Cemetery Blues' for me, and she busted out laughing. 'Boy,' she said, 'what you studyin' 'bout a cemetery for? You ought to be out in the park with some pretty chick.' Every time I saw her from then on, Bessie kept kidding me about the kinky waves in my hair; she'd stroke my head once or twice and say, 'You ain't had you hair fried, is you, Boy? Where'd you get them pretty waves? I get seasick every time I look at them.'"
Bessie Smith was also, in the show-business way, excessively generous,

to the point, indeed, of virtually not being able to hold onto money. But drinking transformed her. Sidney Bechet, who worked with her in the early twenties, wrote, "Bessie could be plenty tough; she could really handle her own. She always drank plenty and she could hold it, but sometimes, after she'd been drinking a while, she'd get like there was no pleasing her. She had this trouble in her, this thing that wouldn't let her rest, a meanness that came and took her over." The singer Ida Cox put the two Bessies together: "Bessie Smith was an old, old friend and everybody loved her, which was why they was so shocked when she died in that accident. Of course, she *did* have enemies. Who don't? She was a very high-tempered person, and she didn't take anything from anybody. But she was a good girl, on the whole." She was, as Van Vechten points out, a majestic and hypnotic performer. She never used a microphone, but her voice literally filled the largest hall, and she moved around onstage with the special, awesome grace of very large people. (Some musicians in Memphis who had heard her sing there in a big hall told Norvo that the size and effect of her voice were astonishing.) But the way she looked is not completely lost to us, for, in that eerie way jazz musicians sometimes have of carrying on the images of revered predecessors (Buddy Tate for Herschel Evans, Jimmy McPartland for Bix Beiderbecke, Benny Morton for Jimmy Harrison), she lives on in the royal presence of Mahalia Jackson, who was a child when she heard her but who distinctly resembles her physically, as a performer, and as a singer.

There is no substitute for listening to a performer in the flesh, but the magnitude of Bessie Smith's voice is more than suggested in her recordings. It is, in some of her later and technically better ones, *there*. Her voice unquestionably had operatic possibilities, and in another time and place she might have become a diva. (The fortunate lack in this country of the European tradition of guilds and academies in which the young and talented are classically trained is one of the chief reasons that American folk art has flourished so long and so well. Consider that marvellous folk anachronism Erroll Garner. He cannot read a note and was never taught the piano, but lessons would destroy the uninhibited and immensely inventive primitivism that gives his style its charm.) She had a heavy, almost ominous contralto, a "cast-iron" voice, as Berton Roueché has felicitously put it. But her voice was not dense or inflexible like Paul Robeson's. It had a spacious, easy sound that one can almost walk into. It was warm, bearish, and utterly commanding (compare the cold, controlled voices of Carmen McCrae and Anita O'Day). Even more striking was the way she moved this massive instrument around, for she had, within her limits, a flawless technique. (Her breathing sometimes got in the way of her phrasing.) She landed with both feet on every note, she had exact pitch, her bent notes stopped precisely where she wanted them to, her vibrato was controlled and effortless, and she had perfect diction. She also had a superb sense of rhythm, and she could move her phrases anywhere around the beat she wanted, and in doing so she became the first modern jazz performer—a performer of considerable influence on everyone from Louis Armstrong to Billie Holiday. One difficulty she never surmounted, and that was not of her making. The power of her delivery often flattened her materials. When she sang an undistinguished blues, it was like watching a tack being driven in with a sledge hammer. Her style never changed during the ten years she recorded. (Her attack varied, of course, for she sang pop tunes, gospel-type songs, off-color songs, and novelty numbers as well as blues.) All of it was there in her first recording, and nothing had diminished in her last. Indeed, she probably had another ten or twenty years left within her, and she knew it, for she had said she would not retire until 1960.

Columbia has done a herculean job on the Bessie Smith reissues. It has been able to find only fifty-seven intact Bessie Smith masters in its vaults, so decent prints of the hundred and three remaining sides, some of them in circulation for forty-seven years, have been searched out and borrowed from collectors. The records have been subjected to a new remastering process developed by Larry Hillyer, a Columbia engineer, and the results are a wonder. The pre-electrical recordings (electrical recording came in in 1925) have an uncanny presence and clarity, and the electrical recordings are even better. (Would that Hillyer's process could be applied to the marvellous, seminal 1923 King Oliver Creole Jazz Band recordings, which, with their tinny, distant toylike sound, are all but unintelligible.) The records are being reissued in an odd but acceptable order. The first album includes the first sixteen records she made (February of 1923 to June of 1923), and the final sixteen (April of 1930 to November of 1933). The second album runs from September of 1923 to January of 1924 and from May of 1929 to March of 1930, and the third album goes in like fashion. There is more than enough gold scattered through the three albums, even though one simply has to get used to the clomping, Sunday-school pianists and whinnying clarinettists she was generally offered as accompanists. They seem not to have bothered her much, and they are more than compensated for when she is accompanied by Fletcher Henderson and Joe Smith and Charlie Green, or by James P. Johnson, who was the most sympathetic accompanist she ever had. Of particular interest in the first album are "Black Mountain Blues," "Hustlin' Dan," and a couple of pseudo-gospel numbers in which she is backed by James P. and a bumbling vocal group. The second album includes the classic moaning, subterranean rendition of "Nobody Knows You When You're Down and Out," recorded in 1929 by someone who really was, and the perfect "Dirty No Gooder's Blues." Charlie Green and Joe Smith and Henderson are on hand in the third album, and there are a dozen delights, among them "Weeping Willow Blues," "House Rent Blues," "Spider Man Blues," "Ticket Agent Ease Your Window Down," and the celebrated and funny six-minute "Empty Bed Blues," with its lumbering double-entendre lyrics. (Note also, in this album, the photograph of Bessie Smith, probably taken just after her career began to boom. She is wearing a dark, expensive silk dress, her hair is swept back, and she is fingering a long loop of pearls. Her head is slightly and beseechingly tilted. The veiled, inward-looking expression in her eyes is almost unendurable, and so is her sheer beauty. It is a very great photograph.) But the best moments in the three albums take place during her last recording date, under the direction of John Hammond. It includes "Do Your Duty," "Gimme a Pigfoot," "Take Me for a Buggy Ride," and "Down in the Dumps." (Bobby Short has kept "Pigfoot" alive by singing it rousingly well almost every night when he is at the Café Carlyle.) Hammond put together the best band that ever worked behind her—Frankie Newton (trumpet), Chu Berry (tenor saxophone), Benny Goodman, Jack Teagarden, Buck Washington (piano), Bobby Johnson (guitar), and Billy Taylor (bass)—and it shows in her singing. In many ways these are the finest sides she made, and they probably come closest to how she sounded in front of an audience. She swings, her voice is limber and free (though she seems a little short of breath here and there), and there is a steady and impassioned exuberance. The band is used behind her much as similar all-star groups were used in the Billie Holiday 1935–38 sessions, which Hammond also supervised. It plays loose ensembles or organ chords under her ("Buggy Ride"), the horns provide obbligatos ("Down in the Dumps," in which Teagarden and Newton, working with her in the first and last choruses, respectively, become, in a manner I have never heard anywhere else, startling alter-voices), and there are ample solos. (Newton, using those tremulous bent notes and easy legato intervals of his, is particularly winning in "Do Your Duty" and "Pigfoot.") Hammond recently talked about the recording session: "I was twenty-two, and it was a marvellously productive year for me. I was driven. It was the year I covered the Scottsboro case and made Bessie Smith's last record date. I had found her in a gin mill in Philly, where she was a singing hostess. She was very broke and she was very excited about doing the date even though I told her there wouldn't be much money in it—

two hundred for her and two hundred for the band, all of which I paid myself. I got that band together out of left field, and it was a mixed one, which was still a rarity then. Chu and Frankie and Teagarden had never worked together before, nor had they ever worked with Bessie. In fact, some of them had never even *seen* her. Buck Washington, of the old vaudeville team of Buck and Bubbles, couldn't read, and he wasn't the greatest choice on piano, but James P. Johnson, who would have been perfect, was out of town. I had to use a guitar because she wouldn't let me use a drum. The session was scheduled for ten in the morning—it was probably the only morning record date she ever had, and probably the only one where there was no liquor—and the four numbers were finished by one-thirty. All the songs, which she chose herself, were by Coot Grant and Sox Wilson. We had just one engineer and an old R.C.A. mike, which she stood at least two feet from. She wore a plain dark dress, and I would guess she weighed about one hundred and eighty at the time. She was an absolutely direct black woman. No Tomming, not a shade of the phony to her. The session was held in a small studio at 55 Fifth Avenue. Ethel Waters was in the building that day, and she and Bessie loathed each other, so I made very sure they didn't meet. Benny Goodman, who was then the Columbia house clarinettist, is only on one track because he had to leave for a Ben Selvin record date in the next studio. At the end of the session, the musicians all thanked me, and that doesn't happen very often."

But there are sides to come in the last two albums that are just about equal. They include the numbers done with members of Fletcher Henderson's band and the series with Louis Armstrong (Churchill and De Gaulle doing duets), in which he nearly overpowers *her*. Two of the Smith-Armstrong sides are extraordinary—"Reckless Blues" and "St. Louis Blues." Both also have Fred Longshaw on the harmonium, a wheezing, mysterious, organ sort of instrument. In the first, she sings with a sweet, sotto-voce sadness that is unique in her recordings, and in the second, taken at a slow, stately tempo, she gives a calm, prayerlike reading of that noble blues that is one of the masterpieces of recorded music.

1971

IV
People 1968–1971

It's Detestable
When You Live It

In Los Angeles, midway between Beverly Hills and Watts, there is a
small, factorylike two-story building that is occupied on the ground
floor by the Urban League and on the second floor by R.P.M. International. (The initials stand for Recordings, Publishing, and Manage-
ment.) The building, of gravy-colored stucco, blends easily into a
nondescript, old-fashioned residential area dotted with small stores
and small businesses. It has windows only on the ground floor, it is
rectangular and flat-topped, and, except for its partly glassed-in front,
it is as expressionless as a brick. But its insides, like a poker player's
thoughts, are startling. A flight of stairs carpeted in Florida orange
climbs from the foyer to an orange-and-white reception room containing a switchboard, a desk, an orange-haired receptionist, a leather
sofa, a couple of leather chairs, and a coffee table displaying the newest
issues of *Down Beat, Billboard, Hollywood Reporter,* and *Record
World.* Two facing doors open into yellow halls. At one end of one
of the halls, off which are a dozen brightly colored cubbyhole offices,
is a spacious yellow-and-blue-and-black recording studio equipped
with a piano and an organ, clusters of microphones, and a control
room jammed with glistening sound equipment and resembling the
cockpit of a jet plane. At the opposite end of the hall are adjoining
mogul offices. In the bigger one, three of the walls are painted yellow
and the fourth is made of rough brown cork blocks. The wall-to-wall
carpet is bronze. A dreadnought V-shaped table-desk, set before a
high-backed leather chair, faces the door, and arranged around the
walls are an upright piano, a television set, a long leather sofa, and
a card table ringed by chairs. An enormous moonlike lighting fixture
is set into the ceiling. The smaller office is a frenetic twin: the desk

and the cork wall and the sofa are black and the floor has brilliant red carpeting. This one is occupied by Joe Adams, the executive vice-president of Ray Charles Enterprises, which is the heart and mind of R.P.M. International, and the bigger office is occupied by Adams' friend and boss, Ray Charles, the unique, blind, thirty-nine-year-old singer, pianist, composer-arranger, music publisher, recording executive, and promoter.

Charles *is* the American Dream. He is wealthy and world-famous and inordinately gifted. But none of this, his talents excepted, was given him. He was born in sub-log-cabin poverty in the Deep South at the start of the Depression, he went blind when he was seven, he was an orphan at fifteen, he has been harried by drugs, and he is black. Despite all this, he has solved the Midas-touch-versus-artistic-integrity problem with extraordinary grace. He is, in his naked, powerful manner, in a class with Billie Holiday and Bessie Smith and Louis Armstrong, and, in a country that has never counted jazz as one of its blessings, he is revered by every class, color, and creed. (In the past couple of years, this reverence accounted for three million-sales albums.) There is no one explanation for this miracle. Perhaps it is because Charles almost *touches* his listeners' emotions with his voice, perhaps his wild, down-to-the-bone singing offers a safety valve, a purgative in a turbulent time, perhaps the iron honesty of his voice helps offset our haywire morals, or perhaps it is simply because he is a zealously concentrated performer whose singing and presence and timing form a flawless hypnotic force.

Charles' style, fed by a bottomless emotional well, has many sides. He can sing anything short of lieder and opera. He has recorded standard popular songs, country-and-Western music, down-home blues, American anthems such as "Old Man River," novelty numbers, rock and roll, the Beatles, and folk music. He works with equal ease in front of a small jazz band, a big band, vocal groups, choruses, and strings. (The sound of his pinewoods voice tearing along over violins and a choir is one of the wonders of music.) He can shape his baritone voice into dark, shouting blocks of sound, reduce it to a goose-pimpling whisper, sing a pure falsetto, yodel, resemble Nat Cole at his creamiest, and growl and rasp. He is always surprising. Yodels follow deep-throated rasps, he dwindles from stark recitative to a soft, fleeing moan, he rocks along way behind the beat and then jumps into metronomic time, he shouts asides to his accompanists or the audience between words, he bends and cracks and splits notes in treasonous places, and he is a master of melismatics. Insofar as it is humanly possible, he never repeats himself; a 1967 performance of "Georgia on My Mind" and a 1970 one are minutely and marvellously different. He is his own best accompanist, playing a piano that ranges from the backwoods blues to a clean, Nat Cole single-note style, and he is a competent, swinging alto saxophonist. His compositions, gospel-flavored and often funny, are a natural extension of his singing, and so are his arrangements, with their economy and their affecting voicings.

His appearance is deceptive. From a distance, he looks frail and spidery. He has a shuffling, bent-kneed walk, and at the piano he sways wildly from side to side or rears back to the point of falling over. A steady smile and big, ever-present dark glasses mask his face and make him seem smaller than he is. But close up he is tough and campact. He has wide, boxers' shoulders and a flat, trim waist, a high forehead, close-cropped hair, flaring cheekbones, and a jutting, stony chin. His speaking voice is deep and guttural and hand-hewn. He talks quickly and his language moves between sunny, sprawling Southern colloquialisms and lofty Northern abstractions. He is startling on the telephone; he literally barks and grunts. And he is in constant motion—reading from a Braille notebook with one hand and holding a telephone with the other, lifting his head and shooting out his chin, wringing his hands or clapping them softly together, and standing up for no reason to do a little hopping dance and then abruptly sitting down.

In recent years, Ray Charles the singer has become the cork bobbing on top of the Ray Charles Show, which appears, on a concert basis, in night clubs and concert halls around the country and in Europe. This generally opens with his big band, a seventeen-piece group that is the equal in precision and fervor of any current big band. The band plays a batch of instrumentals, and the Raelets, a comely female vocal quartet, sing several numbers. After an intermission, and with the audience kneaded and ready to rise, Charles himself appears, and sings and talks plays his way through a dozen or more numbers. Joe Adams comes onstage for some you-quit-now-no-I-won't badinage with Charles, and the two men depart arm in arm, leaving a limp, grateful house. It is a dazzling, expensive, moving, clockwork show.

In January, February, and March the Ray Charles Show rests. But Charles spends most of this time in his office at R.P.M., arranging bookings for the coming year, managing his small stable of young talents, memorizing lyrics, walking down the hall to record, consulting with Joe Adams, holding staff meetings, editing tapes, considering new songs to record, talking on the telephone, and granting interviews.

"Most days I get here late, but I stay late, till nine or ten," he says. "I can get more done between 5 and 10 P.M. than I can during the day. Actually, one of these days I might run for senator or governor and get a bill passed to make the working day from about

11 A.M. to 7 P.M. The way it is now, most people don't go to bed until twelve or one anyway, and the next day they walk into that office at eight-thirty or nine evil. My way, you'd read your papers and drink your coffee and leave your house nice and new about nine or ten. I live in an area called View Park. It's about fourteen minutes from here and sixteen minutes from the airport. I do a lot of coming and going to the airport and to my office and I like to get there without a lot of hassle. My house is a three-level structure and it's built up against a steep hill. You have an upstairs and the next floor is even with the ground and then there's another part downstairs. I never counted them, but with all the bathrooms and the den and the playroom and the bedrooms, it's gotta have fifteen or twenty rooms. Roughly that. It's a yellow house and when you come in the front door there's a lot of glass and high ceilings. We have a tennis court and a swimming pool. You couldn't pay me to live in New York, which is just the nerve center, the money center. I like the slow pace out here, which is more like the pace of Europe.

"I've never been able to understand why the people where you live should be any problem. Anyway, what the hell difference does it make if you're colored or white? I just want to be treated fair. And I don't want to be treated better because I'm blind. When I went to school, there just weren't any books about us. It was George Washington and it was just like a dictatorship. We were told what we could learn and that was it. Hitler couldn't have killed all the Jews he did by himself. He had to condition other people. It's the same with black people. That nappy hair. You've been taught it's bad. You're conditioned. Same thing, why is it *black*mail instead of *white*mail? I've seen a commercial on television where they have these two cars testing gasoline, and the white one always goes the furthest. When you have people who have been *made* to feel imperfect, the problem is how to teach them they *are* good, that it has nothing to do with color. After all, a lot of the whites who first came over here were outcasts, religious or from prisons, but people just want to control other people, they have to control other people. Now the Northern people always say, 'Did you see what they're doing to the Negroes in Alabama or Mississippi?' but they're doing the same thing up here, only they're sneaky about it. Down South, at least they're open. They *tell* you. I wonder what would happen if Christ *was* black. 'His face shall shine like patent leather and His hair be like the wool of a sheep,' it says somewhere in the Gospels. I would like to see what would happen if He came back and He came in the wrong color."

The telephone rang. Charles answered it, stood up, and rocked back and forth: "Yrrrrh. Yeh. Yeh. Yeh-yeh. All right, sweetie, all right. Yeh." He banged the phone and sat down. His left hand swept the desk top until he found a package of cigarettes. He took one out and lit it.

"It's a cinch something's going to kill you, whether you smoke or not. I told myself I'm going to quit, but it's just a question of how you enjoy the time you have. I'm not one who worries about coming back. I don't quite believe God is going to take the good people and raise them from the dead, but if He did I don't picture Him needing to take the nothings of the world and raising them, too. The bad people would just be the dust the good people walked over. That was my wife, Della, on the phone. We have three boys, and we've been married about fifteen years. Ray, Jr., is fourteen, David is eleven, and Robert is ten. Then I have a daughter by a previous marriage— Evelyn. She's twenty. My wife and I are about as average as you can get. We have many happy moments and we have our fights. But it's got to be fifty-one forty-nine in a marriage, and I'm the fifty-one, as long as I'm out there making a living. My wife understands that. A woman *wants* a man to be a man. It's the same with kids. They really *want* guidance. When we say 'No!' they know it's authority speaking. I met my wife in Houston. She has a big family, but I don't know that much about them. I'm not that interested in having my house overrun by family, and Della is very considerate about that. She sees her father and mother from time to time, and last Thanksgiving, when I was on the road, she had a dinner for forty or fifty, with all the little cousins and the aunts and all. But that would have been all right with me. I like to see people happy. When I'm on the road, I'm home in pieces—two or three days here, a week there. It's not so bad. It used to be a lot worse. I'm fortunate enough to have my own plane. I can do four hundred miles to a gig in an hour instead of spending the whole day in a bus.

"We have a Viscount turboprop—a four-engine prop jet with Rolls-Royce engines. The way we have the configuration of it, I have a lounge and sleeping area in the back, and in the rest of the plane we took out a lot of the seats and spaced the remaining ones plenty far apart. There are roughly thirty-five of us on the road, but the plane could hold sixty-four. We bought it year before last, and before that we had a Martin 404, a two-engine job, which could carry about forty. And we have a little twin-engine Cessna 310, which holds about five people. I like to fool with radio and engineering when we're flying, but I believe I could set down a plane if I had to without killing myself. I might tear a wing off, but I don't believe I'd kill myself. Anyway, we have two full-time pilots, and we've been lucky. Once, we were in the Cessna—there was the pilot and co-pilot and a couple of friends—and we were coming into the Oklahoma City airport. It was freezing outside and the heater that is supposed to defrost the windshield broke and the windshield was coated with ice and we literally couldn't see a damn thing, even when we got down to two hundred feet. So we circled and circled, and of course the more we did the more ice the plane picked up and the heavier she got, and on top of that we were running out of fuel. Then suddenly a hole appeared through the ice on the windshield. It looked exactly like somebody had taken an icepick and made it. It was a miracle. So the pilot could see the strobe lights and he brought us in. The pilot I had then, Tom McGarity, like to broke his neck on the ice on the ground when he got out of the plane, but he didn't panic up there. We've never had any trouble with the Martin and the Viscount. Lightning hit the Martin once and went straight through the plane. It made a *bang* and scared the hell out of everybody, and you could see it come out the other side."

There was a knock on the door, and Joe Adams came in. He is over six feet tall and slim and Broadway-handsome. He has arching eyebrows and a small mustache. His hair is combed flat. He is a clotheshorse, and he was wearing a green V-neck sweater, a turtleneck shirt, and olive pants. His voice is low and even, and he speaks with B.B.C. precision.

"I have the band list," he said to Charles. "Contract time is coming up. You want to put your thoughts on who you want and who you don't?"

"Go ahead," Charles said, and lit a cigarette.

Adams sat down on the edge of the desk, swung one leg slowly back and forth, then began to read the roster. (Some of the names have been changed.) "Leroy Cooper."

Charles nodded.

"Wallace Davenport."

"He's all right," Charles said.

"George Jay."

"I'd like to do a little research on that."

"Fred Rooney."

"Yeh. I'd love to have him back. He's a preacher, that one."

"Albert Scullen."

"I could go either way."

"Teddy Romaine and Barklie Henry."

"I *have* to have them."

"John Masterman."

"I'm going to do a little research on that, too."

"David Griffin."

"I believe we can live without him."

Adams read the rest of the list, Charles made his yeas and nays and maybes, and Adams left.

"Out of seventeen guys in a band, it always works that you have just six or seven who are the key men—the men who concentrate and work with the younger cats and keep the outfit straight and sharp. It's very hard for a guy in the band to skate on me. I can hear every horn, every note. Musicians are not the easiest people to handle. A lot of times I make people nervous in the band, so I try and be a little close with them. If there is something personal a musician has on his mind and he can't handle it, he can come to me, and fine. I've always wanted a big band to work behind me. I like the sound. You can make a small band from a big band, but you can't make a big band out of a small band. I'm a person who takes his time, and when I could afford a big band I put one together. And I've been fortunate enough to maintain everything new I've tried. It was my mother who taught me that patience.

"Her name was Areatha and my father's name was Bailey Robinson. My name is really Ray Charles Robinson. Sugar Ray Robinson was a powerful man when I was coming up, so I took my first and middle names and dropped the last. Then, of course, later I ran into the other Ray Charles, the choir director, but it hasn't been any trouble, outside of getting each other's mail once in a while. I was born in Albany, Georgia, in 1930. September 23rd. But my parents moved to Florida when I was two or three months. We moved about forty miles east of Tallahassee to a little bitty place called Greenville. My father worked for the railroad, cutting and repairing the crossties and connecting the steel. But he was also a mechanic and a builder. He could build anything. In the South in those days, you learned to do many things to make a living. We were poor people in every sense of the word. My father taught me if you ever get your hands on a dollar you always keep enough to get home on and you never let that dollar become your word. If your word is no good, your money isn't, either. He could go downtown and give his word anywhere, and that was it. If he said he'd be somewhere on Monday at eight in the morning, it was Monday at eight, not Tuesday at ten or eleven. I try and do that. I work maybe three hundred jobs a year, and in the last fifteen years I've missed just three jobs and I've only been late six times. My father was what they used to call a 'good nigger.' But he was no Uncle Tom. He just wanted to be left alone, and he was not interested in chasing some white woman. He was very well respected. If a white man liked you, he liked you and he'd do anything in the world for you, and that was the way my father was treated. My mother was a sweet lady. She cooked and worked for white families, and she made all our clothes. And she had a strong feeling about independence. Just because I was blind, she'd tell me, didn't mean I was stupid. 'One of these days I'm gonna die and you're gonna have to take care of yourself,' she'd say. So I was taught to wash and scrub and cook and rake the yard and make my own bed. I'd cut wood, too, which caused a situation in the church, where they got to saying that my mother was making that poor blind boy cut wood when a piece of wood might fly up and hit him in the face, so she went and told them that even when a man with sight cut wood sometimes a chip flew up and hit him in the face and even if he saw it he couldn't move fast enough, and that quieted them. If I hadn't of been taught by my mother, I wouldn't be anywhere. I was brought up not to beg. Even now, I wouldn't beg nobody for *nothing*. If we had a little extra, we knew it, and if we didn't, we knew it, and nobody said a word. I think my mother killed herself working with my father to make ends meet, and I'm sorry she didn't live long enough to see me become something.

"I was born with good sight and I didn't start having trouble with my eyes until I was five. It started by my eyes running like hell all the time. Not tears—it was too thick. It was more like mucus, and when I'd wake up in the morning it was so thick I'd have to pry my eyes open. The pressure began to build up behind my eyes and there was a pain like the pain you get in your head when you stay up for two or three days and don't sleep. Then my horizon began to shorten up. The local doctor was not a specialist, but he did the best he could. He gave me drops and told me to stay out of strong light. But it got worse and worse, and when I was seven I was stone-blind. I often think of my parents having to watch all that. It was probably glaucoma. At least, that's what doctors I've talked to since say it sounds like. Glaucoma used to damn near kill people, but now thirty per cent get their sight back and forty get partial sight. I remember many things about seeing: the way the sun looks, the moon looks, my mother looks, and the colors, the standard colors, the mother colors—red, green, black, white. I remember the sunsets. I only use my memory of seeing if an occasion calls for it. If I want to buy some clothes, I can get a true picture of the colors using my memory of the mother colors. Normally, I don't look to the past for instruction. There are so many things you can see without the eye, and ninety-five per cent of seeing is unimportant anyway. I know what this desk is like and what this chair is like and what a woman is like. I don't have any trouble with food or taste, and I've never been a heavy eater anyway. I like a good cup of tea and about a gallon of milk a day. And there are things I don't want to see, like people lying in the street with their heads bashed open. I know what my kids look like to me. I suppose that if there was anything in the world I really wanted to see before I die it would be them. I see as much through touch as most people do through seeing. The majority of the time there is someone with me, but I'm not sure that wouldn't be the same if I could see. The first time I came to New York, I came alone, and before I had money I did everything by myself. Now, I don't drive a car, but I don't ever care about driving a car. I ride bicycles and motor scooters. I've been known to do that. I'd love to ride a bicycle in Central Park when I'm in New York next time—go out with two or three people and they'd ride right near me and talk. We used to ride bikes in the hills around home, but I don't recommend it for everybody. Your senses don't become better by theirselves. You develop them. I used to shut myself up in a hallway and take a golf ball and throw it against the end of the hall and try and catch it before it passed me coming back. I'd judge where it was by the way the sounds bounced off the walls, the same way when I was walking down the street by myself, my step would make an echo and the echo would get louder and louder when I approached something big, like a building. *Every*thing makes a sound, even crêpe-rubber soles on a rug, but you have to train yourself to pay attention all the time. If I came to a very busy intersection, where the traffic sounds got mixed, I'd get myself in among a bunch of women, and when they crossed I'd cross with them. And I caught the trains and buses and planes by myself. If you hand the ticket man a one-dollar bill for a five-dollar ticket, he'll let you know, and I'd always ask for my change to be counted out in singles. I don't think in all the years I was out there by myself that anybody beat me for a penny.

"We were tough kids then, stuck in that little town in the woods in the South, where they gave you castor oil for everything. It was different from now and it helped you later in life. If we fell out of a tree and knocked our wind out, we got up and kept running. If we got cut, we'd stick some clay dirt in the cut, or a cobweb, and that would clot it. If we had boils, we'd take the thin skin from just inside the shell of an egg and put it on the boil, and it would burst, or we'd take a hot brick from on top of the stove and pee on it and create steam and the steam would burst the boil. We'd make tea out of honey and lemon and sassafras, and it would sweat out a cold, and if we ate too much candy we'd take castor oil and a few drops of turpentine, and, baby, it worked. And we ate a lot of hard foods—raw sweet potato and hard pears and coconuts and the meat from sugarcane. They'd exercise your gums."

Adams came in again. "I thought you'd like to hear this little piece from the Chicago *Tribune* about the John Bishop Trio, which we handle." Adams read it.

"Thass nice, thass very nice," Charles said.

Adams went out, and Charles leaned back in his chair and lit a cigarette, lifted his glasses slightly, rubbed his eyes, and pushed the glasses back in place. He seemed to be staring at the light in the ceiling.

"I love to work with young people. I wished it was that one day a week, Sunday or something, the big newspapers would devote space to what the young people do *right*. Let the young people *know* that they don't have to rob a bank to get in the news. If I was in charge of a newspaper, I'd find out what the young people are doing that's *good*, and print it, so they'd know we care about them. It's like my feeling about drugs. What I did is done and that's that. I've been talking about drugs to the papers and everybody for the past two or three years and I could continue to talk about it for thirty more years. But if you make a mistake and rectify it, you don't want to hear about it the rest of your life. I'm no missionary or pope and I'm not trying to reform anybody. I did it and it's done and over and that's that."

Charles picked up the telephone and asked when the Sony people were coming to demonstrate a portable motion-picture camera. He put the phone down, missed the cradle by an inch, and jiggled the receiver into place.

"Well, I didn't start school until I was seven, when my parents sent me to the St. Augustine School for Deaf and Blind Children, in St. Augustine. It was a state school. Before that, my mother, who was not the most educated woman in the world, taught me. She taught me the ABCs and a little arithmetic, and she taught me how to print. I can still print today. I can't write, but I can print. I was treated very fair in school. I was normal there, happy there. In September, the state bought your train ticket to get you there, and in June they bought you another one to get you home, but at Christmas your parents had to buy the tickets. Somehow, my mother always got the money. I remember leaving at Christmas, and there would be two or three kids left at school who wouldn't get home. I didn't want to leave them there alone and I also wanted to see my mother. The school went through the tenth grade, which is what I was in when my mother died. I was fifteen. She had some sort of gastric disorder. She'd eaten a sweet-potato pie or sweet-potato bread and she blew up like a balloon overnight and it stopped her heart and she died the next day. I came right home. I couldn't cry right then, and I couldn't eat for three weeks, and I almost died for it. My father was never the same after that, and he died—they said from diabetes—not long after. My mother was thirty-three and my father about forty. There were just no medical facilities outside of the local doctor. The nearest hospital was forty miles away, in Georgia. If you got sick you went to bed and Mrs. Reynolds or Miss Jones or Miss Williams, ladies in the area, they took turns and stayed up with you at night.

"My mother had brainwashed me to the point where I had to be independent. There was no point in living off this aunt and that uncle, and anyway they was mostly living in places like Baltimore, which was a *long* way away. But I knew some people in Jacksonville through my mother—Lena Mae and Freddy Thompson. I agreed to live with them because I could pay them something. I'd go out and play piano at tea parties and such and make five dollars and give half to them. They fed me and took care of me. I had picked up my first piano at home. There was a little café next to us and it was run by a man named Wiley Pittman. He had a piano there and he was of the boogie-woogie school—Meade Lux Lewis and Albert Ammons and the like. When he played, I'd run in and listen. He must of taken note. He would let me sit on the piano bench next to him and bang on the keys. I didn't know *nothing*. He would tell me, 'Play it, play it. You're doing fine.' I'll always love that man for that. He just let me bang on the piano, and one time when I was about six and I was losing my sight and there were some other people in the café, he called over to me and said, 'R.C.'—which is what people called me—'I want you to play like you played yesterday.' I had the nerve to get shy when I couldn't play a damn thing anyway, but I sat there moving my left hand back and forth and banging with my right and they clapped just to make me feel good. From that point on, I loved to play music. By the time I was seven I could play little tunes, one finger, then two fingers, and I had always loved to sing from the time I was tiny. Mr. Pittman had a jukebox and I'd hear those blues by Big Joe Turner and Tampa Red and Big Boy Cruddup and Sonny Boy Williams. When I got to school, I started studying. I was an excellent musical student. I studied Chopin and Mozart and Bach. Beethoven had a lot of feeling, but Bach was nervous, with all those lines running against each other. Classical music is a great foundation for playing jazz. You play correctly, with the right fingering. With classical music you play exactly what the man wrote, but in jazz, when you get rid of the melody, you put yourself in. So every time I thought my teacher wasn't listening, I played jazz. And I listened to Goodman and Basie and Ellington and Erskine Hawkins and Andy Kirk and Lunceford and Tiny Bradshaw and Artie Shaw. Shaw got me interested in the clarinet, so I took it up, along with the alto saxophone and a little trumpet. Shaw had more feeling than Benny Goodman, and I loved his sound. And of course my favorite pianist, then and now, my idol, was Art Tatum.

"I stayed with the Thompsons about six or seven months. I had worked a little in Jacksonville in Henry Washington's big band, but he didn't need me, so I went to Orlando and got a job with Joe Anderson, who had a sixteen-piece band. I wrote arrangements for him and I sang. I've done a lot of arranging and occasionally I still do one. I can hear the whole arrangement in my head, note for note, and I just sit down and dictate it. We didn't work too often, and there were times when I was sustaining myself on beans and water and crackers, and it came to be a heavy proposition—a malnutrition thing. I can really understand how people can get chained into situations like that, how people can get stuck in a web and can't get out. Men sit and stare and women become prostitutes. I was one of the fortunate ones. I had this little profession and I did get out of it. But it was total hell twenty years ago, with the race thing and being blind, too. It's easy for people who eat warm food and sleep in warm beds to talk about it, but it's detestable when you live it. I stayed with Anderson three or four months, then I went to Tampa. I knew a guy worked in a music store, and one night he took me to this little club and I sat in on piano with a hillbilly group, the Florida Playboys. Their piano player was sick and I got the job. It was a strange thing. They were white, but they were always nice to me. Every night they took me home, and when the girls came up and talked to the fellows I didn't feel left out. I wasn't interested in chasing no white girl. My only interest was music and getting my hands on some money. I always loved hillbilly music. I never missed the 'Grand Ole Opry.' It was honest music, not cleaned up, and it still is. They don't sing, 'I sat there and dreamed of you'; they say, 'I missed you and I went out and got drunk.' I learned how to yodel by being around the Florida Playboys. Then I went with a small combo led by Manzie Harris, and after I had saved my money with him for seven or eight months I decided I wanted to get out on my own, go to a nice-sized city the furthest from where I was. I was afraid of New York and Chicago. I had a friend, and we took a map of the country and he traced a straight line diagonally as far as it would go and it hit Seattle. I didn't know anybody there and nobody had sent for me, but I got on the bus. I got to Seattle at five in the morning. I went to a little hotel near the bus station and I was so tired I slept twenty-one hours. When I woke up, I asked downstairs what time it was and the lady said two o'clock, I thought it was two in the afternoon. She straightened me out and I asked where could I go to hear some music and she told me about a place, a private club called the Rocking Chair. I took a cab and knocked on the door and told the man I'd heard they was having a talent night. I pleaded with him and he said, 'O.K., you look older than eighteen. Come on in.' When I got my chance I sang 'Driftin' Blues,' and they went wild. People from various clubs in town were there and the man from the Elks Club heard me and two days later I had a job there. I put together a trio—the Macson Trio, with Gossie-D McGee on guitar and Milt Garritt on bass. I'd known McGee in Florida, so that was one of those strange coincidences. I never thought of calling the group the Ray Charles Trio, and when we got our first money—three hundred dollars—I divided it evenly, even though I was the leader. I didn't know anything. We worked at the Elks three weeks and then the Rocking Chair man approached me and asked me to come and work for him, and instead of giving two weeks' notice, which I didn't know about, either, I told the Elks man the whole story and he said, 'All right, you have told me the straight of the thing and I am very happy for you and you go.' I spent most of my time in Seattle in the Rocking Chair, but I also worked the Black and Tan, the 908, and the Washington Social Club. And I got married, but it didn't quite work out. We had a little trouble with the girl's mother. She thought I'd never amount to anything, and rightly, I guess. I don't blame her. But once we were married and every time there was some disagreement between us this girl she'd call her mother and her mother would lay it on me on the telephone. I didn't have any poise and I wasn't as nice as I am now. So I said some wrong things. But I think it could have worked out if the mother had said, 'Settle your own fights; it's between you-all now.' "

The Sony people were announced, and Adams ushered in a blond girl, a white man, and two Negroes. Charles stood up, swayed from side to side, and moved into the middle of the room, his right hand extended. Adams introduced the girl, Miss Becker, and the white man, Mr. Rice. The Negroes, Terry Wilcox and Howard Moorehead, are friends of Charles. Charles shook hands all around.

"I first met R.C. in a little country town in 1955," Wilcox said to Miss Becker.

"I remember," Charles said.

Rice was unpacking a big camera, a portable tape recorder, and several other pieces of equipment, and he was down on his knees.

"Come on over, Ray," said Moorehead.

Charles squatted. Rice said, "This is the battery charger and it has instructions."

"I don't like instructions," Charles said. "I like to find out myself how things work."

"This is the plus post and this is the negative," Rice said, and guided Charles' hands. He moved them quickly and lightly over the area, and Rice explained how everything worked. Charles nodded and began loading the tape machine himself. "Stay still, sweetie," he said to a reel of tape. "If I can get you on, we'll have some action."

Then Rice showed Charles the camera. His hands scuttled over it like big hermit crabs.

"The lighting is kind of poor in here," Moorehead said.

"I like it that way," Charles said. "Generally, I don't have any lights on at all. This is the one place in the building where we save on the electric. O.K., people. I appreciate all this. You get everything fixed up and I'm gonna take some pictures."

The Sony people shook hands with Charles.

The phone rang. "Yehrr," he said. "Tell the car to wait. I'll be there in five minutes."

Charles went into Adams' office. A chunky, elderly man was sitting on Adams' sofa. It was Al Williams, of the old Stepp Brothers dance team. "Joe, I'm going out a little while. I'll be back in about half an hour," Charles said, and the door closed after him.

Adams sat down behind his desk. It was gleaming and completely bare except for a couple of pens and a blotter. There was an abstract painting on one wall and photographs of Charles' planes on another.

"In 1959 Ray Charles was going out on the road and he asked me to go with him as the m.c.," Adams said, in his low, manicured voice. "They wanted a little dignity for the show. Then he asked me to go overseas with him. I went. And then he asked me to join him on a personal basis. I agreed. The first six weeks I never heard a word from him, so I quit. Two weeks later he sent for me, and I'm still with him. I've never been hired in the sense of a contract. A handshake between gentlemen. Eventually, he started forming his companies, and I now serve as his personal manager and the general manager and vice-president-treasurer of all of them. He's never told me what to do or how to do it. We have the kind of relationship where he's so astute that I should be paying him.

"I was born in Watts when no one had ever heard of Watts. I wanted to take public speaking in school, but they said, 'No, you'll never get a job in radio because you're a Negro.' I used to walk all over Los Angeles looking for work, and some of the people who turned me down are working for me now. I was the first Negro announcer in coast-to-coast radio, and I started with the disc jockey Al

Jarvis. I was with N.B.C. ten years, and when I quit I quit at the top, with a Number One rating. It was 1957, and there was no more creativity in the work for me. Along the way, I've worked as a speech-and-diction coach at M-G-M and done a lot of pictures and television shows. I was with Pearl Bailey in 'Carmen Jones.' Otto Preminger hired me. And David Merrick put me in 'Jamaica' with Lena Horne.

"I design all of Ray Charles' clothing as well as the gowns the Raelets wear. I designed this building, which we built in 1963, and I did all the interior decoration. I'm kind of blessed. I have the good fortune to have good taste. I like things clean and pure. The members of the band have eight changes of uniform and we carry ninety-seven shirts, so that they have a clean shirt every day. When I hire a man for the band I give him an instruction sheet, so he will know how I want him to dress and behave. No drinking on duty, no narcotics, and I will not allow profanity in public. I teach them pride in their work. You can set your watch by the time we start our shows. Once we took a job and were told to hit at eight o'clock. There were only four or five people in the hall. The man who hired us had figured on a half-hour leeway for himself. Well, he begged me to stop the show and I did, but I gave him hell. On the road, I have a road manager ond a stage manager and two bandboys, and there are outside people, like seam-stresses and tailors. I have learned to fly and I am now studying for my instrument rating. During the Second World War, I was with the 99th Fighter Squadron, the first all-Negro squadron, but I washed out. After I had joined Ray Charles, I was always ordering and buying airplane parts, and I wanted to know what they were for, so I took up flying. But I'm a cautious pilot, a scared pilot.

"Ray Charles is a strong man, a remarkable man. He didn't have much help, but he was a millionaire at thirty and he could quit work-ing now and be independently wealthy the rest of his life. People never used to think that he could even talk. But he can talk about any-thing. And he reads a great deal. He sees with his fingers. Once a little piece of equipment had to be replaced in the engine of one of our planes. The mechanics worked five hours on it and couldn't get it properly in place. Ray Charles said, 'Let me see what I can do with that. In five minutes he had the job done. He will never compromise himself or his materials. We were sitting in the office of the president of A.B.C. records in New York a while ago and the president—he's Larry Newton—said, 'Ray, I know how you can make a million dollars. Record an album of spirituals.' Charles refused. He felt it was wrong to tamper with religious music that way. He often works from impulse. One night I was leaving here around eleven, and when I went in to say good night he said, 'Get me a Corvette.' 'I'm sorry,' I said. 'What did you say?' 'Get me a Corvette. That's a car, a Chevrolet, and I want it in gold.' Luckily, I found an all-night automobile dealer who happened to have a gold Corvette. And he used to drive a scooter. There are two Cadillacs sitting out there in the parking lot, but I think he'd rather ride a scooter. I would sit behind him on it and apply pressure to his shoulders to tell him what direction to steer in, and sometimes, on an empty road, we would hit fifty-five. I've seen him go in a strange building and take a flight of stairs three or four steps at a time. If he wants to wear his green tuxedo instead of his black one, he appears in the green one. He tells the difference by finding some little thing on each suit—a loose thread, a button that is a bit off center, a pocket with something different about it. He is a good cook. And he can type seventy words a minute and he plays a good game of chess. He can do more than most people with sight. When we were making a recording of a tune called 'I Believe' and the Raelets were held up by bad weather and couldn't make the session, Ray Charles sang his part and then he sang all four of the Raelets' parts, in falsetto. It turned out beautifully."

Charles opened the door from his office and stood there swaying and smiling. "I'm back, Joe." He turned, went into his office, and, skirting his desk, sat down heavily. "You know, it's *rainin'* out there. Rains here, and everything comes to a stop. But it's better than Seattle, which I left in 1950 when I moved permanently to L.A. I'd made my first records earlier in the year, for a little record company called Swingtime, run by Jack Louderdale. We made them with the Macson Trio. I got an apartment on the west side of town, and I thought I wanted to stay. Lowell Fulsom, who had the first big hit of 'Every Day,' was here, and Louderdale thought I ought to go out on the road with him, so I did, as the added attraction. It was the first time on the road in my life. We went to Arizona and New Mexico and Texas. We went out there and tried our best to stay out there. It was exciting to me. It had a gloss. I stayed with Fulsom a year and a half, and once when we were going through Texas, Howard Lewis, who was a big promoter in that part of the country, told Lowell he should have an agent. He called Billy Shaw in New York, and they arranged a contract. Not long after, we went to the Apollo, in New York, and the Shaw agency came and heard us and they signed me and Billy Shaw told me, 'When the day comes that we don't produce for you, you don't need us. And when the day comes that you don't produce, we don't need you.' It sounded cold to me. I was young and enthusiastic, but later, when I got to understand business, I understood what he meant. Lowell began having his problems of various kinds and I decided I wanted to suffer through my own problems instead of his. I wouldn't downgrade him. He was essential to me, and so was Wiley Pittman and Howard Lewis and Jack Louderdale and Billy Shaw and the fine gentlemen at Atlantic Records, where I had my first big hit, in 1954. They were all links in the chain of my success. Shaw booked me as a single attraction, which meant they would send me to a little town and I'd play and sing with whatever musicians was there. I did it a couple of years, but it was hard. It was necessary for me to try and find out what it was like on my own, but playing one-nighters with all those different musicians . . . Man, I *love* music and I hate to hear it played wrong. Early in 1954, I went into a club in Philly and the band was so bad I just went back to my hotel and cried. That band couldn't read and they couldn't hear, either. I called the Shaw agency and told them I couldn't play the job. It was the first time I literally refused to play. They sent someone down to Philly, and the next day we found some musicians and I was able to finish the gig. I needed that job. I didn't have any pocketful of money. I couldn't afford to work with that band and I couldn't afford to work without it. But everything happens for a reason, and if it hadn't been for that experience I might have gone another long while without my own band, because it was a hell of a lot easier to book a single at seventy-five a week than someone with a whole band. I pestered the Shaw people to death and they loaned me the money to buy a station wagon, and I had enough money to make a down payment on a car for myself. I went down to Dallas and put a band together out of people I had heard one place or another. It had Leroy Cooper on baritone, David Newman on tenor, a couple of trumpets—John Hunt and a guy named Bridgewater—and Jimmy Bell on bass, and Bill Peoples on drums. I'd met my second wife, and after I got the band together we were married and moved into an apartment in Dallas. That was a damn good band, and we had our good times and our bad. We were on the road three hundred or three hundred and fifteen days a year, sometimes travelling seven hundred miles one day and a thousand the next, through hot July, or going the two hundred and forty miles between Dallas and Houston on pure ice, at five miles an hour and getting hit anyway by a car and only being forty-five minutes late for our gig. Our first big hit record was 'I Got a Woman,' and then there was 'A Fool for You' and 'What'd I Say' and 'Hallelujah I Love Her So.' My percentage of successes was extremely good. If you can count out seventy-five to twenty-five in your favor, you shouldn't gripe too much. I dearly loved the people at Atlantic. Their engineer, Tommy Dowd, was a marvellous man, and they never told me I had to record *nothing*. They'd submit materials, but I was always my own boss and sometimes I'd send all the tunes back. But this caused me to write my own things, like 'Hallelujah I Love Her So' and 'What'd I Say,' and I did all the arranging for the band. In 1957, when I felt ready to buy a house, my wife and I moved out here. We left Atlantic in 1959 and went with A.B.C. Paramount, where we had our first million-album seller. There were no bad feelings. It was just an honest business arrangement. A.B.C. does our distribution now. Beyond that, it's *no*body's business. The contract we have with them is forty pages long. The way things are set up here is we have Ray Charles Enterprises, which is composed of the band and the show and transportation and salaries, including mine. Then we have our recording company, Tangerine Records, and two music-publishing companies—Tangerine Music, which is B.M.I., and Racer Music, which is A.S.C.A.P.—and there is R.P.M., which runs this building. All the other companies pay R.P.M. rent. We record ourselves on Tangerine and we handle new young talent like Rita Graham, the John Bishop Trio, Andy Butler, Alexandra Brown, and Jimmy Lewis. Joe Adams is my executive business manager. He's been with me over ten years. He was a disc jockey with KOWL here and he was very big. Between twelve and three every day, there was no place you could go in Los Angeles and not hear Joe Adams. He first came out on the road with us as an m.c., and I began to study him. He struck me as articulate and very intelligent. He's tight with money and he's got the business where it's manageable. I feel I'm only a small businessman. I'm content to let the business grow as long as I can see a little improvement each year. This is a very slippery business. You have to be careful. It's constantly changing, and you've got to move with it. I remember when there were only a handful of recording companies in the whole country. Now there are three or four hundred.

"I'm not even sure I'm a singer. You certainly need some luck. I've been able to take a pop song, and it paid off, and a country-and-Western, and it paid off, and a blues, and it paid off, and standards like 'Old Man River' and 'Georgia on My Mind,' and they paid off. But I've tried to find songs *I* can get feeling out of. I must please myself first before I sing a song in public. The song must strike me some way in my heart. Now, I love 'Stardust,' but I'll never record it. Every time I sing the song to myself, I can't get the feeling out of it. The same with the national anthem and Nat Cole's 'Nature Boy.' I loved that record, but I can't sing it to sink. But I'd like to sing 'America the Beautiful.' The lyrics of a song are vital. You become the person the writer is talking about. It's like a dramatic actor. People have come up to me and said, 'That girl Georgia you sing about must have really meant something to you.' Hell, I never had a girl named

Georgia, I never *knew* a girl named Georgia. I can be very angry or very sad when I go onstage, but I love music so much I forget that. I refuse to get entangled in something that will make me perform bad. I start to work, it's like a different machine takes over. Tempos are important. I set the tempos, and 'Georgia' may be a hair faster one night or a hair slower the next and it can have a profound difference on the way you sing the words. The melody is your guideline, your radar, but music would mean very little to me if I had to sing it the same way day in and day out. What I do is try and improve on it each time. Change a note here and there, make a twist in your voice, bend a note—take liberties like that. You won't become stagnant if you can change a little each night. I'd have to *make* myself sing the same song the same way twice a year, which some people do every night without any effort at all.

"I can't give any reasons why the public likes me. Of course, one time I might be up and the public might not feel a thing, and another time they might cry and I might consider myself down. The only thing is I have tried to be honest and I cannot be a disappointment to myself. I've felt that way all my life. I've often wondered, Who am I? What am I that people would spend the money to come out and stand in the rain to hear me, come out and spend the money on tickets and baby-sitters and carfare to hear me? But if I can tell myself I did my best, I know in my heart I feel satisfied."

1970

A Walk to the Park

I went down to the Chelsea Hotel one afternoon to visit Elvin Jones, the unique and brilliant drummer whose ferocity and originality and subtlety on his instrument have in the past six or so years changed the entire nature of jazz drumming and, to a degree, the nature of jazz itself. He met me in the hallway outside his first-floor room and ushered me in. The room was long and narrow and dark, and it was clearly a bachelor's nest. The bed hadn't been made, and on a small dining-room table were a box of cornflakes and a used cereal bowl with a spoon in it. The bed was flanked by night tables, on one of which was a Welch's Grape Juice jar of water and on the other an overflowing ashtray and a copy of "The Voyage of the Space Beagle." The bureau was littered with aspirin and Band-Aids and a travelling clock, which had stopped. Wedged between a bass drum and a snare drum in a window alcove were a pair of shoes and a bow tie.

Jones rummaged around in a bureau drawer and pulled out what appeared to be a thick sheaf of hotel bills. "I'm the world's worst bookkeeper," he said, in a sturdy, rasping voice. "I've been living here for several months, and, man, the seventy-some dollars a week I pay is expensive for me. And Pookie's Pub, where I'm at now, is not the highest-paying club in town. I make about scale, or about a hundred and fifty a week. This morning I got a letter from my wife, who lives near the Haight-Asbury district in San Francisco—she's no hippie—and my kid, who is two, is sick again, which means more doctor bills. Everybody wants that bread all at once." He got down on his knees, pulled a box from under the bureau, and took out a copy of his newest album. He wrote something on the back of it and picked up one of the hotel bills. "Let me just lay this album on the man downstairs. Maybe it'll keep him quiet for two or three days." He opened the door and collided with a large chambermaid.

"How's your towels?" she asked. "There's always a 'No Disturb' sign on the door, so's I never can get in here."

"I know it," Jones said, "but I forget it, and I'm not here that much to remember and take it off."

When he returned, the maid handed him some fresh towels. He put them on the table, then went into the kitchenette, got a bottle of Löwenbräu, and sat down on the bed. He picked up a package of French cigarettes and lit one. He was wearing a striped sports shirt, rumpled pipestem khaki pants, and unshined Italian shoes. He is an arresting-looking man. His head is large and his face is winged by his cheekbones. He has a generous mouth, a firm chin, and a broad smile which is heightened by a missing canine tooth. His eyes flash. He is six feet tall and has wide shoulders and a Scarlett O'Hara waist, and he hasn't an ounce of fat on him. His hands are big, with long, thick fingers.

Jones puffed up a couple of pillows and stretched out on the bed. "There. The hecticism of the day is dying down. I've been uptown and back already. I don't get to bed until about four-thirty, but I wake up like a firecracker at ten-thirty. I guess that's what happens to you when you turn forty. But I take a nap around four or five in the afternoon and then I'm all right. Tomorrow morning, at nine-thirty, I have to go out to the Gretsch drum warehouse in Brooklyn and pick out some cymbals. I use K. Zildjians, which are made in Turkey. The last time I was out there it took me a whole afternoon to find just one. I must have tested five hundred cymbals. My head was ringing for days." Jones waved his cigarette around. "I've been smoking these things since Duke Ellington, who was with a Norman Granz tour in Europe, sent for me. It was about a year and a half ago. I joined him in Frankfurt, and my stay with him lasted just a week and a half, through Nuremberg and Paris and Italy and Switzerland. I was new. It was difficult for the band to adapt to my style and I had to do everything in a big hurry, trying to adapt to them. Then the bass player started playing games with me by lowering and raising the tempos to make it look like I was unsteady, and finally I had to speak to him and he stopped. Hodges and Cat Anderson and Gonsalves and Mercer Ellington knew what was going on, but Duke didn't. And I guess I didn't connect with the anchormen, because they complained about my playing to Duke. I don't know whether Cootie, who kept giving me the fisheye, wanted me to call him Mr. Williams and shine his shoes or what. Also, Duke had a second drummer in the band and he was an egomaniac. So Duke and I talked at Orly Airport and I told him to send a telegram to Sam Woodyard and tell him to get himself over there, because he knew the whole book. I saw Duke later, after he'd found out what had been going on, and everything was fine—no sweat. He told me I could come back with the band any time I wanted. He's such a great man. Given more time under different circumstances—being left alone and all—it might have been a beautiful thing for me. After I left the band, I holed up in a hotel room and slept for three days. I didn't want the terrible headaches I'd had out on the Coast in my last days with Coltrane."

Jones swung his legs over the side of the bed and lit another cigarette. He held it cupped in his hands between his knees. His eyelids suddenly drooped, giving him a secret, almost drunken expression, and his voice became low and husky. "I joined John Coltrane in 1960. Of all the bands and all the people I've worked with, the six years with him were the most rewarding. It seemed that all my life was a preparation for that period. Right from the beginning to the last time we played together it was something pure. The most impressive thing was a feeling of steady, collective learning. Every night when we hit the bandstand—no matter if we'd come five hundred or a thousand miles—the weariness dropped from us. It was one of the most beautiful things a man can experience. If there is anything like perfect harmony in human relationships, that band was as close as you can come. You felt so close nobody ever wanted anything destructive to happen to anyone else. Coltrane was humble in the finest sense of that word. He was a man of deep thought. He would never say anything trivial. He was honest with people *and* with himself. He was religious. I think his grandfather was a Baptist minister. I'm a Baptist myself, but I quit going to church years ago. Yourself is the church.

"During my time with Coltrane, I could investigate my quest of how to play with other instruments. He left me absolutely alone. He must have felt the way I played, understood the validity of it. There was never any rhythmic or melodic or harmonic conflicts. At least I never felt any, and you can spot those things coming a mile away. I was never conscious of the length of Coltrane's solos, which sometimes lasted forty minutes. I was in the position of being able to follow his melodic line through all the modes he would weave in and out of, through all the patterns and the endless variations on variations. It was like listening to a concerto. The only thing that mattered was the completion of the cycle that he was in. I'd get so excited listening to him that I had all I could do to contain myself. There was a basic life-force in Coltrane's solos, and when he came out of them you suddenly discovered you had learned a great deal. I didn't want to leave Coltrane, but the personnel had changed. He added another drummer, and I couldn't hear what I was doing any longer. There was too much going on, and it was getting ridiculous as far as I was concerned. I was getting into a whole area of frustration, and what I had to offer I felt I just couldn't contribute. I think Coltrane was upset, and I know in those last weeks I had a constant migraine headache."

Jones lifted his head and opened his eyes and cleared his throat. "When I heard about him being dead, I didn't believe it. Billy Greene, my piano player, called me early in the morning and told me. Later on, I called Bob Thiele, who recorded Coltrane, and he confirmed it. You know how you react when someone close and dear passes away—that bad feeling comes on you.

"But I've been very fortunate in the variety and number of great musicians I've worked with. When I started out in Detroit, in 1949, there were a lot of clubs and a lot of musicians working—Barry Harris, Billy Mitchell, Paul Chambers, Kenny Burrell, Tommy Flanagan, Milt Jackson, and Doug Watkins. It was a revelation to me, because Pontiac, my home, was like out in the country. I got my first professional gig through Art Mardigan, the drummer, with a five-piece group in a bar on Grand River Street, and everything was fine until Christmas Eve, when it was time to get paid, and I looked out the window and it was snowing like hell and there was the piano player, who was also the leader, running down the street with all the money. So I went back to Pontiac and took a job in a little roadhouse that had a floor show with a Sophie Tucker-type singer. She didn't have *any* music in her, but she was the owner's sweetheart, and when she told him *I* didn't have any music in me I got fired. Then Billy Mitchell called me from Detroit and wanted me to come into the Blue Bird with him. It was a small place owned by three sisters and a brother, and it had delicious food. I stayed about three years. Tommy Flanagan came in on piano, and Thad, my brother, who'd been on the road or in the Army since 1939, came in on trumpet. Pepper Adams, the baritone saxophonist, sat in, and so did Sonny Stitt and Miles Davis and Wardell Gray. Then Thad went with Count Basie, and six months later I went into the Rouge Lounge. I also played a lot of concerts and all the after-hours places where you could jam. I don't know any other city like Detroit was then. It got behind its musicians and supported them. At the Rouge Lounge, I was working with Kenny Burrell backing Carmen McRae, and one afternoon Ed Sarkesian, who ran the place, got a call from New York from Benny Goodman, who was putting together a big band and wanted me to come and audition. Sarkesian was a great Goodman fan, and when I came to work that night he was ecstatic. His face was lit up like a Christmas tree. He told me about Goodman and then he asked me did I need any money, did I need any clothes, did I need anything at all, and I took off for New York the next day—right in the middle of the week. The audition was at the old Nola Studios on Broadway and Fifty-second Street, and I walked in and the whole band was there. The only person I knew was my brother Hank, on piano. Budd Johnson was in the band, and I think Buck Clayton, but I didn't know them then. Benny wasn't there. They got out the music for 'Sing, Sing, Sing,' and if there's one number I've *never* liked that's it, and anyway they wanted all this heavy four-four time on the bass drum. We started, and I just didn't belong in it. Nothing came out right. Then, in the middle of the next number, the bass player had to leave, and I began noticing the guys in the band looking at their watches. When the audition ended, the manager gave me a nice pep talk and Benny called me later and thanked me for coming and gave me a lot of encouragement. But I didn't get the job. I did get a gig, though, in a quartet with Charlie Mingus and Teddy Charles and J. R. Monterose, the tenor player. There was never a dull moment with Mingus. Eccentric as he seems, it's mostly a put-on. He's really an almost shy man and he tries to be boisterous to cover it up. Half the time he's frightened of one thing or another, like a little boy. But when he stops talking and starts playing, the virtuoso, the genius, comes shining out. That's a different Mingus. We made a short tour to Newport and Toronto and Washington, but Mingus and Teddy Charles argued all the time, and so Mingus had one of his crazy ideas: I'll fire you, he told me, and then I'll quit, and we'll go to Cleveland and play with Bud Powell. We did. When Mingus left the group, Tommy Potter joined, and we stayed with Bud for a year and a half."

Jones sat up and said, "I'm hungry. Let me order a couple of sandwiches and some more beer." He telephoned and then got up and walked around the room.

"Bud was very shaky, very sick," he went on. "He was almost completely withdrawn, but we got along fine. It ended up that I became the leader and was consulted about setting up and various routines. And during the day I'd visit with him and take him to the movies or on long walks. He would open up and be very rational. His thing by then was alcoholism, and all he needed was a couple of drinks and he'd go berserk. I rationed him to two bottles of beer a day and he was all right. But every once in a while he'd get away from me—like once, when some people poured some wine into him and he was found the next morning in an alley in his underwear with even his shirt and tie stolen. Then one night at Birdland during an intermission he took off and I didn't see him again for two years. Before he died, a couple of years ago, he came by an apartment I had on Sixteenth Street on my birthday and brought me an auto-graphed picture of himself as a present. He was the most mistreated man I ever knew—by managers and bookers and club owners and police. Somebody told me that Cootie Williams believes Powell's troubles started when he was in Cootie's band in the forties and they were playing a gig in Philadelphia. Powell got drunk or something and was picked up by the police, and they beat him up so badly—mostly around the head, probably causing brain damage—that his mother had to come down from New York to get him. And he couldn't have been more than nineteen. Man, he never had a chance.

"After that I worked with Tyree Glenn, and then with Sweets Edison. Sweets is a real cat, in the true meaning of the word. As slick as grease. Hip. And what a trumpet player, what a beautiful tone—a tone as pure as mountain water. There's no trumpet player living can play a ballad like Harry Edison. It was funny travelling with him. We had a contract to play a jazz festival in this resort at French Lick, Indiana, in I think it was October of 1959, and so all five of us—Jimmy Forrest, Tommy Potter, and Tommy Flanagan were also in the group —squeezed into this station wagon, and because there wasn't any room inside I tied my drums on top and we drove eight hundred miles non-stop through rain and hail—the drums out in it all—and when we get there we get the greeting 'Where have you been? You were supposed to play *yesterday*.'"

Jones laughed in a loose, swinging way. The sandwiches and beer arrived, and he spread his sandwich out beside him on the bed and put his beer on the floor. I asked him if he had ever had any trouble with drugs.

He looked hesitant. "I've had my turn," he said softly, and took a swallow of beer. "I guess it got started in 1949, after I came out of the Army and began going to Detroit. I developed a secret desire to see what everybody was enjoying so much. I wanted to be one of the crowd, to be hip, down, part of that image. Also, there are times when you just don't want to think of certain things. You want to escape from being a liberal or a conservative or a Democrat or a Republican or a Negro or anything else. You just want to live. And later I'd get in trouble when I wasn't working. I'd suffer from despon-dency and boredom and general depression. Slowly, you learn the de-lusions about what you think you are under drugs and what you really are. Whenever I was under the influence it would make me play terrible. It would make me sluggish and slow me down. It destroyed what could have been great performances. I've been drastically em-barrassed by being high on the job. It was embarrassing to me and my associates. It seemed that I had let myself and my friends down—the people who depended on me. Oh, I wouldn't be hostile, but I'd sit there and go to sleep in people's faces when they talked to me or walk around in a kind of part oblivion. When drugs really get hold of you, you move into a whole different world—an area where you associate with nobody but other users. You're taking drugs and they're taking drugs and that's your relationship, and you begin to think of them as friends, until you find out they're boosters or thieves or pimps or whatever. You suddenly discover you're involved in criminal activity, that you're about to get involved with the legal branch of the government, which happened to me in Detroit and happened to me again in New York in 1959. I'd been walking around the city all day and I had this little bag of heroin in my watch pocket. I'd been sniffing on it off and on. I'm all dressed up and I go to a hotel on Forty-ninth Street to visit a friend who'd played with Lionel Hampton, and I forget all about that little bag in my pocket. I get in the lobby and this guy sticks a gun in my back and tells me to come upstairs. It was a cop. When I get to my friend's room, there are other cops, and they've got him stripped and up against the wall and they're going over his clothes like a vacuum cleaner. I think they found some benzies—nothing worse than that. Then they started patting me down and they find the bag, and that's it. Man, I felt queer—like I was suspended in the air in that room, watching all this happening down below to two cats I never saw before."

Jones crumpled his sandwich wrapper and put it in the ashtray on one of the bedside tables. "They sent me to Rikers Island for six months. That was depressing, being locked up, and particularly being locked up with all those repeaters. Those guys have worked out this life where they go out in the streets for six months or so and hustle or push and then they get busted and are sent back to Rikers Island, probably to the same job they had before, and after they've eaten three meals a day and gotten their health back and their terms are up they go back to the streets until they get busted again. But what was worst about it was the rats. I have a great fear of rodents. These guys would take food and candy and stuff into their cells, and at night— there wasn't much light—the rats would come and I'd stay up half the night watching and trying to keep them away from me. So that was the last time for me. I've been clean ever since, and I intend to stay that way. I'm not going to abuse myself, I'm not going to get in that groove. I was never on the stuff more than six or seven months altogether in all those years, and in a way I'm glad it happened. I learned from it. I also learned that I could never get a cabaret card to work clubs in New York. I filled out all the forms I don't know how many times and nothing, no card. So what I finally did was go down there and apply under the name of Ray Jones—Ray is my middle name—and I got one. Of course, now they've wiped out the cabaret-card law, which is the best news I've heard in years."

Around eight that evening, I picked Jones up at the Chelsea after his nap, and we took a cab down to Sayat Nova, an Armenian restaurant on Charles Street. He looked refreshed. He had changed into dark pipestem pants, a clean tan button-down shirt without a tie, and a vestlike cardigan sweater. "I wish my wife would come on East," he said, "but she hates New York. She won't live here. She came from North Dakota and she's smart—college-educated—and sensitive and calm. I get lonely." Jones laughed. "One thing—I was never lonely when I was a kid. I was the youngest of ten children, and I was a twin, an identical twin. But when my brother and me were eight or nine months old we got the whooping cough, and he died. His name was Elvin *Roy.* I can remember the little wooden box sitting on a table in the parlor. I have been challenged on this but have proved it by pointing out the exact spot where the coffin was, so it wasn't just that I was told about it later. My oldest sister and the oldest of all the children, Olivvia, drowned when she was twelve. There was a lake down at the end of our street and she was skating and fell through the ice. The kids she was with got frightened and ran home and nobody told my mother until late that night, and they went and found her under the ice. She was very talented. She was already composing music and, even at her age, giving piano lessons. My brother Hank was born next, and there was Melinda and Anna Mae and Thad. Right above me was Edith and Paul and Tom. Edith still has our house in Pontiac, and she has four children. It's a big old place with three stories and eighteen rooms.

"My father came from Vicksburg, Mississippi, and he died in 1949. He was about six feet four and very lean. He was a lumber inspector for General Motors and a deacon of the Baptist church, as well as a bass in the choir. I'm told I resemble him more than any of the other boys in the family. To me he was a very fine man. His example was in his living. The way he lived—he was as straight as could be—made you want to be like him. He loved to bake. He was up at four every morning and he'd go down to the kitchen and start our breakfast and sometimes pack our lunches. He'd pour coffee into this enormous cup, and when I came down he'd let me drink the spilled coffee in the saucer. Twice a week he'd make a big three-layer cake and put some of my mother's jelly—mulberry or blackberry or strawberry—between the layers. And he'd bake bread and gingerbread. My brother Tom and I would take a piece of gingerbread and make it into a hard ball and I'd put it in my pocket and when we went out we'd pretend it was chewing tobacco. I'd break off a piece and ask Tom, 'Here, you want a plug?' or 'You want a chew?' He'd stick it in his cheek and bulge it out and we'd break up. My mother was a big warm woman and the greatest lady in the world. She gave me every kind of encouragement. She'd tell you to make up your mind at what you wanted to do and then just *do* it. When I finally decided I wanted to be a musician, that was it to her. But she tried to make you into a man before anything else, so that you learned how to take care of yourself, you learned how to survive. That was especially valuable to me in the beginning as a musician. She died of a heart attack in 1951. She had a weak heart but she never let on and she'd never go to doctors."

At Sayat Nova, Jones ordered a beer and egg-lemon soup and shish kebab. "I never learned any prejudices at home," he said. "In fact, I never knew anything about that until the Army. Our schools were unsegregated, and my father and mother taught us you met people as individuals, that you judge a man as a man. They both came from Mississippi, so they must have had good reason to think differently, but they didn't pass any of it down to us. I grew up in the Depression, and I guess we were lucky, because my father always worked. There was plenty of food even though I never saw any *money*. We weren't allowed to go to the movies, because it cost ten cents. And instead of toys from a store I'd go into the woods near our house and make a slingshot or a bow and arrow.

"I quit school after the tenth grade and went to work at General Motors in the truck-and-coach division, unloading boxcars and stacking assembled motors. I already knew how to do everything in the dry-cleaning line. I had gone to work in my uncle's dry-cleaning shop when I was six or seven. School didn't give me what I wanted. The only interests I had there were music and recreation—sports. I was on the track team, and I set records that still stand. I could high-jump six feet, and I ran the four-forty and could do the hundred-yard dash in nine-five. It would take me nine *minutes* now.

"I started playing drums in junior high. I got a practice pad and sticks and a Paul Yoder method book. When I first looked at those notes it seemed so complicated. I didn't have the least idea of note evaluation. I asked a kid I went to school with about it. He took private lessons for fifty cents and I thought he must be rich. He taught me about whole notes and half notes and quarter notes, and suddenly it dawned on me. I walked around all the time counting— a-one, a-two, a-three, a-four. I went through the whole book and I learned all twenty-six rudiments. I learned that book upside down and back and forth. I was moved from the junior-high marching band up to the high-school band, and in a week I was in the first chair. If anybody really influenced me on drums it was the band director, Fred N. Weist. He made me to realize that the drum is not something to bang on, that it is not a round disc to be pounded. He told me you can hear incoherent sounds in a traffic jam and that music should go far beyond the reproduction of traffic jams. We had quite a collection of records at home, and I'd try and play along with them. It was very unsatisfactory, but I learned how valuable it is to keep time, that that is the drummer's primary function."

Jones spooned up some soup and doused the bowl with pepper. "I listened to all the drummers I could, on records and in person. I'd hear Buddy Rich, say, do something on a record and I'd wonder if he was doing that snare-drum pattern with one hand or two, and finally I'd get a chance to *see* him, with Tommy Dorsey, and I discovered he was using two hands. I saw Jo Jones with Basie, and on records I heard Chick Webb. He takes a little solo at the beginning of 'Liza,' which was made, I believe, around 1938, and it's so melodic and clean and modern it's unbelievable. It could have been recorded last week. I heard Sid Catlett on 'Salt Peanuts' with Dizzy Gillespie and Charlie Parker, and he was flowing and flawless. And I listened to Dave Tough and Max Roach and Kenny Clarke and Tiny Kahn. I began to develop my theories on drums. I figured that a lot of things drummers were doing with two hands could be done with one—like accents with just the left hand on the snare, so you wouldn't have to take your right hand off the ride cymbal. And it didn't seem to me that the four-four beat on the bass drum was necessary. What was needed was a *flow* of rhythm all over the set. I never learned any tricks, anything flashy— like juggling sticks or throwing them in the air. That kind of thing stops me inside. After all, Artur Rubinstein doesn't play runs on the piano with his chin."

Jones covered his shish kebab with pepper and ordered another beer. "Of course, I learned from my brothers Hank and Thad. When Hank came home in the forties from being on the road with Jazz at the Philharmonic, I'd ask him a lot of questions. He'd tell me different things to listen for in a performance, or he'd tell me to get my wire brushes and play along with him. You don't realize how much you are learning at times like that until much later, when it hits you like post-hypnotic suggestion. I didn't see much of Thad until he joined our band in Detroit. Both Hank and Thad are C.B.S. staff musicians now, and they live in New Jersey. We don't see each other that much, but we're close, particularly in times of crisis, when there seems to be a kind of telepathy between us. To me, they're both perfect. I don't know anything bad about them. Hank is the greatest pianist in the world and Thad is the greatest trumpet player. Hank has stubby fingers and hands, but they spread out like wings when he plays. He doesn't feel right if he doesn't practice three or four hours a day. I can understand that. He wants to have that response when he needs it.

"Around 1946, when I was nineteen, I took off for Boston with my brother Tom and a friend. I worked in a dry cleaner's there, and then I went down to Newark, New Jersey, by myself and enlisted in the Army. They sent me to eight weeks of music school at Fort Lee, Virginia, after basic training, and then I was sent to Columbus, Ohio. Part of the time I travelled all over the country with a Special Services show called 'Operation Happiness,' but I was a stagehand rather than a drummer. I went along just to watch. And I began to play at dances on the post and I gained confidence. I never got that many compliments and I never got that much criticism. The men I played with liked me enough not to repudiate my shortcomings. They wouldn't do anything deliberately to hurt me. You give kindness to human beings, you allow them to grow."

Jones took a sip of Armenian coffee, and I looked at my watch. It was going on ten. "We'd better get down to Pookie's," he said. "The owner is nervous, and he gets upset if I'm not on the stand by ten. Maybe he's nervous because he just got married. Before I got married, six years ago, I asked my wife—we'd been pretty close—if she would change afterwards. 'Oh, no. Oh, no.' Man, the words 'I pronounce you man and wife' were still ringing around the room when she started telling me to do this, do that." He laughed and went up the stairs from the restaurant two at a time. We found a cab on Charles Street.

"My drums are my life," Jones said, resting his head against the back of the seat. "Sometimes what happens to you during the day affects your ability and shows up in your work. But once you get to your set, you can obliterate all the troubles, which seem to fall off your shoulders. If you aren't happy before, you are when you play. Playing is a matter of spontaneity *and* thought, of constant control. Take a solo. When I start, I keep the structure and melody and content of the tune in my mind and work up abstractions or obbligatos on it. I count the choruses as I go along, and sometimes I'm able to decide in advance what the pattern of a whole chorus will be, but more often five or six patterns will flash simultaneously across my mind, which gives me a choice, especially if I get hung up, and I've had some granddaddies of hangups. If you don't panic, you can switch to another pattern. I can see forms and shapes in my mind when I solo, just as a painter can see forms and shapes when he starts a painting. And I can see different colors. My cymbals will be one color and my snare another color and my tomtoms each a different color. I mix these colors up, making constant movement. Drums suggest movement, a conscious, constant shifting of sounds and levels of sound. My drumming can shade from a whisper to a thunder. I'm not conscious of the length of my solos, which I've been told have run up to half an hour. When you develop a certain pattern, you stay with it until it's finished. It's just like you start out in the evening to walk to Central Park and back. Well, there are a lot of directions you can take—one set of streets going up, then in a certain entrance and out another entrance and back on a different set of streets. You come back and maybe take a hot bath and have some dinner and read and go to bed. You haven't been somewhere to lose yourself, but to go and come back and finish your walk."

Pookie's Pub is on the northeast corner of Hudson and Dominick Streets, a block north of the Holland Tunnel and a block south of the Half Note, a bar and spaghetti palace with jazz.

Jones groaned as he got out of the cab, for the owner of Pookie's Pub was striding back and forth in front of it. He buttonholed Jones and talked intensely into his ear. I could hear the words "time" and "late" and "people inside." Jones said softly, "Now, man, cool it. Don't bug me. When I *get* here, I *work.*" The owner charged through the door, and Jones raised his eyebrows and laughed. We followed the owner in.

Pookie's is long and narrow and dusty-looking. A bar is on the left and banquettes are on the right, with closely packed tables between. At the rear, between the end of the bar and the men's room, is a tiny jerry-built bandstand two feet above the floor. Jones headed for the stand, and the rest of his quartet—Billy Greene, Joe Farrell (tenor saxophone), and Wilbur Ware (bass)—got up from a table and followed.

Jones' drums are strictly functional. They include an eighteen-inch bass drum, two tomtoms, a snare drum, two ride cymbals, and a high-hat. He hung his sweater on a hook by the upright piano, sat down, and tapped his way around the set with his fingers. He tightened his snares and his bass drumhead and picked up a pair of sticks. Then he looked at Farrell, said something, counted off, and the group went into a medium-tempo blues.

The center of Jones' beat shifts continually. Sometimes it is in his constantly changing ride-cymbal strokes and sometimes he softens these and bears down heavily on his high-hat on the afterbeat. Sometimes swift, wholly unpredictable bass-drum accents come to the fore and sometimes the emphasis shifts to left-hand accents on the snare, which range from clear single strokes to chattering loose rolls. Jones' hands and feet all seem to have their own minds, yet the total effect is of an unbroken flow that both supports and weaves itself around the soloists.

Farrell started quietly on the blues and Jones set up light *tic-tic tic-tic-tic tic tic-i-tic tic-tic* strokes on a ride cymbal, while his left hand played five behind-the-beat strokes on the snare, followed by softer irregular strokes and a shaking roll. The high-hat jiggled unevenly up and down and the bass drum was quiet. Farrell grew more heated, and Jones began throwing in cymbal splashes, bass-drum accents, and complex, charging left-hand figures. His volume rose steadily, though it never eclipsed Farrell, and suddenly one realized that Jones' quadruple-jointed rhythmic engine was in high gear. Pookie's was rocking. At the end of Farrell's solo, Jones abruptly dropped his volume to some sliding cymbal strokes which shimmered below the opening of the piano solo. Jones scuttled and rattled behind the piano. His snare-drum accents were light and loose, and the center of his efforts fell on the ride cymbal, on which he would run softly ahead of the beat, fall exaggeratedly behind, then catch up and ride the beat before shooting ahead again. During Ware's solo, Jones whispered along on the high-hat, dropped occasional bass-drum beats, and made Ware's tone sound fat and assured. Farrell returned, exchanged some four-bar breaks with Jones, and the number ended with a shuddering rimshot.

Jones' face was as elusive as his motions—a boxer's assortment of jabs and feints and duckings, supported by steadily dancing feet. At first it looked tight and secret; his eyes were shut and a dead cigarette was clamped in his mouth. Then he opened his eyes, which appeared sightless, and nodded at Farrell and Ware. Smiling widely, he closed his eyes in a pained way and turned his face toward the wall. A slow version of "On the Trail," from Ferde Grofé's "Grand Canyon Suite," came next, and it was converted into an intense marching blues. The set closed with a delicate reading of "Autumn Leaves." Jones put on his sweater and jumped down from the bandstand, ordered a beer, talked to a couple of admirers, and came over to my table. He was mopping his head with a limp handkerchief, and his shirt was so wet it was transparent. "Wait a minute," he said. "Big Jim's at the bar and I just want to check in with him. I don't know what he *does*, but he's always got plenty of bread and he supports the musicians, follows them around to all the clubs. He makes you feel good." At the bar he pounded the back of a chunky, well-dressed man sitting with a platinum blonde. The man jumped off his stool and started shadow-boxing. Jones put up his hands and the two men weaved and bobbed down the bar and out onto the sidewalk, boxing back and forth in front of the door for several minutes, then slapped each other and laughed. A jukebox went on and Billie Holiday started singing. The owner said in an intense way, "Do you know who that is? Do you know what that is? That's Billie Holiday singing 'My Yiddishe Mama.' Tony Scott, the clarinettist, taped it at a party not long before she died and put it on a record and gave it to me. You won't find that selection on any other jukebox in the world." He darted away, and Jones sat down at the table. "Oh, my. I dig Big Jim." He took a long swallow of beer. "I think this will be one of those rare nights that seems like they're over before they begin, with everybody in the group *listening*, everybody in the group *hearing*. I want to build my group into topnotch quality. I want it to make a significant contribution. I'm not interested in flash-in-the-pan activity, and I think the men I have with me feel the same. It takes a lot of the agony out of things. Occupying your time for yea amount of dollars just doesn't work. Jazz is infectious. There's no way to avoid it. If you're going to play music—any kind of music—you can't avoid it. It just naturally takes over. This is my first group and I like being a leader, but then I guess I've been sort of a leader in most of the groups I've worked in. A drummer should conduct."

The owner appeared and touched Jones' shoulder, and he made a face. "All right, man, all right," he said. He turned to me. "Man wants some music, we'll oblige him."

The first number, built around Jones' wire brushes, was a fast version of "Softly, as in a Morning Sunrise." Farrell soloed on flute and Greene and Ware followed. Jones handles brushes the way a great chef handles a wire whisk, with fast, circular, loose-wristed motions. He began almost inaudibly, with polishing, sliding, ticking sounds on the snare, broken by silvery cymbal strokes. Slowly he rent this gentle flow with bass-drum beats and with jagged, irregular wire-brush strokes on the snare and the big tomtom. These were multiplied and intensified until it sounded as though he were using sticks, and the solo ended. It was a short, perfectly designed warmup. The group went into "Night in Tunisia." It started in a high, intense fashion, and by the time Farrell had finished a ten-minute solo Jones had switched to sticks and Pookie's was ballooning with sound. Then Jones took off. He began with heavy rimshots on the snare, which split notes and split them again, then broke into swaying, grandiose strokes on his ride cymbals, accompanied by lightning triplets and off-beat single notes on the bass drum. Switching patterns, he moved his right hand between his big and small tomtoms in a faster and faster arc while his left hand roared through geometrical snare-drum figures and his high-hat rattled and shivered. He switched patterns again and settled down on his snare with sharp, flat strokes, spaced regularly and then irregularly. He varied this scheme incessantly, gradually bringing in bass-drum beats and big tomtom booms. Cymbals exploded like flushed birds. Jones had passed beyond a mere drum solo. He was playing with earsplitting loudness, and what he was doing had become an enormous rolling ball of abstract sound, divorced from music, from reality, from flesh and bone. It trampled traditional order and replaced it with an unknown order. It delighted the mind and hammered at the guts. Jones waded through his cymbals again and went into a deliberate, alternately running and limping fusillade between his snare and tomtoms that rose an inch or two higher in volume. Suddenly he was finished. Farrell played the theme and Jones slid into a long, downhill coda that was a variation on the close of his solo, paused, and came down with a crash on his cymbals and bass drum.

There was a shouting silence. Jones was back from the Park.

1968

Like a Marriage

Though it is newer and smaller, the Modern Jazz Quartet, which is made up of John Lewis on piano, Milt Jackson on vibraharp, Percy Heath on bass, and Connie Kay on drums, has much in common with the Duke Ellington band. Both groups are shepherded by gifted pianist-composers who use their ensembles both as canvases and as test pilots for their compositions. (Lewis and Ellington, though original and moving performers, have been steadily underrated as pianists.) Each group has a unique collective sound which has as much to do with the ultimate effect of what it plays as the composition itself. Both groups have refused to compromise, and both have made sizable sums of money. Both have altered and elevated the course of jazz and of Western music itself. And both have remained constant: Harry Carney has been with Ellington since 1927, and the M.J.Q. has had one personnel change in its seventeen years of existence. But the Modern Jazz Quartet has accomplished things that even the Ellington band has not. It has invented a semi-improvised collective approach, hinted at roughly in New Orleans music, that has rescued jazz from the banality of the endless solo and the rigidity of conventional arrangements. It has developed a musical interplay and sensitivity that only great string quartets can rival. And it has perfected a subtlety that has misled the unknowing into regarding it as a cocktail group and the knowing into scoffing at it as staid and stuffy.

The Quartet, because of its instrumentation and its constant inter-weaving, is tintinnabulous. It shimmers, it rings, it hums. It is airy and clean. Like any great mechanism, its parts are as notable as their sum. Lewis' style is single-noted and rhythmic. His simple, seemingly repetitive phrases are generally played just a fraction behind the beat, where much of the secret of jazz lies. He is an emotional pianist—in a transcendental way—and he succeeds, where most pianists fail, in transmitting that emotion. Jackson is more than a consummate foil. He is profuse, ornate, affecting, and original. His solos, inspired by Charlie Parker and Dizzy Gillespie, are open at both ends; they seem to have started long before we hear them and to go on long after they have actually stopped. Whereas Lewis has a dry, belling tone, Jackson reverberates and rolls, continually threatening to slosh over onto the rest of the group. Heath moves through and under Lewis and Jackson, supporting them with exactness and a beautiful tone. Kay is much the same. He is precise yet driving, and he gets a resilient, measured tone on his drums and cymbals that both embellishes and strengthens the total sound.

Onstage, the M.J.Q. often resembles, with its solemn, dark-suited mien, the rostrum at a morticians' convention. But this is only a collective mask; closeups reveal life and variety. Heath is tall and thin and patrician. He has a high, receding forehead and a Pharaoh's nose. Kay is taller, with a full, monolithic face that conceals sharp, lively eyes. Jackson is a gnome. He is short and bird-boned, and is dominated by an askew owl face. Lewis looks like a Teddy bear, and when he moves he runs, even from room to room. But he has the good, untroubled eyes that professors of philosophy should have. Even the voices of the Quartet jostle one another. Lewis speaks softly, allowing his constant smile to carry half the weight of his words. Heath's near-shouting is rounded by continual laughter. Jackson's speech is quiet and almost subliminal, while Kay sounds like his bass drum.

If the Modern Jazz Quartet ever recorded an autobiographical piece, it might sound like this:

I. Masters of the Music

Lewis: The original Quartet was made up of Milt and Ray Brown and Kenny Clarke and myself, and we decided to try and become a group after a record date early in the fifties for Dizzy Gillespie's recording label. There were things wrong in the music around us that we all agreed on, and some of them were long, long solos and that formula on a tune of everybody playing the melody in the first chorus, followed by a string of solos, and then the melody again. We didn't work together steadily until 1954. We lost Ray Brown before we really got started, because he married Ella Fitzgerald and we couldn't afford him anyway. Then I went back to school—the Manhattan School of Music—and after I'd graduated Milt didn't know whether he wanted to be just a member of a group or the leader, so while he was deciding I took a job with Ella as her accompanist, during which time the Quartet, or a quartet, with Percy Heath and Horace Silver on piano and Clarke and Milt worked the first Newport Jazz Festival. We made our first record in 1952 and had our first gig late in 1954 at the Showplace on West Fourth Street. Kenny Clarke left us in 1955. He was sick and we talked about it and he said he knew he'd be better off on his own just then, so he left and Connie Kay came in. Kenny is still my favorite drummer of all time. He's the most unique drummer I ever heard. He's profound. You can listen to him all by himself, without anything else. And I think he plays even better now in Europe than he did then.

Kay: I joined the Quartet in February of 1955. Lester Young, who I'd been with, was out of town with Jazz at the Philharmonic, and I was thinking of taking a job with Sonny Stitt, the alto player, until Lester got back, but Monte Kay, the Quartet's manager, called me one morning and said the Quartet had a concert that night in Washington, D.C., and then a two-week gig at Storyville, in Boston, and would I like to go along? I met John at Penn Station and he filled me in on difficult pieces like "Django" going down on the train. I knew Milt real well and I'd met Percy and John. I understood it was a two-week gig, but when it was over nobody said anything and nobody has yet and that was fourteen years ago.

Jackson: The Quartet will never break up. The only way we'd break up would be somebody getting sick. The way things are now, most of the musicians around are barely making it. We think alike on staying together. It's been like a marriage, a seventeen-year marriage. It's become a way of life. You get to know each other's habits and mannerisms. At all times, each one knows what the other is going to do. John and I are more active than Percy and Connie musically. In fact John is more than active, he's reckless the way he runs from place to place. He's been hit a couple of times by cars. He's got to be more careful of himself. John is always coming up with new ideas, and that keeps it from getting monotonous. Of course, there are times when I like to straighten out and just swing, get away from that controlled thing and play that old-time music. I generally take a group out in the summer—maybe Jimmy Heath, Percy's brother, and Cedar Walton and Bob Cranshaw and Mickey Roker. That's how those rumors about the group breaking up always get started. I took a band out a couple of years ago and there was quite a lot of work, but things are slow now, so I've given up on it. I make records on my own, and I've thought of setting up a studio and teaching, just as a means of coming off the road. But as long as the Quartet is going the way it is, I don't have the time. So when I'm not working, I'm home playing pool and learning to swim.

Heath: I guess I took over the job of handling the Quartet's money because I handled the contract for our first gig at the Chantilly, which is what the Showplace was called then. I'm supposed to give out the checks every week, just as Connie is supposed to make hotel reservations and take care of transportation, but we have an attorney and a road manager and a booker and a travel agency now, and they take care of most of those details. But we used to do it all, and I suppose you have to go through that discipline at first. We probably make as much money as any jazz group. Our payroll is about seventeen hundred dollars a week. Twenty-five thousand dollars a year goes into just moving us around. In Europe, they generally pay your travel, and some festivals do here, but most of it is on us. And we spend a good deal of our pocket money on the road just to live right. We consider that we're of such calibre and station that we should stay in the best places and eat the best food. Some years the Quartet has a little money left over, and one year we invested it in a new ski resort in New York State, which was fine until they foreclosed the lift. I understand the enterprise is a great success now. But we've kept aside enough to start a pension plan and we have our own publishing company, but none of us could live on that. Milt and John probably make twice as much as I do. John has his movie scores and royalties, and Milt has royalties and recordings and the separate gigs he takes every summer. But I have no complaints. June, my wife, hasn't had to work since 1949, when we first moved to New York and lived on Sugar Hill, where we had some fish-and-chip days. But the whole thing with the Quartet is that we have made some money, but we have never conformed. We have built up seventeen years of prestige, and been paid for doing it.

Lewis: I got out of the Army in 1945, and when I went back to the University of New Mexico they told me I might as well go to music school. I'd met John Hammond through David Sarvis, who taught in the drama department at the university, so I went to New York and entered the Manhattan School of Music, and John helped me financially and every other way. Before I'd left home, in Albuquerque, I'd heard radio broadcasts from Billy Berg's in Los Angeles, where Charlie Parker and Dizzy Gillespie were playing with Ray Brown and Milt Jackson, and it was unbelievable. When I got to New York I played one-nighters while I was waiting out my union card. I worked on Fifty-second Street with Allen Eager and Eddie Davis and with a band that Hot Lips Page and Walter Page had. Joe Keyes, a most remarkable trumpet player, was in it. In the meantime, Kenny Clarke had come back from the service and through him Dizzy hired me as a pianist for my summer-school recess, and then he asked me to come and play with the band. I had to make a decision about the school and Dizzy. I decided I'd learn more from Dizzy, so I joined him in September, 1946. Kenny was in the band and Ray Brown and James Moody. We went on ninety one-nighters in a row, and it was a very emotional tour—always a lot of fun and a lot of crying. Ray Brown left and we lost two drummers and the pianos were always half a tone out of tune and the audiences weren't too great because they didn't know how to dance to that music. It was really a concert band, which we found out when we went to Europe in 1948, where we left everybody's mouth hanging open. Dizzy was marvellous to work under. He was never late and that was when I learned not to be late. You have to get that over with.

I was disgusted with my playing at the time and I told Dizzy he better get someone else. But he talked me into staying. He always looked after me. Once when I got sick on the road he brought me all the way back to New York to the hospital. He's not as funny as he used to be, and I guess there's a good reason: It's a very strange country we live in now. I finally left Dizzy because I wanted to go back to Paris. If you ever go to Paris, you'd leave anything because of it. It's the jewel of jewels. I stayed there for five months, then came back to join Miles Davis's little band, with Gerry Mulligan and Eddie Bert and Max Roach. It was exciting, something new. Then Miles got me a job with Illinois Jacquet, who had his brother Russell and J. J. Johnson and Joe Newman and Jo Jones. I was with the band about eight months and I never saw so much money. Jacquet was making suitcases of money. We had to play "Flying Home" about four times a night, but I always found something in it. Norman Granz wanted me to come with his Jazz at the Philharmonic, but I decided I wanted to go back to the Manhattan School of Music, and I got all the way to the airport on the way to meet Granz before I turned around and came back. Norman is a hard man to stay no to and we weren't the greatest of friends for five or six years. But I got my Bachelor of Music, and in 1953 my Master of Music.

Kay: Sid Catlett was my man, my idol. The first time I heard him I was working after school and on Saturdays in a Chinese art gallery in the Fifties, and one day I passed Café Society Uptown, which was between Lexington and Park on Fifty-eighth Street and is now the Fine Arts Theatre, and the door was open and music was coming out. I stepped in and Teddy Wilson's band, with Big Sid, was rehearsing, and when I heard Sid that was it. I got to meet him a while later, when he was working on Fifty-second Street at the Down Beat Club. He was out on the street after work trying to get a cab to go home and I offered him a ride in a little raggedy 1935 Studebaker I had. "O.K., Bub," he said, which is what he called everybody. I drove him to One Hundred and Fifty-sixth and Amsterdam, where he lived, and after that I'd drive him all over and he'd always tell me to stop by anytime—ground floor, right at the back. One night we drove around to a lot of clubs. We went into Nick's and he sat in, we went somewhere else and he sat in with a bebop band, and then he sat in with a swing group. He could play with anybody or anything. He was a happy-go-lucky person. Nothing bothered him. I think the secret of his playing was in his attitude toward things. He wasn't fazed even when he took a job at Billy Rose's Diamond Horseshoe. These showgirls would each bring a part of his drums onto the stage, singing something about him while they did, and then leave him up there all alone, where—bam!—he was supposed to play an unaccompanied solo absolutely cold, the lights on him and on his tuxedo, which was covered with sequins. He taught me little things. He'd stop by where I was working and tell me my left hand was too inactive or my beat on the ride cymbal was too loud, and he'd show me things at his house. But I learned the most from him in his attitude—his quiet, beautiful way toward things, whether it was the world situation or just people.

Lewis: I was less influenced by piano players than by other instrumentalists, like Lester Young and Coleman Hawkins and Ben Webster, and trumpet players like Roy Eldridge and Harry Edison. I was formed more from hearing horn players. I learned some things from Earl Hines, not too many, and some of Count Basie's things, and of course one of the greatest pianists was Art Tatum. I'm happy it happened that way. I didn't get trapped into mechanical things, piano things.

When I take a solo, I try not to look at my fingers. It distracts me from the music-making. And after I learn a piece, I stop thinking about the rules—the bars and the harmony and the chords. I think about other things, even other music. If you break through those mere rules, destroy them, that's good, and it can become quite a marvellous experience. It's not just sadness or joy, it's something beyond that, perhaps exhilaration, but that's rare. A year or two ago, at Monterey, I played with Illinois Jacquet and Ray Brown and Ray Nance, and that was exhilarating. When you start to play, an idea comes along, and that dictates where you have to go. Sometimes things go wrong, and many times you find a nice way of getting out of a phrase that is better than the original way you were going. But you have to be a musician first and an instrumentalist second. It's more important to be a master of the music than a master of an instrument, which can take you over.

Kay: I don't like to take drum solos at all. Drums are a flat instrument, and besides Catlett is gone and there's only one Buddy Rich. I know how I feel when other drummers solo. It seems like you've heard them all before. There just aren't that many original people around. But when I do solo I think of the tune I'm playing. I try to fit what I'm playing into the composition rather than do just twelve bars of rudiments. The melody goes through your mind and you go along with it, fitting yourself to it. Also, my solos are always short, which I learned from Lester Young. He never took more than two or three choruses and neither did Charlie Parker, but they always managed to say all they had to say.

Jackson: When I solo I come down from the melodic line and the chords that are being played, or anything else, like a phrase the drummer might play, which can turn what you're doing into something lyrical. And I keep the melody in mind. I always remember the melody and then I have something to fall back on when I get lost, and with the human element I do get lost, but I've always been able to find my way back. Of course, your troubles and pleasures will come out in your music. But you do the best you can to entertain. Jazz is an art, but it's in the form of an entertaining art. I'm most relaxed in the blues or in ballads, which are my criterion. I get the most results from myself then and I reach the audience quicker. My blues comes from church music and my ballads from the fact I'm really a frustrated singer. Lionel Hampton was the only influence I've had technically on the instrument. I heard him one night at the Michigan State Fair in 1941, when he had Dexter Gordon and Howard McGhee, and that night really got to me. In style and ideas, I adapted myself to Charlie Parker and Dizzy. I can get around the mechanical feeling of my instrument by making glisses and grace notes, so that it sounds more like a horn. I still use a prewar Deagan vibraharp, and every two or three years the Deagan people take it apart and put it together again for me.

Lewis: When I'm working behind Milt, I try and be out of the way and at the same time supply something that might even improve on what he's playing. And I try to supply patterns that are strong rhythmically. It's easy to underestimate rhythm-making. I can never guess what Jackson is going to do next. I'm supporting him but I'm also moving along parallel to him. I learned to play collectively in Dizzy's band. I was trying to find a way to function, to add something, since most of the time I could play anything and no one would hear me anyway, and one night it happened up in Boston behind Dizzy when he played "I Can't Get Started." My discovery was related, too, to the way Kenny Clarke played drums in Dizzy's band. He complemented everything that was going on.

Kay: My drums are black pearl, but the fittings and stands are brass, which looks like gold. They're Sonor drums and are made in Aue, Germany, by people named Link. They're the oldest percussion-makers in Europe. We had a German bandboy who had worked for Stan Kenton and once he brought me a Sonor snare drum to try, and when we were in Europe next he took me down to Aue to meet Horst Link. He didn't speak English, but I got across a few things I didn't like—the response of the snare and such—and they worked it out. The snare they made me is wider and deeper than most people use, and I have calfskin heads instead of plastic. Plastic is fine when you have to play out-of-doors or in a lot of dampness. My floor tomtom is fourteen by sixteen inches and my side tomtom is eight by eleven and the bass drum is fourteen by twenty. I use a timpani head on the beater side of the bass drum, which gives more ring, and I use a big soft full beater ball, like a marching band's. There's a rod coming up from the top side of the bass drum, and on it are a little cymbal and a triangle and chimes. I designed the rod and I call it a sound tree. I've tried to get it patented, but have been told I can't. I also have two timpani drums that Sonor makes for me. They're smaller than usual and they don't have any pedals. I used to have two small Syrian drums mounted on top of the bass drum, but I don't use them anymore. We no longer play the pieces that called for them, and anyway they were hard to tune and had goatskin heads, which were difficult to get. I have six cymbals, including the two high-hat cymbals, and they're A. Zildjians. I've had them eight years and I don't think I'll ever change them. Sonor also makes my drumsticks, which I designed. They're very light and thin and are made of white ash finished with a black lacquer. Even though they look fragile they have the same strength and tone as heavier sticks and they don't chip or break as easily.

Lewis: Ideas for compositions pop into my head all the time and I write them down in a notebook. The things you hear and see go back in the brain and eventually something comes out—melodic fragments or an opening for a piece or ideas of how something I've already written could be improved. Indirectly, the music I've heard inspires me, but it works negatively. The music I've heard suggests music I've never heard. It points to something that doesn't exist, that might be a little better, and I try to supply that. A piece can take a few hours or a couple of days to write. My writing and my playing are connected. I can take ideas I have written or maybe not written down yet—ideas just floating around back there. I can take those ideas or written things and expand on them each time I improvise, so in that way the pieces I write are never finished, never complete. The reverse—taking an idea or a phrase from a solo of mine and letting it inspire a new composition —is trying to happen to me for the first time, and I don't know whether to let it happen or not. In fact, there's something from a solo of mine on our new record that keeps running through my head. It's terrible, like a mosquito you can't get get rid of.

The group dictates what I write. I think in dramatic terms. Anyone playing the solo part in the concerto is dramatic, and it's the same thing with our little tiny group. In a piece like "Three Little Feelings," the star characters are Percy and Milt and Connie. They are given things to do that focus on them. I have written a lot of pieces based on the commedia dell'arte. I find the idea of the commedia attractive. They had to do the same things as jazz musicians. They never wrote things down. They developed pieces based on the prominent characters or events of the town they were working—things which would attract their audience. So they *created* their jobs, just as jazz musicians do. And, of course, I love the blues. Blues pieces are easier to write. You have a little form to fill out. I try to find blues in all non-blues— just in the way a group of notes goes together in a particular short phrase. I keep feeling those elements in non-blues music—the music in southern Yugoslavia, in Hungary, the music in North Africa and the Middle East, and in flamencan music. I don't believe in too much form. Music should have surprise in it, and too much fugue or any formula like that takes away the pleasure, which is what bothers me about the Third Stream and what Gunther Schuller has been trying to do. I'm not interested in that. But I am interested in the classical *orchestra*—particularly the stringed instruments, which still have to be brought successfully into jazz.

II. Beginnings

Heath: I was born April 30, 1923, in Wilmington, North Carolina, but when I was eight months old we moved to Philadelphia. I have an older sister, Betty, and two younger brothers—Jimmy, the tenor player, and Albert, the drummer. Pop was an automobile mechanic. He was a wild little guy, a great guy, and sharp and handsome. He played clarinet with the Elks. It was part of a weekly cycle. On Mondays he'd pawn the clarinet and get twenty dollars and pay his bills, and on Saturday, when he got paid, he'd get the clarinet out of pawn and play with the Elks on Sunday, and on Monday, back to the pawn shop. I said to him once, "Pop, if you just keep the clarinet out of pawn one week you'll be all right and you won't have to pay that dollar interest." But it was his thing, his habit, and he never kicked it. He had Bessie Smith records, and every once in a while he'd pull out his clarinet and do Ted Lewis or his own Silas Green routine—Silas Green from New Orleans. In the early thirties, he rented space in a garage and had his own shop, and up until then we had money. Then the Depression ran the small businesses out, and he took a W.P.A. job for a couple of years, and went back to being a mechanic for somebody else. My mother was a hairdresser. She was a choir singer, and her mother before her, in the Baptist church, where I spent a lot of time when I was growing up. Those old sisters screaming and falling out in church, you felt something going through you when you watched them. We had a family quartet. My grandmother sang bass and my mother soprano. I used to sing on a sepia kiddie hour on the radio, and the kids who made it on the show got special passes to the Lincoln Theatre, where we would get to go backstage and shake hands with Fats Waller and Louis Armstrong and Duke Ellington.

I went to school in Philly until the last two years of high school. There was an all-colored school across the street from my grade school and the Italian and Jewish kids in our block had to walk three blocks to their school, which we all thought was a joke. From junior high on it was integrated, but six years of separation and the damage was done. Being thrown suddenly together couldn't undo it. I played a little violin in junior high and I had the second chair in the first violin section at graduation. But it was rough getting home through the streets—you know, a little skinny guy named Percy carrying a violin. I chopped and hauled wood after school, and hauled coal and ice in the summer. I'd bring home four or five dollars a week, which was all right in those days. My father's mother had a grocery store in Wilmington, and we used to go there for the summers, and so I stayed down there and finished up high school. I came back to Philly when I was seventeen and went to work with my father, and the two of us enrolled in a night school that specialized in mechanics. This lasted a year or so, and when I saw I wasn't getting anywhere at the shop—I'd be upstairs really involved in a carburetor job when they'd call up, "Hey, Percy, come on down and wash this car or do this grease job"—I said, "O.K., Pop, maybe I'm a dummy, but I'm going someplace else." I went to work for the railroad and ended up handling big equipment, moving engines around the yard, and I earned a boiler-watcher's rating. I started going out with girls and I had a car. I was making a lot of overtime and I'd get these fat paychecks—eighty dollars and more every two weeks, which beat the twenty bucks I was making with Pop. Then after a year or so I got a bright idea—volunteer for the Air Force and get into aircraft mechanics school. I took the physical. Underweight. They told me to come back in thirty days. I went home and slept late and ate bananas and went back. Still underweight. My number came up and I was drafted and I realized why I was underweight: They didn't have any colored aircraft mechanics school.

I made a great score in the mechanical part of the aptitude tests they give you and one day I was asked, "Do you want to be a pilot or a navigator or a bombardier?" I was amazed. I remembered reading about some guy standing up in Congress when this program was announced and saying, "This is all very well and they've come a long way but they aren't ready for *flying* yet." I has sent to Keesler Field in Biloxi, Mississippi, where we lived in tents in a low area way over on the wrong side of the base, separate and unequal. The closest we got to an airplane was at Saturday parades when somebody would look up and say, "Hey, there goes a B-24." Then we were shipped to the Tuskegee Army Air Force Base at Tuskegee, Alabama. I graduated in January, 1945. Seven hundred of us started out and twenty-eight graduated. I was a lieutenant and had my wings and my boots and everything but a forty-five, which is the last thing they issue before you go overseas. I never got my forty-five. The European war ended and I got out and there I was with all that training and no place to use it. There were umpteen million white guys with multiple-engine ratings coming back and I was a Negro with a single-engine rating. So I had to find something captivating to me. Having become an officer and a gentleman, I naturally didn't want to go back to all that dirt and grime. I'd heard a record with Coleman Hawkins and Sid Catlett and John Simmons, the bass player, and decided that's for me. I decided to go back to music. I went to the Granoff School of Music in Philly and studied harmony and I took lessons on the bass from a little old guy named Quintelli. I learned the C scale and how to read stock parts and I joined the union. I'd already worked in non-union places in some really funky neighborhoods in Philly. Then my brother Jimmy came home from Nat Towles' band. He'd heard Charlie Parker for the first time, and Johnny Hodges and Cleanhead Vinson just weren't it anymore. So we had continuous practice sessions at home. My mother was a great woman to put up with it. We even wrote out Parker's "Billie's Bounce" for Pop to play on clarinet. He made it sound just like a march. So we learned bop and had gigs. I worked with a Nat Cole-type trio for five or six months and then became part of the house rhythm section at the Philly Down Beat Club, along with Red Garland

and Charlie Rice. Everybody played with us—Coleman Hawkins and Eddie Davis and Howard McGhee. I worked in a rhythm-and-blues band led by Joe Morris and joined McGhee in 1947, and I was with Fats Navarro and J. J. Johnson and Bud Powell and Art Blakey and Miles Davis after that, and in 1950 I went with Dizzy.

Kay: My parents lived in New York, but my mother's brother lived in Tuckahoe, and I was born there on the twenty-seventh of April, 1927. I was the only child. My parents are West Indians who came from an island named Montserrat. Their name is Kirnon and I was born Conrad Henry Kirnon. Originally the name was Kiernan, which was the name of one of my great-great-great-grandfathers, who was Irish. My father had a tailor shop in New York, and when that didn't do too good he got a job as an elevator operator, which he did until he retired. My mother had odd jobs doing housework and down in the garment center. She was musically inclined. She played piano and organ in church and she sang a little. She taught me how to play piano. She insisted I learn, but I didn't like it. My father played a little guitar. My mother used to let me stay up and listen to Cab Calloway broadcasts and I'd take the wooden bars out of coat hangers and shape them into drumsticks and play on the hassock. A friend of mine had an uncle who kept a snare drum under his bed and we'd sneak it out and play it. So I always loved drums. I had my first gig right around the corner from where we lived in the Bronx, at a place called the Red Rose. All the guys were young and the only seasoned professional was the piano player, Jimmy Evans. He'd grown up in Monk's neighborhood, in the West Sixties, along with Elmo Hope and Tiger Haynes. The drummer at the Red Rose got sick and they had heard me practicing out of the window and asked me if I wanted to go to work. My parents said yes, and I stayed there weekends on and off for a couple of years. After the Red Rose, I was at Minton's in Harlem in a trio with Sir Charles Thompson and Miles Davis. We'd play one set and generally that was it. The rest of the evening it would be people sitting in—Charlie Parker and Dizzy Gillespie, Milt Jackson, Georgie Auld, Red Rodney. I remember when Ray Brown first came there. Freddie Webster came in all the time and he showed Miles how to get those big oooh sounds, those big tones Miles uses now. I was with Cat Anderson's band after that and then I toured the South with a rock-and-roll group led by Frank Floorshow Cully. I wanted to see what it was like down there. Cully was a tenor player and he was just like his nickname. He'd jump up and down when he played and stick the saxophone between his legs and do splits. Randy Weston, the pianist, was in that band, and it wasn't a bad band. The bass player hit all the wrong notes, but he had a hell of a beat. You just closed your ears and felt the beat. We travelled in a seven-passenger Chrysler, and we went as far as Lubbock, Texas, and both coasts of Florida and Mobile, Alabama. I wasn't too surprised because I'd heard how things were down there, but it was still a revelation. We worked at a big roadhouse for several weeks that used to feature people like Blue Barron and Horace Heidt—we were the first colored band that had ever played the place—and during intermission we were supposed to go back in the kitchen and stay there. But you'd be offered drinks by customers and you didn't know whether to accept and stay out front or get on back. In those days it didn't pay to be a pioneer. We'd pull up at a restaurant and be told to go around to the kitchen and there you'd find a regular booth with a Formica-top table and all, which was fine with me because they always piled your plate up. At orange-juice stands you'd have to drink your juice off to one side, and if we stopped at a grocery store they'd sell us cold cuts and canned stuff, but we had to eat it in the car. Once we ate in a restaurant owned by a colored cat and I told him if we get together, organize and the like, maybe we can *do* something about all this crap. Well, he wanted to fight *me*. He had two restaurants, he said, and everything was *all* right. It was a two-month tour, and later I took another one with Lester Young's band. Joe Louis and Ruth Brown and Buddy Johnson's big band were on the same bill. Louis had this routine with a straight man of cracking a few jokes and throwing some fake punches and doing some Shuffle-Off-to-Buffalo-type dances. It was pathetic.

By this time I could get a job with anyone. My main asset was I could keep good time. I had made a whole lot of rock-and-roll records for Atlantic Records. I was with Young off and on for five or six years. Lester and I were like buddies. When I joined him, I already knew him, but he didn't know *I* was joining him. I met him down in Penn Station and asked him what he was doing, and he said, "I'm waiting for the drummer, Lady Kay," which is what he always called me. "Well, I'm the drummer," I said. "What! You're the drummer?" and he fell out. He was a sweetheart to me. He was very shy. He didn't love crowds or to be around strangers, and he didn't like to eat. All that alcohol. He'd leave home for work with a fifth of Scotch every night and everybody in the band would work on it to keep Lester from getting too drunk. It was terrible I drank so much Johnny Walker. Later, the doctor told him to switch to cognac—a *little* cognac —so it was a whole bottle of cognac every night. He had a funny, codelike way of talking, with nicknames and strange names for everything. Everybody was Lady So-and-So, a chorus was one long and two choruses two longs, and he had nicknames for all the different songs.

A lot of the jive talk you hear now on TV I first heard from Lester, and when he and Basie and Old Man Jo Jones got together they all talked it. He wasn't a forceful person, but he'd get fed up. One time he had a trumpet player who took the same solo on a certain tune every night, and when he'd start Lester would look at me and say, "Damn, Lady Kay, there he goes again," and we'd sing the whole solo note for note right along with the trumpet player. Lester didn't feel he was getting the recognition he deserved and finally he got to the point where he didn't care whether he lived or died. I used to ask him why he didn't play his clarinet once in a while, and he'd always say, "Lady Kay, I'm saving that for my old age."

Jackson: There were six boys in my family and I was the second. I was born in Detroit on January 1, 1923. My mother was from Georgia and my father from Winston-Salem. She had a very religious background—the Church of God in Christ, which we call the Sanctified Church. She was a housewife and she worked in a defense plant during the war. My father was quiet but very lively, always on the go. I guess that's why I stayed so small—always moving so much. Also, it's a trait of Capricorn. My father was a factory worker with Ford and Chevrolet, and he played three or four instruments—piano, guitar, and so forth. I started on guitar when I was seven, and I was completely self-taught. I didn't study anything until I took piano lessons at eleven from a Mr. Holloway. I took them two years. I've lost track of him completely, which I regret. I like to check those things out. By the time I got to high school I was playing five instruments—drums in the marching band, timpani and violin in the symphony, guitar and xylophone in the dance band—and I sang in the glee club and choir. But I was concentrating on drums. Then the music teacher asked me if I wanted to take lessons on the vibraphone, as something else to do. I'd finished the drum course and was even helping other kids on drums, so I tried vibraharp and got hung up on it immediately. I gave up the drums altogether and concentrated on vibes. By 1939 I had two things going. I travelled all over on weekends with a local gospel quartet, the Evangelist Singers. We broadcast every Sunday over CKLW from Windsor. I got into it through my playing in church. If they needed vibes, I made that; if it called for drums, I made that; if it called for guitar, I made that; if it called for piano, I made that. The other thing was I started playing vibes with Clarence Ringo and the George E. Lee band. Sugar Chile Robinson was in the first group I played with. I had met Dizzy Gillespie in 1942 and through him I had an opportunity to join Earl Hines' big band, which he was with. At least there were about to be negotiations to join the band, but I got drafted and ended up in Special Services in the Air Force. I never went overseas and I got out in 1944 and went back to Detroit, where I organized a little group called the Four Sharps. It had guitar, bass, piano, and me, and we were backed by the Cotton Club. Detroit was full of musicians —Howard McGhee, Al McKibbon, the Jones brothers, a good alto named Burnie Peacock, and Lucky Thompson. Yusef Lateef and I went through high school together and Billy Mitchell and I grew up together.

The Four Sharps stayed alive a year and then Dizzy came through and sat in one night and persuaded me to go to New York, so I went in October of 1945. He had Ray Brown and Max Roach and Charlie Rouse. We worked the Brown Derby on Connecticut Avenue in Washington, went back to New York, and out to Billy Berg's in Los Angeles. We had Stan Levey on drums, Al Haig on piano, Ray Brown, Charlie Parker, Lucky Thompson, Diz, and me. We took the train. Man, four and a half days. We left on a Tuesday and got there Saturday. I guess we stayed out there six or eight weeks. Slim Gaillard had the other group at Berg's, and they wound up as the stars. People went for the new jive language he sang, and anyway Slim is a very entertaining man. And Frankie Laine would come in every night for his two numbers. The audiences couldn't understand what *we* were doing, but it didn't bother me. I'd just turn my back on them and listen to Charlie. That was all I wanted to hear. When we got back to New York, Dizzy organized his big band, and that's where I first met John Lewis. Klook —Kenny Clarke—was responsible for bringing John in. I stayed with Dizzy until 1947 and then worked with Howard McGhee and Jimmy Heath and Percy, and in 1949 and 1950 I was with Woody Herman, and then I went back to Dizzy.

John and Ray Brown and Klook and myself had actually played as a group as early as 1946. We'd play and let the rest of the band rest. I guess it was Dizzy's idea. I stayed with Dizzy until 1952, when we tried to get the Quartet going. Ray Brown left, so we hired Percy Heath. John suggested the name of the group.

Lewis: I was born in La Grange, Illinois, a suburb of Chicago, on May 3, 1920, but by July I was sitting in Albuquerque, where my grandmother and great-grandmother lived. They'd come from Santa Fe and my mother from Las Vegas, New Mexico, which was there long before that other one. My people came down from the Cherokees —the Virginia Cherokees. I don't know much about my father, Aaron Lewis, except that he came from Chicago and was an interior decorator and played good fiddle and piano. He and my mother were divorced not long after I was born, and my mother died of peritonitis when

I was four. I remember that. So I was raised by my grandmother, who is still alive and comes to see us once a year, and by my great-grandmother, who died in 1953. Except for my mother, they were strong women. My great-grandmother knew Pat Garrett, who shot Billy the Kid, and I think she even knew Billy. And she knew Geronimo, the Apache chief, who was a remarkable man, a very clever, intelligent man. My grandmother was a caterer and my grandfather had a moving-and-storage company. I never knew him. He accidentally shot himself in the foot duck hunting and developed tetanus. And my great-great-grandfather had owned the Exchange Hotel in Santa Fe. I had a good childhood. Albuquerque was a town of just forty-five thousand souls in those days and everything was so special—the Spanish culture and the air and the cleanness. We lived right in the middle of town and there were very few Negroes. It was the people of Spanish extraction, or Spanish and Indian extraction, who had the hard times, not the Negroes. I went to the public schools and the atmosphere was very competitive. Once you got on the honor roll, you had to *stay* on it.

Everybody played something in my family, so I started on the piano at five or six. It was drudgery, and I tried to revolt on the grounds the lessons cost so much, but failed. I took lessons forever. When I was ten or so I was in a little band. We were Boy Scouts winning music-achievement badges. Our first gig was in a real night club. We played from nine to twelve and were paid a dollar apiece and all we could eat, and someone came along to watch over us. There were local bands around and a lot of Southwest bands came through town. Eddie Carson had one of the local groups and I had cousins who played in it. Sticks McVea, who was a fantastic drummer, would bring his band in from Denver. Freddie Webster was in it, and he had a wonderful piano player named John Reger. John Hammond wanted Reger to play with Benny Goodman, but Reger's wife wouldn't let him go East. I'd take Reger's place some nights. And the Bostonians would come through, with Jay McShann on piano and Howard McGhee on trumpet. Lester Young sometimes played in town. He knew my whole family. He was a very gifted, talented genius-type person. He was like a poet. Everything came out as poetry when he talked. By the time I was fourteen or fifteen I was working in dance halls and night clubs. I had to learn Spanish music to play the fiestas. When I went to the University of New Mexico, I became the leader of a dance band there, and Eddie Tompkins, the trumpet player who had been with Jimmy Lunceford, would sit in. I took arts and sciences for two years, then became fascinated with anthropology. I devoured everything on the subject, and kept my music going at the same time. Then, six months before graduation, I was drafted. It's the only thing I've ever had against the Japanese people. I was in the Army four years, in

Special Services, and the best thing about it was that I met Kenny Clarke in England in 1943 or 1944. At the time, there was a surplus of pianists and drummers, so Kenny and I took up trombone. It was all right. In fact, I can still play it.

III. Room to Live in

Jackson: I built my house in Scarsdale a couple of years ago. My wife, Sandra, and I moved up there with our daughter, who's four, from Hollis, Long Island, where we'd lived for nine years. It's been beautiful. No hostility. The people around us have some money and they're not concerned with whether you're a Negro. We have all kinds —Jews, Italians, Negroes—and they just aren't concerned with it. I've handled the race thing fairly well. I've been pretty outspoken. I don't know whether it helps or hurts, but it gives me a clear outline on life and myself. The first thing a man has to do is take stock of himself. You have all these people who go to school and study and still don't know themselves or what they want in life. I never had that trouble. From the age of seven I knew I would play music. There was never any doubt in my mind. I've always had my feet on the ground, had a good idea of where I was going. Like in high school, I wanted to learn something about my ancestry. I wanted to know where my forefathers came from and what they did. I was regarded as a troublemaker, asking questions like that. And in 1943, during the Detroit race riots, I wanted to organize and go back to Detroit from the Army instead of going to Europe and fighting somebody else.

Heath: We live in a big old white 1902 house in Springfield Gardens, in south Queens. It's near Farmers Boulevard, where the farmers used to take their stuff up to market. I bet we live on the only block in the city limits that has just four houses on it—ours, an old Colonial house whose owner, a lady, was born in our house, and two others. There aren't any sidewalks out front and we have fruit trees in the backyard. The neighborhood was a model integrated one when we moved there in 1958, but it's changed. The white families have begun moving out and the area has become one of families where both parents work and the kids have keys to their houses to let themselves in, which is where the trouble starts. We never go out when I'm home. I seldom go in to New York anymore, unless it's to rehearsals or if we have a gig there. It's too much to go and see all these cats standing around, half of them without gigs.

Lewis: We take a vacation in the summer, guaranteed July and August. It's based mostly on Percy. He has the older children and he wants to be with them when they are out of school. And Connie, who lives with his wife near Lincoln Center, has two boys, and he likes to be with them. We work steadily the rest of the year, and it has to be that way, with the vacations. The group is a coöperative and always has been. We have a corporation, the Modern Jazz Society. I'm president, Milt is vice-president, Percy is treasurer, and Connie is the secretary. We pay ourselves a weekly salary, and we don't have any such thing as a leader, in the old-time concept of a leader. I serve as artistic director and musical director. Occasionally I *have* to make the group do something, and later they generally see it's what we should have done. Sometimes I cut things so fine trying to make everyone happy it frightens me. We've gotten along well or we wouldn't still be together. We're smart enough and clever enough to give each other room to live in, to have respect for each other's personalities. It's not a perfect marriage by any means; it's normal travelling by sea, with stormy periods and all. The time we see of each other outside of our work is reduced even more than it was. We see enough of each other when we're out on the road, where we always have separate rooms. Milt gets up early and I do, too. Percy and Connie don't. Some of us, Connie in particular, like to watch TV and some don't. We have a fine for lateness. It's fifty dollars for the first five minutes and fifty dollars for each fifteen minutes thereafter, unless there's a sufficient excuse, which traffic and such isn't. You just start early enough. If anyone were to be late, it would probably be Percy or Connie. Milt and I generally come early. It would be impractical to break the group up. We're way past the point of no return financially. It's too late for all of us, trying to make it on our own.

I bring in the music and the arrangements and the group starts learning. Every now and then I put something in a piece that they can't play, so there isn't any dullness. They are fair readers. It takes us a long time to learn things, but they're much faster than they used to be. It generally takes us three hours to learn a piece, which is the length of a standard rehearsal. The whole thing on my part is to anticipate this or that musical difficulty, which means spending more time writing and thinking. We have over three hundred numbers in our repertory, and it grows and changes all the time. Sometimes I change certain passages in numbers, and tempos automatically tend to get faster through the years. And the group grows steadily and understands the music better, and that contributes to change. When we haven't played a number for a long time, we have to sit down and start all over with it. Gradually each piece comes to sound as if it is improvised all the way through. Some actually are and some are almost all written. "The Jasmin Tree," which I wrote as the sound track for a government documentary, starts with six choruses of pure improvisation. Milt plays three choruses and I play three, and then the end of the piece is all written. The length of a piece is pretty much dictated by where it is in the concert program, and the program is figured out, balanced out, from the first number to the last, so that it has a design and structure. So the program as a whole comes first, the pieces next, and the solos last. We don't have any prearranged signals, aside from somebody just looking up from his instrument, for letting each other know when he's finishing a solo. Jackson almost always takes the same number of choruses and I just seem to know when he is finishing, and it's the same with him when I solo. We abhor long solos. If good things don't happen in the first chorus of any solo, they're generally not going to happen at all.

Heath: The group didn't take its first vacation until seven years ago. I guess I pushed hardest for it. My wife and I have three boys—Percy, eighteen, Jason, thirteen, and Stuart, eight—and this business of working all year for ten years, it was *nothing*. It was ten years of double existence. If I'm out there on the road worrying about what's going on here, I might as well not be there. So I had to tell June, "Whatever comes up is on you, Snooky," and she's handled it ever since—everything, all the cuts and bruises and sicknesses that come along with kids. When I first brought up the vacation idea, it was "Oh my . . . Hmm . . . Well, I don't know, the Quartet comes first." Damn! Anyway, we took our first vacation out on Fire Island, and it was not the vacation we had hoped for. I lugged all this electrical gear out there— hi-fi, tape recorder, toaster—and trundled it down the broadwalk to our house, the people I passed nodding their heads and mumbling about what a great generator we must have, and of course we got there and no electricity. Then I discovered David Amram and some other cats were staying nearby, so I ended up jamming every night. On top of that, fishing—particularly surfcasting—is my thing, but nothing happened. I don't think a fish passed that beach all summer. So the next year we went out to Montauk and we've rented a house there ever since. I have a camper, and I let the air out of the tires about halfway and we drive down the beach and fish and never see anybody for miles. There's a great group of people doing surffishing. They're from all walks. Sometimes I go to the Rockaways just south of where I live and once at dawn I was fishing and I noticed this figure way down the beach. We moved toward each other slowly and finally I thought, he looks familiar, and when we got near enough to see each other there was Ed Shaughnessy, the drummer on the "Tonight Show." We fell out—two jazz musicians meeting up at dawn on an empty beach. I don't see how people *don't* fish. To get that close to the fish in Montauk and not get involved—I don't see how people do it. Just to realize that big bass are swimming in between them in the water—unbelievable. I'm looking forward to the time when I can be by the seashore and in the sun chasing fish all year. Then if I take any vacation, it'll just be from fishing. Right now, messing around with all that salt water isn't the best thing for a bass-player's hands. It softens them up. But I start rehearsing a week or two before we come back and my hands are generally O.K. by the time we play our first gig.

Lewis: I met Mirjana, my wife, in Yugoslavia when the Quartet was on tour there. Her sister was going around with a Yugoslavian jazz pianist who worked in a group patterned after ours. I spent a lot of time with him and one night we went to Mirjana's house and I met her. She was going with someone else. I liked Yugoslavia very much. I liked it so much I went back every year to the jazz festival they have in June, and I'd spend most of my time with Mirjana's sister and her boy friend. Then in the summer of 1962 Mirjana and her sister the pianist—they were married by now—came to visit me in the South of France, where we were playing. They spent two weeks, and two weeks later Mirjana and I were married. You can only get married on Wednesdays and Saturdays in Zagreb, so we got married on a Wednesday and on Thursday I had to leave for a South American tour, and it took two months to get all the papers so that Mirjana could join me. Both she and her sister are pianists, and their father is a voice teacher. He is a remarkable, great human being. He is teaching now at the New England Conservatory. Her mother was an actress on stage and in films and she worked in the Underground during the war. We have two children—Sacha, who is four and a half, and Alex, who is a year old. I think we live where we do, in an apartment looking over the Hudson back of Lincoln Center, because the view always reminds me of one in Yugoslavia.

Heath: June is one in a million, one in eighteen million. She comes from Philly, and when I met her she was working in a record shop. She had a falling out with her family over things like having pictures of colored musicians on her walls. But she loved the music and she found the players were pretty human people. She'd stop by when we were practicing at my parents' house after the war, and I wouldn't even know she was there. She'd be sitting in the corner reading a book. It wasn't a matter of my choosing another race. It was a question of finding a good woman. I quit shaving back then—I couldn't stand all that scraping and chopping every day—and she didn't mind. She was willing to go to New York with me in 1949 and willing to take a gig as a nurse's aid at thirty dollars a week while I sweated out my union card. I guess what finally drove us out of Philly was one night when we were walking home from a movie or something and this cop pulled up beside us and says, "Are you all right, Miss?" June looked at him and said, "What do you mean?" "Well, I'm just doing my job," the cop says. "Of course I'm all right," June said, and we went on. And you know, that cop was a neighborhood cop and he knew who I was.

Kay: I still love to play, but it's not like when I was younger. I don't seem to see and hear that fire—that musical fire—that was all around us then. I don't seem to hear that kind of music anymore. Generally the people I like to play with just aren't around. They're in the studios or out of town or they have their own groups. But when I get the chance I like to play with Ray Brown and Bill Evans and Sonny Rollins and Jimmy Heath and John—John Lewis. To my mind, John plays very underrated piano. I like to play with Dizzy and Miles and I like Idrees Sulieman and Oscar Peterson. And Sonny Stitt and Cannonball, and I like Clark Terry and Sam Jones. I like to play with big bands, too. I don't think it's any harder. I play the same way as with a small group. A lot of drummers make the mistake with big bands of being louder and heavier, but all that does is bog things down. Playing with the Quartet can get a little monotonous, night after night, week after week. Sometimes you have to play the same numbers over and over to please the people. But no one in the group ever plays the same thing twice. It's always new, always different, and I have just about complete freedom. Sometimes John writes out a drum part to give me an idea of what he wants, but then I can change it around to the way I want it, and I'm absolutely free behind the soloists. I can feel by what they're playing when a solo is coming to an end. I can feel that they've just about run out of what they want to do. And I can feel when someone might want to change the rhythm or double the tempo.

Lewis: I think that the young primitive rock people have something going. There'll be new developments, some attractive ones. The music is getting better and better. A lot of their guitar players sound better to me than most of the thousand-note jazz guitarists. There are more good young jazz players in Europe than there are here—Jean Luc Ponti, a French violinist, and a bass player from Copenhagen, Nils Henning Ørsted-Pederson. He's pretty terrific. He's only twenty or twenty-one and he used to hang around Oscar Pettiford when he was a teenager. I've heard an eleven-year-old drummer in Yugoslavia with a great sense of time. And when you go to a festival in Europe it's not like it is here. Everybody *watches* everybody play, whether they're good or bad. Youngsters get up there on the stage, their faces as red as beets trying to play, and everybody watches. There's no question more is happening in Europe than here.

Heath: A group sound is one thing to work for and individual virtuosity is something else. I don't worry about the virtuosity thing. This recent bringing of the bass into the front melodic line is a mistake. Most bass solos, particularly if you don't know the tune, sound the same. The bassists figure out certain sounds and patterns and just fit them to whatever it is they're playing. I used to hang around with John Simmons a lot and then with Oscar Pettiford. O. P. and I would play bass and cello duets all night. Ray Brown showed me how to hold the bass properly. I always considered Ray the walker, the rhythm man, and Pettiford the soloist. But I'd rather be part of a group. I have to play certain parts as written, but you can hand a group of notes to ten different players and each one will read them differently. It's up to me to make those notes say exactly what they have to say, in a particular spirit. What we have over most groups is simple: We've played together for seventeen years. Another advantage is doing exactly what we want to do by creating music and selling musical entertainment. We've taken jazz into the concert halls of the world, even into the Mozarteum in Salzburg. We've performed with a lot of symphony orchestras, and respect for jazz has grown among symphony players. Some of them have even become jazz players. For a long time white Americans only understood polkas and foxtrots and waltzes, but through rock they're beginning to understand the jazz feeling, even if it comes from listening to an imitation of Muddy Waters from England. Jazz has always been considered a dirty music, an evil music, a colored music, and the country is still ashamed of it.

Jazz is a funny thing. Once you let the externals dominate—classical music or Eastern music or Brazilian music—you have something else. But as long as you can incorporate little bits and pieces from the East or Vienna or Brazil and still keep the special feeling of that dotted eighth, that pulse, that afterbeat, then it's fine. It's the same thing with the long solos, the Coltranes. I'd go hear Coltrane and after the set, which might be one long solo, I'd say, "Hey, 'Trane. How are you, man? You sound good," and I'd beat it out of there. That music is just one facet of existence; all that music does is shout Help! But all you have to do is look away from the chaos it's staring at and you'll find the ocean still there, the beauty and peace still there.

The way you play has to do with the way you feel that night. You hear that your kid was hit in the face three thousand miles away or you're lonesome and haven't found anybody to talk to or you're tired of the town and sick of each other; it all comes out in the music. After all, those people up there on the stand or the stage are *men*. You have to know how it feels to be miserable, how it feels to be sad, how it feels to be in the dumps before you can project it. When that slave cried out in the field, he wasn't just making music, he *felt* that way.

1969

Ecstasy at the Onion

I arrive in Denver on a Thursday afternoon to attend the preliminaries of Richard Gibson's seventh annual subscription jazz party, which begins on Friday at five-thirty in Aspen and ends on Sunday at six. All the news about the party that has filtered East in recent years has been good. A highly considered musician who has played it four times has told me that the music "ranges from the excellent to the exceptional." Moreover, in the process of hiring his musicians, Gibson has brought out of near-oblivion Joe Venuti, the astonishing seventy-year-old violinist, raconteur, and wit; Maxine Sullivan, the gentle, precise singer; Ernie Caceres, a fine and long-underrated baritone saxophonist; and Cliff Leeman, a former big-band drummer with an effortless, metronomic beat. Most important, Gibson persuaded Red Norvo to appear at the party in 1968, when Norvo, deeply troubled by hearing problems, had decided to quit music. Norvo and the rest of Gibson's reclamations have been working ever since.

Gibson meets me at the airport. He is a big, fast-moving, fast-talking, enveloping man of forty-three who is given to superlatives and laughter, and who favors sneakers and open-neck shirts. We take a cab to his house in Denver, and he talks about the party: "I gave my first jazz party in 1963. My wife, Maddie, and I were sitting around our living room one night having a drink, and she asked me if I missed New York, where we lived until eight or so years ago. I said all I missed were the ocean and jazz. I couldn't do a damned thing about the ocean, but maybe I could do something about jazz, and so the idea of the party sprang full-panoplied that night. We wrote letters to everybody we knew in Colorado, and at first the response was poor, but I brought in ten musicians from New York and we held the first

184

party, with about two hundred guests, over a September weekend in the old Hotel Jerome in Aspen. We charged fifty dollars a couple. The next year, we had eighteen musicians and two hundred and seventy-five guests, and we charged eighty-five a couple, but the party didn't really catch on until the following year, when we had twenty-three musicians and over three hundred guests. It was awesome how bereft Colorado was of jazz. Most Coloradians had never heard, let alone seen, a jazz musician. We kept the party in Aspen four years, and when the Jerome was shut down for legal reasons we moved to Vail, a new ski resort about a hundred miles away. Now the place we played in in Vail is padlocked and we're going back to the Jerome. Even though I charge a hundred dollars a couple now, I lose several thousand a year on the party, but that's my privilege. It's meant to be strictly a *players'* party, and the audience is there only as a necessity, as a kind of warming mirror for the musicians. Aspen is a perfect place, and I'm hung up on it. It's away from everything, and it has wit, beauty, imagination. The people who live there are very individualistic. It provides the ambience for what I want, which is an isolated experience—an experience that is intense and extraordinary and that when it is over takes on a did-it-really-happen dream quality for all the participants. The musicians—I simply choose the ones I know and like—react accordingly. Nobody loafs, because they sense that it is something special, that it's their party. Yet they have *time* to have a hangover or a bellyache or to waste a set. I decide who plays with whom in each set, and generally the musicians don't know who will be on the stand until they get up there. Marvellous surprises result. And the audience reacts in turn. Few people leave the room during the music, they are quiet, almost nobody gets drunk, and when the party ends, on Sunday, they scream for more. This year we'll have about five hundred people, including paying guests, guests of the party, and thirty-three musicians. Roughly half the guests are coming from Colorado and the rest from Sweden and Rome and Mexico and Toronto and from a good twenty or thirty states, including Hawaii, and I'm bringing Phil Woods, the alto player, from Paris."

Gibson lives in an old section of Denver, on the sort of mean but opulent street that turn-of-the-century *nouveau-riche* Americans exulted in. The street is narrow and heavily guarded by tall Chinese elms, and both sides are lined by mud-colored brick-and-stone mansions set shoulder to shoulder and decked out with massive eaves and high stoops. The inside of Gibson's house, with its dark, hand-carved panelling, parquet floors, distant ceilings, and stone solarium, is equally formidable. But every room is filled with musicians when we get there, and they have a cheering, softening effect. Teddy Wilson, sitting at the kitchen table and drinking a beer, talks about the late Coleman Hawkins' love for the unexpected, the unplanned. Bob Wilber, in tennis clothes, trots through the foyer, which is piled with musical instruments. Phil Woods is in the living room telling Joe Venuti, who is just back from a round of golf, that a cop, mistaking him for a hippie because of his long hair and Mod dress, grabbed him backstage at this year's Newport Jazz Festival, and that Dick Gibson, standing nearby, grabbed the cop and in turn was grabbed by another cop. Al Cohn and Zoot Sims are upstairs playing a tumultuous game of pool. Maddie Gibson, slender and brown-haired and attractive, moves from room to room, and the four Gibson children, ranging in age from fourteen to six, are underfoot everywhere. There is a pot of beef stew on the stove, and liquor bottles forest a small pantry. Maddie Gibson announces that everyone has been invited to the Flanagans', at the opposite end of the block, for cocktails and a buffet supper, and around six-thirty the migration begins. Musicians pour out of the Gibsons' house and out of half a dozen other houses, where the Gibsons' neighbors are putting them up. Zoot Sims, whose flowing hair and gap-toothed smile and bowsprit features give him a kindly Rasputin look, runs down the front steps, grabs a child's bicycle from against a tree, and pedals furiously up and down the sidewalk, his knees up to his ears, his hair standing out behind. An onlooker snaps a picture of him from across the street, and waves to the Gibsons. The Flanagan mansion, a forty-two-room behemoth, is already filled with tailored, glacéed Denverites. Seven or eight musicians, among them Toots Thielemans, Dave McKenna, Larry Ridley, Gus Johnson, and Woods, are playing at one end of an enormous living room. The party is loose-jointed. After supper Mrs. John Love, the Governor's wife, takes a chair in front of the band, and is immediately surrounded by acolytes. People stretch out on the floor, digging the music, and once in a while a child shoots down the bannister of the main stairs, sails into the living room, and collapses on the floor. Musicians wander in, play, and are replaced, but there aren't many sparks, and around eleven the music peters out. Gibson spreads the word that the bus for Aspen will leave from in front of his house at ten sharp the next morning.

The bus trip takes six hours, including a lunch stopover in Vail, and it is hair-raising. It begins with a grammar-school-outing air. We have gone only a few blocks when Gus Johnson shouts, "Stop the bus! Stop the bus! I forgot my teethbrush!" which provokes loud hilarity. And just before we board, Joe Venuti, round and implacable and cement-voiced, poses straight-faced for photographs in a derby jammed so far down on his head it splays out his ears and pushes his glasses halfway down his nose. Laughing musicians are all over the sidewalk. Around eleven o'clock we begin the long climb to Loveland Pass, which is just under twelve thousand feet. We move at twenty miles an hour because of our load, and once we are above the timber-line we wind endlessly along a narrow two-lane road, the mountains rearing up on our left and bottomless chasms falling away on our right. "They don't put any guardrails on this road because of the snow-plows," Teddy Wilson says offhandedly. "This way, they just push the snow off the edge." Gus Johnson moans, "Oh, man, why did I have to sit on *this* side?" and someone else shouts, "Don't look up! Don't look up!" Gibson, sitting near the front and verbally spurring the driver on, laughs and says, "Funny things happen on these weekends. Billy Butterfield, the trumpeter, can get very excited, and when he does he's apt to bite. He bit Zoot Sims one night in my living room in Denver, and Zoot said to me later, 'You know, Dick, I can't figure it out. When he bit me, it hurt like hell, but he didn't leave any marks. Do you think his teeth are made of rubber?' And once when we were flying back to Denver after the party with the musicians on Sunday night and bumping the hell all over the place, I noticed Cliff Leeman sitting there in the dark and rubbing Noxzema all over his face. He didn't know anybody was watching him. Then he took out a big alarm clock and set it and put it in front of him, and the moment the wheels touched ground it went off, and he said, 'Right on time,' wiped his face, and got up. There have been spooky times, too. A couple of years back, we took the bus home on Sunday, and when we got to Loveland Pass, which is just ahead, we were hit by a flash snowstorm. There had been an accident moments before in the pass, and it was com-pletely blocked. I was terrified, but I don't think any of the musicians knew what was happening. There we were, with very little air to breathe and a lot of aging musicians, and I thought, 'God, what if we're trapped up here five or six hours, how many of these great old men will keel over?' It was the worst moment of my life. Well, they cleared the wreck in half an hour, and, miraculously, we were on our way."

We grind through Loveland Pass, escorted by a mountain blue-bird, and roar down toward Vail. We heel the wrong way into hairpin turns ("She won't tip over," the driver says, turning all the way around and smiling. "She just feels that way"), flush beautiful black-billed magpies, and yaw and bounce over straight bumpy stretches, like a jet landing too fast on a poor field. I keep my imaginary brake pedal pressed flat on the floor. But we make it to the hotel at five, and on the dot of five-thirty the party begins.

A bandstand has been set up in a corner of the Jerome's dining room, which is small and high-ceilinged and already filled with guests.

The room is homogenized Victorian (red wallpaper, globe chandeliers, transparent scalloped drapes) and the audience homogenized Nixonian (blazers, frosted hair, tweeds). Hard-core jazz fans tend to be an absorbed, nervous lot, given to skinniness or fat, and I spot a sprinkling in the room. Gibson greets his guests briefly over a microphone and pulls the first set out of his hat—Bob Wilber, Lou McGarity, Yank Lawson, Bud Freeman, Dave McKenna, Bob Haggart, and Sol Gubin—and we are back at Nick's again. Teddy Wilson, accompanied by Jack Lesberg and Cliff Leeman, who gives a fascinating exhibition of faking on the fast tempos, pedals easily through the next set (all the sets, it turns out, are about half an hour long), and he is followed by a group made up of Clark Terry, Woods, Kai Winding, Sims, McKenna, Ridley, and Johnson. A neo-bebop head of steam is built up, and during the second number, a funny, swaying "Donkey Serenade," Sims plays the first of what is to be, during the weekend, an astonishing number of driving, beautiful solos. He begins in "Donkey Serenade" gently, like a good tutor beginning the morning's lessons, and works his way into an ascending five-note phrase, breaks it off, repeats the phrase, breaks it off again, repeats it, and then effortlessly finishes it with half a dozen perfect ascending notes which fall off into a fast, turning run. Ben Webster growls and flutter notes creep in, and Sims closes with a drawn-out wail. McKenna, a huge, lowering man who often constructs crashing, two-handed solos down in the dark lower registers, flies off Sims' catapult, and the set ends with a fast "Perdido" driven by Sims, Woods, and McKenna. Gibson spins his lottery wheel and out come Bobby Hackett, Peanuts Hucko, Al Cohn, Carl Fontana, Ralph Sutton, Milt Hinton, and Morey Feld. The set is lighted largely by a silver Hackett solo, in "In a Mellow Tone," and the first concert is rounded out by a group consisting of Billy Butterfield, Matty Matlock, Caceres, Vic Dickenson, Lou Stein, Lesberg, and Johnson. Butterfield is irresistible in his solo and in the closing ensemble of "Swing That Music," and Caceres ambles easily around in a medium-tempo "Rose Room." It is eight o'clock, and dinner is a ravenous prospect.

The proceedings resume at ten o'clock in the Red Onion, a dark, rambling, low-ceilinged night club and restaurant three blocks from the Jerome. There are seven sets in all, starting with a Lawson-McGarity-Wilber-Freeman-Buck-Pizzarelli-Haggart-Sutton-Leeman group and ending with a Butterfield-Winding-Wilber-Caceres-Cohn-Thielemans-Hinton-Stein-Gubin group. After a time, I feel I'm watching a long freight slock slowly by, and it is a relief when originality and invention break through. This happens in "Lazy River," when Wilber, an excellent soprano saxophonist, plays two majestic choruses, and it happens again in "Now's the Time," when Thielemans, on amplified harmonica, lets loose chorus after swirling chorus, each full of good, odd notes and neo-Charlie Parker phrases. His exuberance strains his instrument to the point at which it loses identifiable tone, and the music, freed of instrumental limitations, suddenly seems absolutely pure. Sims, working with a Fontana-Cohn-Terry-Woods phalanx, gets off a champion solo in "Lester Leaps In," and Venuti, in company with Hucko and Norvo, plays a stamping "Sweet Georgia Brown." (By this time something awful has happened to the sound system, and Norvo's vibraharp becomes inextricably entwined with Stein's piano, producing a new, ear-shattering instrument, the vibrapiano.) Caceres, playing a lolling solo in "In a Mellow Tone," provides the evening's final stimulation. We have been treated today to six and a half hours of music, and almost ten hours are scheduled for tomorrow. But Gibson, hustling around and scribbling personnels on a thick sheaf of papers, appears tireless, and so does Maddie Gibson, who, ceaselessly nodding her head all evening, never drops a beat.

The music starts Saturday at quarter to one, back at the Jerome, and I walk around town before it begins. Gibson is right; Aspen has it. The air is thin and sweet and clear, and everything is unbelievably peaceful. We are in the lacuna between Aspen's summer cultural bustle and the skiing season. There are no traffic lights, and the wide, empty streets line away and disappear at the foot of the mountains. The buildings, low and well spaced, look as if they have sprouted from the ground, and they range from weird, almost geometric sandstone or brick structures put up in the eighties and nineties to new no-nonsense condominiums. (Aspen, a native informs me this morning, has successively been a gold-mining town, a ghost town, a silver-mining town, a ghost town, a cattle town, a ghost town, and a ski resort. It will, he says, never be destitute again, for its skiing is now widely regarded as the best in the country.) Mountains ring the town, which is eight thousand feet up, and they lean back, letting in a non-stop Wagnerian show of mint-white clouds, black thunderheads, and topless blue skies. There are hippies around, and a few ten-gallons, but dogs seem to run the place. They're of every size and description, and they lounge on the corners, crisscross the streets, block doorways, snooze on the floors of bars, and wait in heaps in their owners' parked jeeps. Like most politicians, they ignore each other but bark a lot.

Going back into the hotel for the first set is like being called in from the ball field for a violin lesson. The dining room is jammed, so I find a seat at the back of a bleacherlike platform set up in the lobby. The acoustics are surrealistic. Most of the music that squeezes out of the dining-room door is lost in the lobby, which is almost as high as the main concourse of Grand Central and is full of jabbering musicians. Butterfield, Matlock, Sims, Fontana, Dick Hyman, Ridley, and Leeman take the stand, and Butterfield and Sims are faultless, in a down, searching way, in "Willow Weep for Me." In the next set, Gibson's mix-'em-up tactics pay off. He puts Wilber and Caceres together with a rhythm section. The tonal similarities and differences of the two horns are fascinating, and the two men, clearly digging one another, play intense duet ensembles ("Poor Butterfly," "Rosetta"), rubbing along contrapuntally, letting an octave or two of air in between them, harmonizing briefly, and throwing off pleasant dissonances. Their solos form an unbroken flow of ideas and seem the work of one man, and they close with a slow, affecting "New Orleans." A Lawson-McGarity-Freeman-Hucko Nicksieland set jounces by, and Teddy Wilson, backed by Hinton and Bert Dahlander, a longtime associate of Wilson who now lives hereabouts, slides through half a dozen Gershwin tunes. I lose most of it in the hubbub, but manage to catch a medium-slow wire-brush solo by Dahlander that is full of easy staccato patterns and humming cymbals. Cohn joins Wilson for a couple of numbers, and there is a good set by Hackett, Matlock, and Dickenson, who is funny on a fast "Sweet Georgia Brown" and sinuous and moody on an unfamiliar ballad. (Most unfamiliar ballads have open-ended titles like "Here We Are Now" or "Tomorrow Will Be" or "If You Only Could.") I look at the clock in the lobby and it is four, so I get a sandwich in the bar. I also have a Coors, which is the best beer in America. Two dogs are asleep under the bar rail, and another is stretched across the door to the street. I get back for the ninth set, which has Sims and Fontana and rhythm. (Zoot is fond of Fontana, who is a brilliant trombonist. Yesterday, after lunch in Vail, Sims was wandering back to the bus ten or so feet behind Fontana, and, passing a parked jeep without a cap on its gas tank, he leaned over and called into the pipe, "Hello, Carl.") The set equals the Wilber-Caceres duet. There is a fast "Man I Love," with good solos by all, Fontana picks his way delicately through "The Shadow of Your Smile," and Sims plays an aching "Gee Baby, Ain't I Good to You?" The so-called World's Greatest Jazzband (Lawson, Butterfield, Wilber, Freeman, McGarity, Fontana, Sutton, Haggart, Johnson) closes the afternoon, and Butterfield and Lawson play a fine growling-and-moaning duet in "St. James Infirmary." The festivities are to resume at nine-thirty at the Onion, and I step outside to catch the last of the afterglow.

Gibson's whim tonight is black tie, and everybody looks like a swell, Aspen being basically a gum-boot-and-lumberjacket town. Five sets step by, and I wonder why Gibson keeps them so short. The party, he says, belongs to the musicians, but when musicians hit a groove they

like to stretch out—an indulgence generally forbidden in night clubs
and at festivals and in recording studios. The five sets are notable only
for two Wilber choruses on "Crazy Rhythm," for Sutton's solo rendition of a rare Bix Beiderbecke piano piece, "In the Dark," and for
Fontana's playing with Winding and rhythm. Fontana is gentle, meticulous, lyrical, and subtle on all three numbers, and Winding, a
shallow, bravura performer, must feel superfluous. Then the remarkable Venuti, accompanied by Hinton, Stein, and Feld, comes on. He
is a first-class violinist who carries off his technique with humor and
imagination (one celebrated device: he unhooks the frog on his bow,
puts the bow stick beneath the violin and the bow hairs across the
strings, and rehooks the frog, which enables him to play all four strings
at once). His ideas never cease, and he swings unbelievably hard for
a musician who came up in the twenties and early thirties, when jazz
was still finding its rhythmic legs. He warms up with a fast "I Want
to Be Happy," and in a blues he uses his four-strings technique, producing all sorts of dark, marvellous chords. Then Sims unexpectedly
appears from backstage. Venuti roars into "I Found a New Baby,"
carrying the melody while Sims plays close counterpoint. Each man
solos with exhilarating fervor, and the two go into a long series of
four-bar exchanges in which Sims plays astonishingly hot and funny
parodic figures. The final ensemble, jammed as hard as any collective
improvised passage I have ever heard, is unique, for the two instruments are so close tonally and melodically and rhythmically that they
sound like one instrument split in half and at war with itself. The
number ends, and Ira Gitler, an editor of *Down Beat,* appropriately
shouts "Jazz ecstasy!" Sims retires, Venuti and McGarity play a polite
violin duet, and Venuti, just before unpacking "I Got Rhythm," calls
out, "Where's Zootie? Where's my Zootie?" Sims reappears, and the
two just about match their first performance. We cool off for the rest
of the evening with the World's Greatest Jazzband; a Norvo-Hucko
set, which is drowned by Morey Feld's flashy, unsteady drumming
("His girl friend was in the audience," a musician explains the next
day); and a good, funny version of Dizzy Gillespie's "Owl" by Terry,
Woods, Wilber, and Caceres. The Venuti-Sims explosion neatly im-
poses form on the weekend: two days to reach the peak, and one to
get back down.

I have seen something yesterday and today that I have never seen
before. At the end of nearly every set, the musicians smile and shake
hands with each other.

I go for a swim in the Jerome pool after breakfast on Sunday and
watch an eagle casing Red Mountain, and then I run into Gibson in the

lobby. He is wearing the guest badges for all seven jazz parties on the left side of his shirt, and he looks like a five-star general. We sit down, and I ask him to tell me about himself. He demurs, saying it is the musicians' party, and so on, but then the autobiographical gates open: "Well, I was born in Mobile, Alabama, and I was an only child. My father, a strange, witty, secret man, left when I was three to work in a brokerage house in New York, and my mother left not long after to be one of the early supervisors of hostesses for what was to become American Airlines. So I was raised largely by my maternal grandparents. At seventeen I joined the Marines, was wounded, and was out in a year. Public Law 16 enabled me to go right through the University of Alabama, where I got a degree in psychology and played left end on the football team. Then I hung around, taught a little creative writing, coached football, and ran the university's white-rat lab. One day I looked in the mirror—I guess I was twenty-four—and asked myself what the hell I was doing, and a week later I was in New York, beating the streets for a job. I ended up a space salesman for *Town & Country,* and went on the *Herald Tribune,* where I became the financial manager. That led to a vice-presidency with the Lehman Corporation. The last couple of years there got to be meaningless; I made a lot of money but spent every cent, and the commuting was an endless nettle. One two-degrees-below-zero morning I was waiting for the eight-two or whatever it was at the Larchmont station, and a railroad man came ambling down the tracks and said, 'It ain't coming today.' Well, *it* had run off the tracks in Stamford or somewhere. I thought, 'Somebody is trying to tell me something.' I went home and called my office and said I wasn't coming in, and the next day I quit. I searched the country, looking for both the best investment-banking firm and the best place to live, and Boettcher & Company and Denver won, both of which led to my involvement with the Water Pik. A Denver friend told me about this contraption a man had invented and was manufacturing in the basement of a bungalow in Fort Collins, which is sixty miles north of Denver, and that he was looking for financial backing. I knew enough about investment banking to know that you never loan money to inventors, but I drove up for a look. Four people were turning out several hundred of these strange boxes a year, and the place looked like Santa Claus's workshop gone wild. They gave me one, and I put it on a closet shelf and forgot about it. Well, it turned out that my gums were in bad shape and I was in grave danger of losing my front teeth. I came across the Water Pik one Saturday afternoon and started using it twice a day. When I went to my dentist five or six weeks later, he was astounded. My gums were perfect and my teeth saved. I found a president, Al Kuske, who is probably the finest businessman in the country, for the company, raised some money, and eventually quit Boettcher and became an executive vice-president of Water Pik. Everything went so well that the whole works was sold two years ago to a conglomerate for twenty-three million dollars. Now, at last, I'm doing exactly what I want to do, and I'm consumed with it. My life is devoted to getting the World's Greatest Jazzband on its feet, and to related, even more important matters, and there's nothing surprising about this, because the single, constant, gathering thread in my life has been my love for jazz. In fact, my addiction, predilection, immersement in jazz precedes my memory. There was a colored settlement around the corner from where I was raised, and I can't recall the first time I went over there. Maybe it was 1930. The houses didn't have electricity, and I can still remember the smell of the candles."

Maddie Gibson appears, and her party badges are pinned across the front of her waist. I thank Gibson, and she takes him away on urgent business. I wander over to the Red Onion, where the final session is to start at quarter to one. A musician says to me outside the Onion door, "Man, I don't know if I'll make this next year. It's *too* much music. After the first half hour, the audience starts listening with its eyes, and even the musicians go off to the bar or take a walk when they're not up there." There are ten sets, but the shadows of Venuti and Sims are everywhere, and the few bright spots are provided by Wilber in "Beale Street Blues," by a handsome Hackett-Dickenson set and a driving Sims-Cohn set, and by a lucid, calm Woods in "Here's That Rainy Day." Norvo, badgered by one thing and another all weekend, finally comes into his own with an exquisite, ad-lib, staccato version of "The Girl from Ipanema." The fifteen musicians still on the premises climb up on the stand for the last number and boom their way through "The Saints Go Marching In." The crowd screams for more, and the party is done.

The musicians' bus, half empty now, leaves the Jerome on Monday around ten-thirty, but I fly back to Denver over the Rockies in a little two-engine Cessna. We spend most of the flight in a snowstorm, stirred from below by peaks, and we get up to seventeen thousand feet. The oxygen mask feels good. Then we slide out of the soup and down over brown, sunny plains and into Denver, back from Shangri-La.

1969

The Music
Is More Important

"Please don't call it a vibraphone," Red Norvo admonished me. "I play the vibra*harp*, a name coined by the Deagan Company, which invented the instrument in 1927 and still supplies me with mine. Of course, I started on the xylophone and marimba in the mid-twenties, and up until then they were vaudeville instruments, clown instruments. They differ from one another chiefly in range, like tenor and alto saxophones. The xylophone is higher than the marimba, but both have piano-like keyboards, with three registers. The bars, or what would be the keys of a piano, are made of rosewood. The vibraharp has the same keyboard, but it is lower in range than the marimba. It's an electronic instrument, and its bars are made of aluminum. It's electronic because the resonator tubes that hang down underneath the bars, like an upside-down organ, have little paddle-shaped fans in them called pulsators that are driven by a small electric motor. When they're in motion, they enable the performer to get that rolling, mushing-out vibrato you hear from most vibes players. Vibraharps also have loud or damper pedals, similar to the piano's, which lift the bars off felt pads, and when you use the damper pedal *and* the pulsators you get that *uh-uh-uh-uh-uh* sound. On the vibraharp—if you'll pardon my saying it—you can cheat by using the pulsators and the damper pedal. It's been done and is done. I've never used a motor, but what I do have now is an amplifier, which Jack Deagan designed for me six years ago. It helps acoustically in bad rooms. Before, if you had just one microphone and you set it near the center of the keyboard, the upper and lower registers would be cold. Deagan put little crystal mikes in each resonator tube, but at first I couldn't get even amplification, and once when I flew into Las Vegas for a gig they left the instrument out in hundred-and-twenty-degree heat at the airport and all the mikes melted. The mallets you use affect the sound of the instrument. I have hard-rubber ones for the xylophone, and on the marimba rubber ones with a twine cover, which I use on vibraharp, too. Dixie Rollini, Adrian's widow, still wraps them for me. She doesn't do it for anyone else now. It's a nice gesture and I appreciate it. I also use slap mallets, which I invented in 1928. They're rectangular and flattish and the size of a kitchen spoon, and they're made of cork covered with felt and buckskin, and they cause a dead, tramping effect. The vibraharp is a peculiar instrument because it tends to take on the characteristics of the people who play it. Sometimes the instrument becomes the personality. And it's peculiar because vibraharpists are a pretty warm fraternity. Guitarists are also like that. Certain people choose certain instruments, and vibraharpists in general are gentle, quiet people. Trumpet players and drummers, on the other hand, can be pretty argumentative. But the main thing is to play the *right* instrument. So many musicians go through their lives on the wrong instrument. You hear guitarists who should be tenor players and pianists who should be trumpeters and drummers who should maybe be out of music altogether."

Norvo was sitting in his living room in Santa Monica. The room is big and blue and white, with a fireplace at one end and a Pennsylvania Dutch dining table, surrounded by Windsor chairs, at the other. A sofa and several more chairs, one of them a handsome eighteenth-century corner chair, ring the fireplace, and over the mantel is a forthright painting of Norvo playing his vibraharp. An apothecary's chest is against one wall, and near it, in a bay window, stands a beautiful marimba. The dining area is weighed down by a pine cupboard filled with Staffordshire china and a Shaker dry sink filled with spongeware. Opposite the marimba, a pair of open glass doors lead out into a small patio. It was a smogless ninety-degree southern California day, and the sun itself seemed to be in the room.

Norvo poured himself a cup of coffee from a small espresso pot. "Ralph Watkins, who used to run the Embers in New York, gave me this pot. You can't buy them here, or at least I've never been able to find one. You have to go to New York or San Francisco, and it's the same with the coffee. I used to drink it straight all day, but now I water it down some." He jumped up and opened a couple of windows behind the marimba. "It's hot in here, and I don't see why I have to keep all the windows shut. This is Santa-Ana-wind weather. The wind blows straight from the desert and across the mountains to the ocean. I was up early last Sunday and we went up to the Angeles National Forest to do a little varmint hunting. There were a lot of deer hunters down in the gullies and we were up on the high rocks, and so were the deer. We could see the brush fires starting and the wind was blowing like hell. It's usually very cold up there, but when we got out of the car it was *hot*, in the nineties. It was a shock. I hunt every chance I get. In Vegas you can practically lean out and touch the mountains from downtown, which makes hunting there a cinch."

In profile, Norvo, who is medium-sized, is S-shaped. He holds his head forward and his shoulders are bent from almost forty years of stooping over his instruments. He has a comfortable front porch and his legs bow out behind, like a retired hurdler's. Head on, he suggests a mischievous Scottish saint. His blue eyes laugh, and they are set off by V-shaped laugh lines. His nose is generous but subtly beaked, and he has a beard. The beard is orange-red and so is his receding hair, which is long and thick in back. When he laughs his eyes nearly close, and his teeth, in the surrounding foliage, shine like the sun in a fall maple. His voice is even and rich, and it anchors him. He was dressed in a green-and-white-checked sports shirt—worn outside of olive pants— and leather sandals.

I asked him how he liked the Newport Jazz Festival. He had been in a concert given over to vibraharpists, and he had, with his wit and precision and grace, easily matched his colleagues, among them Lionel Hampton, Milt Jackson, Gary Burton, and Bobby Hutcherson. Norvo sipped his coffee. "It was just fine. I was working down near Disneyland, at the Charter House, and when I got through at two-thirty in the morning I caught a plane which stopped in Kansas City and I think St. Louis. The weather was terrible in New York and no regular planes were taking off, so I flew from LaGuardia in a Piper Cub George Wein had hired. We were dodging clouds and going all over the place on the way up, and the pilot said if he could *see* the airport at Newport he'd land. I remember Providence way over on the left and Newport way over on the right, and we could see the airport, so in we went. There was a car waiting and it took me right to the festival and on I went. I'd been travelling eleven hours and I didn't have time to change my clothes. I didn't even know who I was going to play with, but sometimes it's better that way."

A short, pretty woman with dark hair in a feather cut and a Rubens figure came into the room. It was Norvo's wife, Eve. She was dressed in a nurse's white uniform, with white stockings and shoes, and she had a wide, dimpled smile and serene eyes. She stood in front of us with her hands crossed and said to Norvo, "Can I get you some more coffee?" He said no. "I work at St. John's Hospital near here," she told me. "I used to be in charge of the teen-agers who clean and carry trays and the like. But now I'm in Medical Records. It's five days a week from three to eight, and I love it. Where are you playing tonight, Red?"

Norvo consulted a pad. "In a motel in Huntington Beach called the Sheraton Beach Inn. We start around nine and I don't know where it is, so I better leave at seven. That'll give me time for getting lost and setting up."

Mrs. Norvo nodded and asked me if she could pick me up at my hotel in the morning and take me sightseeing on the way to the house. I said I'd be delighted.

Norvo waited until she had left; then he got up and waved his arms around and laughed. "Eve took this job a couple of years ago, when I was playing a long gig in Las Vegas. I was home one weekend and she said she was getting tired of sitting around, so I said, 'Go out and get a gig.' Well, she did, and I learned more about what she's doing there just now than I ever knew before. When the job in Vegas was over I told her she might as well quit. 'Quit? What do you mean, quit?' She got real insulted. When she got her first paycheck she came home real cool and laid twenty dollars on me, she was that proud. I laughed and told her, 'Some big spender.'

"Eve and I were married in 1946, a year before we moved out here from New York. She's always called me Red, but my first wife, Mildred Bailey, called me Kenneth, and so did John Hammond and my mother. They were the only people who always called me Kenneth. Norvo isn't my real name. I was born Kenneth Norville in Beardstown, Illinois, on three thirty-one oh-eight. Next March I'll be sixty-one. I don't feel it, that's the disconcerting thing. My daughter, Portia, who lives with us, is twenty-two, and she even has a little towhead kid. I got the name Norvo from Paul Ash, in vaudeville. He could never remember my name when he announced me. It would come out Norvin or Norvox or Norvick, and one night it was Norvo. *Variety* picked it up and it stuck, so I kept it. Norville is Scottish, and my family came from around Roseville, which is a little town near Galesburg. I had two brothers and a sister—Howard, Glen, and Portia. They're all gone. My father was a railroader, a dispatcher for the C. B. & Q.—the Chicago, Burlington & Quincy. He worked for the railroad all his life, and we moved around a lot before I arrived. I believe Portia was born in Hillsdale and Howard in Macomb and Glen in East Alton. My mother was eighty when she died out here, eight years ago, and we buried her in Roseville. My father was tall and dark and bald. He was stern but quiet-tempered. He liked to say things like 'It takes you all your life to learn to live, and when you have, you don't have time left to live.' He didn't drink, but he'd smoke a cigar and he was religious. He died a thirty-second-degree Mason. He built the new

Masonic Temple in Beardstown and they gave him the door knocker from the old one. I still have it around the house. He played piano—you know, mainly chords—and he'd sing in a big voice. He died before I was twenty. My mother was blond, always very thin and very proud. And she was astute about people—she never missed. Her name was Estelle, and we all called her Stell. She was always very strong on getting us out of small-town life. Of my parents, she had the edge where humor was concerned. Beardstown had a population of about seven thousand, and we lived on the edge of town. My brother Glen had a pony, Prince, and when he went away to college he kind of passed it down to me, but I never felt it was mine, so once when he was home on vacation I said, 'You should *give* me that pony. I don't feel it's mine.' 'All right,' he said. 'Jump off this porch and onto that pony and open up and get around the block in a minute flat and I'll give it to you.' My mother was in the back of the house, and she looked out the window and saw me streaking by and she came running out and yelled, 'The pony's running away with Kenneth, the pony's running away with Kenneth,' and when I came tearing around the corner of the house she could see—she'd known horses all her life—that I was in control, and we all laughed. I used to go into town on Prince to get groceries, and they'd load me up with a bag under each arm and I'd ride home using just my knees. Prince would stop right by the front door when I had groceries, but if I didn't have any he'd lickety-split it right into his stall and I'd grab an iron bar over the door and let him go and drop to the ground. Every Saturday we rode out into the country, and in the fall I got up real early and went up in the hills to get walnuts and pecans. We were on the Illinois River, and I got to know all the riverboats. The Capitol tied up at Beardstown around six o'clock in the warm weather and everyone piled on and she cruised until eleven. She always had a dance band, and one whole floor, one whole deck, would be a ballroom. There were all-day excursions that started at eight in the morning. Some stores gave out tickets like supermarkets give out trading stamps and the boat would go to a picnic ground and come back around six. Showboats came, too, twice a summer. They were like floating theatres, and they gave all the old clichés—'The Drunkard' or a minstrel show or 'Little Eva.' I remember one night excursion I heard Bix Beiderbecke and Frank Trumbauer. I couldn't have been more than ten or eleven. I was fascinated with Trumbauer. I spent the whole evening sitting and watching. I was thrilled, it sounded so good. And of course it was on the riverboats that I first heard Louis Armstrong."

A boy of around sixteen or seventeen sauntered in, and Norvo said that this was his son, Kevin. We shook hands and Kevin said,

"Howdy." He was dressed in a T-shirt and blue jeans, and he is a miniature Red Norvo. He has an undeveloped S-figure, red hair, pale skin, and freckles. "I've got an orthodontist's appointment at four," he said.

"O.K.," Norvo replied. "But will you pick up my shirts at the cleaners'? I don't have any to wear tonight. The ticket's out on the harvest table by the front door. I'll feed you when you get back."

"Money?" Kevin asked.

"Money! I gave you some money the other day."

Kevin smiled and nodded at me as he backed out of the room.

"Isn't he something? The other night some people were here and he told them I was the oldest beatnik in California. Where was I? Oh, the river. Every spring the river rose, and sometimes the levees held and sometimes they didn't. The water rose as high inside houses as that apothecary's chest, and I can remember fishing off our front porch. Once it rained and rained, and the principal of our school called us into assembly one morning and said, 'Grab your stuff and get home as fast as you can. The levee's broken.' The water was above my knees when I got home. I put Prince on the front porch and got his feed bag and straw and bedded him down. The cellar flooded and the heat and lights went out. It was cold. That lasted a couple of days, and my father decided to send my mother and my sister and me down to Rolla, Missouri, where my brother was in college at the Missouri School of Mines. We got through very slowly on the train, and I guess we stayed down there six weeks or so, and that's where it all began. When I was six or seven I'd taken piano lessons, and I'd had a dozen before my teacher discovered I couldn't read a note of music. I was doing it all by ear. One of my brothers or my sister would play what I was supposed to practice and I'd learn it by ear. My teacher rapped my hands with a ruler when she found out—she didn't mean anything by it—and I got frightened and never went back. But in Rolla I heard a man named Wentworth playing marimba in the pit of the theatre. I got fascinated and watched him every night. I was about fourteen. Then it turned out that Wentworth was in the same fraternity as my brother, and he told me I could go over to his room any time and fool around with the marimba he had there. I did, and when I got back to Beardstown it started eating on me and I thought about that marimba and thought about it. A friend of my father's who played wonderful blues piano got me a Deagan catalogue and I saw what I wanted. So I sold Prince for a hundred dollars and worked all summer on a pickup gang in the railroad yards, loading ties and jacking up the cars so that the wheels could be repaired or ground. The reason I sold my pony and went to work was that my father told me, 'You want this marimba bad enough, you get it.' I guess he was tired of paying for lessons and instruments when nothing came of it—like when one of my brothers came home from college, where he had taken up football, and put his violin away for good because it was considered sissy for a football player to play violin. My father was right. It was the best thing in the world for me because it made me really serious about it. When I'd saved enough I bought a table-model xylophone for a hundred and thirty-seven dollars and fifty cents. I never took any lessons. I taught myself to read as I went along and I learned harmony later, when I was on the road."

Norvo went out to the kitchen and got two 7-Ups. "I'd offer you a beer," he said, "but I haven't had any beer in the house since 1952, when I gave up drinking. And I gave up smoking six years ago. Once when I came home from a gig in Vegas I was smoked out and I just decided that's that. What I did was fast for a whole week. All I took was a little grapefruit juice and hot water or a little grapefruit, and I was so busy thinking about how hungry I was that I forgot all about the smoking. When I started eating again, the desire was gone."

I asked Norvo how he got his celebrated evenness and delicacy of tone on the vibraharp—an instrument that invites a muddy attack.

"It was the training the marimba and xylophone gave me. They taught me about evenness of tone. The notes die very quickly on wooden bars and you have to hit each one just right to get the time value you want. If you need a legato passage you really have to *play* legato and not depend on the damper pedal or pulsators, and staccato or fast things have to be clean and hard. If I want a vibrato effect, I add a little roll or tremolo to the end of the phrase, which has to be perfect and is one of the hardest things to do on the instrument. I can never play anything the same twice. Years ago, when I worked in vaudeville, I used to think I had to play things people could latch onto, things they would associate with me. So I worked out about a dozen figures, and every time I tried one it came out differently. Improvisation is like somebody running. Your reactions are fast and you're listening all the time. One ear's on what you're playing and the other's on what's being played behind you. You develop so you listen at a distance, you listen about twelve feet around you. I use the bass line— the melodic flow the bassist is getting—and I improvise against that. The bass line compensates for the way you are going to roll. Improvising is never dull. Each night is like a new happening to you. Tempos, moods, atmosphere, they vary all the time. One night you might play 'I Surrender, Dear' real legato and another night you might find yourself doubling and even tripling the tempo. I work with the construction of a tune, too. I consider its harmonies and linear design and its bridge. What is characteristic notewise in the tune you're working on can be the key to what you do."

Norvo yawned and shook his head. "Nap time. I'm up early every morning, but I need a couple of hours in the afternoon to get me through the evening. Why don't you come by tonight at Huntington Beach? First nights are uneven, and I have no idea what the place is like, but something might happen." He got up and I followed him toward the kitchen, a spacious, bright room with a gas stove, a wall oven, and a charcoal grill he had encased in brick. "I guess you've noticed all the Colonial furniture and stuff around the house," he said over his shoulder. "At one point we had so much I had to rent a garage near here to keep the overflow in. I started collecting when I was with Mildred, and it has become a kind of madness with me. I drop into junk shops and antique shops wherever I am in the country, and I've picked up a lot of things out here. People from the East bring beautiful furniture and china out with them, and then they die and their kids don't want anything *old* in their houses, so they sell it." We had passed through the kitchen into a formal dining room. "Those candlesticks and goblets on the shelves in front of the window are Sandwich glass. That one's a sapphire blue and that's vaseline and that's canary. Those are green and purple, and we call the milky color clam broth, and that blue is cobalt. Most of the lamps in the house are also Sandwich glass. I generally convert them myself. The corner cupboard is cherry and it's from Ohio. The china inside is Eve's. It's Canton, and the old clipper-ship captains brought it over as a kind of ballast and then sold it when they got here. The other corner cupboard is Connecticut, and you can see how much more delicate it is than the Ohio one. The dining chairs are Queen Anne side chairs with block-and-turn legs and Spanish feet. You wouldn't believe it, but I got them from a *museum*. Museums get overstocked, and I picked them up that way. Come on into the front room. The grandfather clock in the corner is extremely rare. It's from Lebanon, Pennsylvania, and is by a clockmaker named Miety. The wood is maple, and the horizontal stripes in it gave somebody the bright idea of calling it tiger maple. The harvest table is tiger maple, too. That's a tilt-top candlestand, and the graceful little feet are snake feet, and the sofa by the clock is—oh, hell, what is it?—O.K., a camelback Chippendale. And that's a Queen Anne wing chair across from it. Come on into our bedroom." We went through the front room into a small hall and into the bedroom, which was filled with a canopy bed and two highboys—one with a delicate fluted top and one with a heavy, sedate bonnet top. "This is my little room in here," Norvo said, leading me back through the hall. "Eve never touches it, and as a result it's filthy. I keep my

Bennington ware in this cabinet. It was made about a hundred years ago and I've got everything—a footwarmer, which I found covered with dirt in a junk shop in New York, and mugs, pitchers, coachman jugs, picture frames, doorknobs. You name it, I've got it. I'm told it's much sought after now. And I keep my gun collection in this closet." It was a walk-in closet. Part of one wall was hung with rifles, and a long row of pistols, each in a leather case, were lined up on a shelf. Big glass jars held bullets of every size and shape, and on a small workbench were two pistols in repair. "Maybe I love guns the most. There's nothing more beautiful than a beautiful gun used in the right way."

Fred Seligo, a friend, a professional photographer, and an admirer of Norvo, drove me down to Huntington Beach after dinner. "Nothing is measured in distances out here," he told me. "It's forty-five minutes or an hour or an hour and a half. This ought to be an hour's run. I guess Red plays at a lot of places like this all over the West—motels and hotels and the lounges in the casinos at Vegas. Red told me once that the owner of a place in Vegas where he had a gig called him into his office one afternoon not so long ago and said that he had to shave his beard off. In half an hour Red and the band were packed and headed back to the Coast. Not only that. Nobody listens to you in those places. The whole scene is sad when you think of it, but it doesn't seem to bother him. And I think he plays better now than he ever has." The motel was across the road from the ocean—a fair-sized building with wings jutting out on either side. We went through a lobby into a dark, circular room. The floor was carpeted and the walls were carved wood. There were hanging plants, and a circular dance floor, set in a well, was surrounded by tables and a trellis wall. Seligo looked around him. "Early phony Polynesian," he said. "And I'll bet that bar in there is called the Lanai Lounge." We took a table outside the trellis and fifteen feet from Norvo, who was set up in the entrance of what Seligo called the "piano bar." With him were piano, bass, and drums. Norvo was in the middle of "Blue Moon," in cha-cha time.

Norvo is the father of his instrument, and, like most originators, he is a visionary. In 1933 he made a startling avant-garde recording on xylophone that had Benny Goodman on bass clarinet, Dick McDonough on guitar, and Artie Bernstein on bass. One side was Bix Beiderbecke's pioneering "In a Mist," and the other was Norvo's "Dance of the Octopus." Both numbers are full of odd harmonies and notes, arhythmic collective passages that suggest the "new-thing" music of today, and a Debussylike motion. A couple of years later he formed a small band that tidily mirrored a big band, using arrangements and riffs and the like. It was, as Norvo has pointed out, the first non-Dixieland small band. His professional liaison with Mildred Bailey marked the first time a jazz vocalist had a first-rate jazz band built around her. In 1945 he headed a brilliant, groundbreaking recording date that brought together bebop (Dizzy Gillespie, Charlie Parker) and swing (Teddy Wilson, Flip Phillips, Slam Stewart, Specs Powell), and not long after that he played with Benny Goodman and Wilson and Stewart in Billy Rose's famous revue, "The Seven Lively Arts." Then he joined Woody Herman, becoming the first vibraharpist to play full time with a big jazz band, and he made small-band Herman recordings that adventurously echoed his own band of a decade before. He assembled a trio in the late forties, with Tal Farlow on guitar and Charlie Mingus on bass, that was probably the most celebrated group he has led and that remains one of the most celebrated in jazz. It lasted nearly a decade, with varying personnel, and in the late fifties Norvo went into the recording studios again, to make four timeless sides for Victor with Harry Edison on trumpet, Ben Webster on tenor saxophone, and Jimmy Rowles on piano. Since then he has had a steadily changing succession of small groups, each challenging and original, each light on its feet and light on the ear.

Norvo's style owes very little to anyone else. There are suggestions in his minute tremolos and in his admixture of sudden runs and lagging single notes of Earl Hines, whom he listened to in the late twenties, but the rest is his own. He is always improvising. In the first chorus of a number he will lead the ensemble with a refined, airy version of the melody, generally played somewhat behind the beat. He seems to pick out the best notes, suspending them briefly before the listener like a jeweller holding good stones up to the light. When he goes into his solo, everything doubles in intensity. He picks out single notes in the upper register with just his right mallet, occasionally jarring them with contrapuntal left-hand notes, inserts an abrupt, two-handed ascending rush that is topped by octave chords, returns to right-hand single notes (the last of them played flatfooted, with the mallet held on the bar after the note is struck to deaden the sound), plays a two-handed run that covers all three registers in both directions, and finishes his first chorus with a legato snatch of the melody. Norvo's flow of notes is startling; a pianist has the equivalent of ten mallets, but he has only two. His solos are without blur; each note is crystalline, polished, cherished. His rhythms shift constantly, and his choice of notes and harmonies is daring and questing. His solos are extrovert. They are full of good cheer, and when he plays a slow blues the emotion transmitted is clean and gentle and free of self-pity. A first-rate Norvo solo is like a piece of Eve Norvo's Canton china; its color and weight and glaze and design are in fluid balance.

"Blue Moon" was followed by a brisk "Sunday" and a brilliant "I Surrender, Dear," which started at a slow tempo, slipped into double time, with Norvo dodging back and forth between the original tempo and the new one, and ended in a triple time closed by an abrupt, free-fall return to the first speed. "Undecided" came next, and the set ended with a fast blues. Norvo talked to his musicians for a minute and then sat down at the table and ordered a coffee.

"Boy, what a set! Nothing went right. I couldn't hear the piano, and the drums sounded like they were underwater, and the piano and drums couldn't hear me. And the lighting is crazy. Whenever I lift the bars with the loud pedal, the light catches the aluminum and it makes me feel seasick, a little dizzy. It depresses me, but I don't let it get to me. My musicians are all down in the mouth, so I just told them, 'All right, the set was bum, but it's *over,* and there's nothing you can do about it now. You're all good musicians, professionals, and you *know* what the trouble is, so you can fix it in the next set.' If you're a leader, you can't show your feelings about depression and the like. You can't excuse yourself that way, any more than you can let drunks and such get to you. If they do, it's your fault. It's just an excuse to spout off, to insult them. It deteriorates you. The main thing is that jazz should be fun. After all, the *music* is more important than any of us musicians. I'm beginning to think it's not that way anymore, which is too bad. We've come into an age of geniuses, of big musicians swaggering down the sidewalk, and nobody has any fun anymore. I've never done anything musically unless I *liked* to do it. Of course, experience is the most important factor in being a musician. Gradually, through the years, you build a higher and higher level of consistency, and no matter how bad the conditions are—in an impersonal place like this you almost always feel like you're in left field—you never drop below that level. But if things *do* go wrong, you just accept it. You might not like what you are doing, but you accept it, and I've found at my time of life that that's the hardest thing of all. Like with my hearing, which I've had trouble with since I was a kid and had mastoids and the doctor lanced my ears. Then I got a fungus condition in Florida in the thirties, and that took a long time to clear up. Then early this year, in Palm Springs, there were times when I couldn't hear the piano, and one night I discovered that the E-flat I thought I was hearing in my head was coming in my ear a D. It scared me. I came home and my whole left ear—my right one has only had sixty-per-cent hearing since I was a kid—collapsed. It was frightening. I got so

I couldn't hear a dial tone, and I watched TV with the sound off. I stopped playing, and in June I was operated on, and when I was back in my hospital room my hearing was perfect. Since then it has been off and on. Sometimes I have trouble hearing the top and bottom of the keyboard, but the bones in the ear have begun to vibrate again, and that's a good sign. So now I just try to stop second-guessing myself when I play, to stop being so damned critical and just move straight ahead."

The next set began with "Our Love Is Here to Stay." The drummer had tightened his drumheads and he sounded crisp and clear, and the lid of the piano had been propped open. Norvo himself seemed to open up, and his solos took on a fleetness and urgency that were missing in the first set. Even his motions became more exuberant. He stooped over his vibraharp like a chef sniffing sauces. His head was jutted forward, chin up, and it swivelled from side to side. At the same time, he rocked on his feet, his cocked, outrigger elbows seemingly keeping him upright. Occasionally he looked down at his hands, following closely a complex run as if he were an entomologist tracking an ant, but then the head came up again, the beard pointing and the eyes scanning and scanning. A bossa nova and a slow ballad followed, and then Norvo picked up his slap mallets and played a tromping, funny, stop-time chorus. In the next number he sat down beside his vibraharp and played bongo drums, laughing and rocking back and forth. The group caught his cheer, and the final number, "Perdido," with Norvo back in the pilot's seat, was a beauty.

Mrs. Norvo picked me up at ten o'clock sharp the next morning. She was wearing a flowered cotton dress and big dark glasses. It was another hot, klieg-lit day. In half an hour we drove through Beverly Hills, Bel Air, Westwood, and Santa Monica, and saw the houses and castles of Tony Curtis ("He was on a television interview program a while ago," Mrs. Norvo said, "and afterward he got letters from all his old school chums in the Bronx asking to borrow money"), Jayne Mansfield, Fred McMurray, Maxine Andrews of the Andrews Sisters, Gregory Peck, Ella Logan, Pat O'Brien, and Phyllis Diller. We toured a corner of the U.C.L.A. campus filled with open-air garages that were larger than most classroom buildings in the East, and we saw the motel in Santa Monica where the Norvos had stayed when they came to the Coast and he was waiting for his Los Angeles union card to come through. ("We used to sit all day and play gin rummy and listen to the radio and go to the beach. It was a pretty nice life.") Then we turned into Alta Avenue and parked in front of the Norvos' house, which is gray and hugged by shrubs and—because it is clapboard—an oddity in southern California. The street is wide and pleasant. Towering palms and short magnolia trees line it, and the lawns are manicured. The ocean was only a block or two behind us, and a light fog was ballooning up the street. "I don't see Red's car," Mrs. Norvo said, taking off her glasses. "I guess he must have gone out for a few minutes. I'm a transplanted Easterner, too. I guess I don't miss the seasons anymore. If we want snow we can go up in the mountains, and of course we have the ocean. Sometimes I walk over and take a path that runs for three miles beside it. It's never the same. One day it will be peaceful and blue and the next it will be black and angry. And as Red says, New York used to have an atmosphere it doesn't have anymore. He used to feel that if he left town and just went to Chicago that he was camping out. And everyone in New York goes like a locomotive. Here the pace is sensible. I was born in Great Barrington, Massachusetts, and I grew up in Lee, which isn't far from there. My father was a tailor and my mother worked with him. Six months before I graduated from high school they moved to New York, and I stayed in Lee with friends until I was finished. I met Red backstage at the Paramount, where he was with Benny Goodman. Five days later he called me—he already knew my brother, Shorty Rogers, the trumpet player—and asked me to have dinner with him. I had been married before, and I have a son, Mark, who's twenty-seven and who's with Hughes Aircraft near the airport. I think Red's greatest asset is his humility. He is a humble, kind, generous man, and—oh, there he is."

Norvo was standing in the front door of the house. Mrs. Norvo and I got out and he joined us.

"I thought you were out," she said.

"They took the car to put new plugs in it. Come on in."

He led the way into the living room, and Mrs. Norvo went into the kitchen to make some espresso. I asked him how the rest of the evening had gone.

"Oh, we're getting straightened around. We moved the vibes a little forward and opened the piano up all the way and we began to hear each other by the last set. A couple of guys came in late, and one of them asked me if I was the same Red Norvo who played the Commodore Hotel in New York with Mildred Bailey in 1938, and I said I was, and the guy with him told me, 'He turned so fast to get in here when he saw the sign "Red Norvo" out on the road that the car nearly tipped over.' Tonight they're coming back with their wives and families. The same thing happened to me a while ago at the Rainbow Grill. People came up and said, 'Do you remember me? You played a dance in Pottstown, Pennsylvania, in 1936, and that was the night I met my wife.' Well, you can't remember those things, but it gives you pleasure that other people do. The thirties were a bad time for a lot of people, but Mildred and I—we were married in 1930—made it pretty well. I spent the last part of the twenties in vaudeville. I tried college twice—once at the University of Illinois and once at the University of Detroit. But it never took, and by Thanksgiving both times I was back on the road with the Collegians or the Flaming Youth Revue in some vaudeville troupe. I sang and played piano or xylophone, and I worked out a routine where I traded breaks with myself, playing xylophone and dancing. But I was never really happy in vaudeville. I had a Victrola I took everywhere, and I drove everybody backstage crazy playing jazz records on it. Then I worked my way up to being a single, and finally to leading house bands in Milwaukee and Kansas City and Detroit and Minneapolis, and when I went up to Chicago in 1929 I got a staff job with N.B.C., and we played radio broadcasts with Paul Whiteman and backed Mildred, who was with him then. I was already playing vibraharp and even a little timpani. I had my first band in New York with Charlie Barnet, and after that was the summer known as the Maine Panic. We got a gig to play Bar Harbor, and through a mutual friend we borrowed the name Rudy Vallée's New Yorkers. Vallée was big then, and since he was from Maine we arranged to borrow his name. I got together Chris Griffin on trumpet and Eddie Sauter, who were both with Goodman later, and Toots Camaratta, and I think we had Herbie Haymer on sax and Pete Peterson on bass and Dave Barbour on guitar. I was the director of the band, and I'd got arrangements by Fletcher Henderson and Teddy Hill, but the people up there were used to Meyer Davis. They'd never heard wild music like ours, and we didn't get paid because no one came back to hear us, and the only way we kept alive was with little gigs around Maine. We came back from one of them in a pickup truck, and when we got home we looked in the back and all the instruments were gone. We'd bounced them out, so the next day we retraced the road and we'd find a saxophone in a ditch and a trumpet in a cornfield and a snare drum in the bushes. We survived on apple pies made from stolen apples, flounders, and clambakes on the beach, with butter bummed from a farmer. Finally it got so bad, though, that Mildred had to come up and get me. But it was the most enjoyable panic of my life. Not long after, I put together my first real group. It had trumpet and tenor and clarinet and bass and guitar and xylophone. No drums and no piano. We opened at the Famous Door on Fifty-second Street. I had the group a couple of years and we worked the Hickory House and Jack Dempsey's on Broadway, and the Commodore, where I enlarged into a thirteen-piece group. Mildred joined us at the Black-hawk in Chicago in 1936. We were there all winter and came to be known as Mr. and Mrs. Swing, compliments of George Simon, the jazz writer. I had the group until 1940, but I had to give it up when Mildred developed diabetes and had to quit travelling."

Mrs. Norvo brought in the espresso and poured Norvo a mugful. "I got the idea for my trio, which I put together in 1949, after I'd moved out here. I figured a group with just vibes and guitar and bass could go into almost any place on the Coast, which would mean I could spend more time at home. Naturally, what happened was that our first booking was into Philly. We were playing opposite Slim Gaillard, who was swinging hard and making a lot of noise, and I felt naked. I wanted to know, what do you *do* behind a guitar solo with a vibraharp? Use two mallets, four mallets? What? It was awful. But by the last couple of days it began to unfold to me a little. Then we went to New York, and one night I stopped in to eat at Billy Reed's Little Club, where they had this sissy group. The guitarist, whom I didn't know, played sixteen bars of something that spun my head. Mundell Lowe was on guitar with me, and he wanted to stay in New York, but he said he knew a guitarist who would be just right and I told him I'd heard one who would be just right, too. I insisted Mundell hear my man and Mundell insisted I hear his man, and you know what happened—they turned out to be the same guy, Tal Farlow. I took the trio to Hawaii, and when we got back to the Haig here in Los Angeles, my bass player wanted to leave, and one night Jimmy Rowles, the pianist, came in and asked me if I remembered the bass player I had used when we backed Billie Holiday in Frisco a while back. I said I did—Charlie Mingus. We called all around Frisco and no one knew where he was, and finally we found him right down here—carrying mail. He wasn't playing at all and he was big. I'd watch him sit down and eat a quart of ice cream and I'd say, 'Hey, what are you doing?' and he'd say, 'Man, I can eat *three* of these at one sitting.' But he went down in weight with us, and by the time we opened at the Embers he was fine. He could play those jet tempos that most drummers can't touch and he was a beautiful soloist. We stayed at the Embers a year or so, and Mingus was with us a couple of years."

Mrs. Norvo appeared with her daughter, Portia, who was carrying her son, Christopher. Norvo kissed Portia, who in figure and coloring is another replica of the old man, and took Christopher and held him at arm's length. "Well, how is it today?" he asked Christopher. "Have they been feeding you right?" Christopher blinked and looked at Norvo's beard. "You're sort of pensive this morning." Norvo put Christopher on his feet by the coffee table.

Mrs. Norvo and Portia sat down, and Christopher sidled over to his mother, staring at me.

"He's a swinger, when he has a mind for it," Norvo said. He picked up a pair of bongo drums and put them between his knees and began an easy rock-and-roll beat. Christopher smiled and edged his way around the coffee table, stopped, looked at Norvo and then up at the painting over the fireplace. He pointed at it and pointed at his grandfather. Then he giggled, sat down abruptly, and got up again. Norvo continued playing. "Come on, what's the matter with you? Don't you want to swing this morning?" Suddenly Christopher let go of the coffee table and started a tentative Twist. He swung from side to side, arms crooked, and Norvo laughed. "Now we're going, now we're going." Christopher Twisted some more, lost his balance and tipped over, and his mother picked him up. Both women laughed, then Mrs. Norvo got up. "We have to go out and do some shopping, and then I have to get ready for work, so I'll see you later. How did it go last night? How long did it take to get there?"

"It was a drag for a while, but it picked up. It's an hour or so down there, but I didn't have any trouble finding it. It looks like at least a two-week gig."

The women left with Christopher, and Norvo settled back in his chair, holding his coffee cup on his stomach. I asked him what sort of person Mildred Bailey was. He looked at me and then at the floor. "My years with Mildred are a hard thing for me to put together now. They were wonderful years in my life, but it's been so long ago it's almost like I read it all in a book. I met her in Chicago in 1929, and she gassed me as a singer. I really dug her, and we started having a bite together now and then. The first thing we were going together, and after we were married and came to New York with Whiteman we lived in an apartment in Jackson Heights and then we bought a house in Forest Hills, on Pilgrim Circle. It was a great house. It was open in back all the way to Queens Boulevard, and when it snowed— there was a little hill down to the garage—we'd get snowed in. There wasn't much jazz in New York then, outside of a few theatres and the Savoy and a couple of big Harlem clubs, so we had a lot of musicians and music in the house. The Benny Goodman trio came into being there. One night Teddy Wilson and Benny were there and they started jamming. Carl Bellinger, who's with a publishing house in New York now, was on drums. He was at Yale at the time, and on weekends he flew down from New Haven to Roosevelt Field in a little Waco he had and sat in on drums, which he left out on our sun porch. Teddy and Benny hit it off, and they brought in Gene Krupa, and that was that. Bessie Smith and her husband came to the house, too. Bessie was crazy about Mildred. She and Mildred used to laugh at each other and do this routine. They were both big women, and when they saw each other one of them would say, 'Look, I've got this brand-new dress, but it's got too *big* for me, so why don't *you* take it?' and they'd both break up. And Fats Waller came out. We loved to go to his place, too, and eat. His wife and mother-in-law did the cooking. Fats was always a boisterous man. It was no put-on. And Jess Stacy came out, and Hughes Panassie and Spike Hughes and Lee Wiley and Bunny Berigan and Alec Wilder. Red Nichols lived right across the street. Sometimes, in those days, people came up to me and said, 'When did you start playing vibes? You had the Five Pennies, didn't you?' That would get me and I'd introduce myself as Red Nichols, and Red told me that the same thing happened to him, and he'd introduce himself as Red Norvo. Mildred was a great natural cook, and she loved to eat. After she knew about her diabetes and was supposed to be on a diet, she'd say, 'Now I've ate the diet, so bring on the food.' She was an amazing person—very warm, very talented. She had a childlike singing voice, a microphone voice, but what singer hasn't? I think her diction got me almost more than anything. It was perfect. When she sang 'More Than You Know' I understood the words for the first time. She made you feel that she was not singing a song because she wanted you to hear how she could sing but to make you hear and value that song. And she had an emotional thing with audiences. I heard it once at the old Blue Angel when there was an ugly hoopla crowd, a messy crowd, and Ellis Larkins, her pianist, played the intro and she started, and before two bars were over—silence. That crowd was down. Mildred loved to laugh and she was very inventive in language. She nicknamed Whiteman Pops. People's opinions of her were very different. They used to say she was temperamental. Sometimes when people don't do or think exactly what they're told they're called temperamental. Either that or they're called geniuses. Mildred got the temperamental bit. She was just astute. She *knew* what was right and she stayed by that knowledge. The first time she heard Billie Holiday, who was just a kid, she said, 'She has it.' Then later she spotted another kid, Frank Sinatra, the same way. She had imaginative ears. We had some pretty strong brawls. Some of them were funny when you look back on it. Once, in the thirties, Benny Goodman and I went fishing out on Long Island, and every time we stopped at what looked like a good place Benny said, 'Come on, Red. I know a better place further on.' Pretty soon we were out near Montauk. We stayed a couple of days—Montauk was a sleeper jump then—and when I got home I could tell that Mildred was hacked. Things were cool, but I didn't say anything, and a night or two after, when we were sitting in front of the fire—I was on a love seat on one side and she was on one on the other side—Mildred suddenly got up and took this brand-new hat she had bought me at Cavanaugh's and threw it in the fire. So I got up and threw a white fox stole of hers in the fire, and she got a Burberry I'd got in Canada and threw *that* in. By this time she was screaming at me and I was yelling at her, so finally I picked up a cushion from one of the love seats and in it went. The fire was really burning. In fact, it was licking right out the front and up the mantel, and that was the end of the fight because we had to call the Fire Department to come and put it out."

Norvo laughed and went over to a window. The fog was thicker and the light in the room was gray. "But we were compatible most of the time. I don't know what happened eventually. It developed into a thing where there were no children. She wanted children very badly, and it got to the point where we were talking about adopting a child. We lived on Thirty-first Street by then, and I looked around me and it was a madhouse—the maid running around, dachshunds running around, the telephone ringing—and I thought, This is no place to bring kids up in. But it was a slow thing. The car skids a little before it stops, the carburetor skips a little before it stops. I'd move out and we would go back together and I'd move out again. It lasted twelve years before we were divorced. But I always had cordial relations with Mildred. After Eve and I were married, we would take the kids up to Mildred's farm in Stormville, New York. She loved the children and she gave each of them a dappled dachshund. We still have one of the descendants out in the patio. Mildred died on December 12, 1951. I was at the Embers with the trio, and when I arrived for work I got a message to call home immediately. Mildred had wanted me to do something for her in New York, and I had talked to her earlier that evening on the phone. She was in the hospital in Poughkeepsie for a checkup—she had had pneumonia the year before—and when I reached Eve she told me that the hospital had called and that Mildred had died peacefully in her sleep. It was her heart. She was just forty-four."

Norvo was silent for a moment. Then he said, "Let's go out to the kitchen and find some lunch."

1968

The Human Sound

It is quite possible that when the century is over, live entertainment—real people singing, acting, dancing, playing, reciting, and clowning in front of real people—will have disappeared in this country or become an anachronism. (The very existence of the phrase "live entertainment" is ominous; the term would have struck the Victorians as a puzzling redundancy.) Concert halls and opera houses are no longer full. The theatre appears static beside the fluid drive of film. (At that, even movie houses, which have always *seemed* like arenas of live entertainment, are rarely sold out.) The circus and rodeo are obsolescent, night clubs are dwindling, and such diversions as band concerts and the straw-hat circuit are almost at an end. When this decline is complete, something essential will have gone out of human experience. In-the-flesh entertainment at its best is one of the most complex, delightful, and inventive forms of communication. It is a mutually beneficial intercourse between the performer, who plays a god, and the audience, which allows this pretension, knowing delightedly all the while that the performer, beneath the skin of his skills, is human, too. Simply by doing what he is doing where he is doing it, the performer demonstrates great courage, and the audience experiences this courage vicariously. The performer is flattered by the attention of the audience, and the audience congratulates itself for having the intelligence and sensitivity to admire the performer. But electronics is closing off this invaluable two-way street. The performer can no longer play his changes on an audience, gauging his abilities in the mirror of its faces, and the audience can no longer manipulate the performer with its cheers and tears. Yet decline and flowering often occur simultaneously; the form dies and its final moments are phoenix-brilliant. I have in mind the brave excellence of Bobby Short, the forty-six-year-old singer and pianist who, one of the last examples (and indubitably the best) of the café singer or the supper-club singer or "troubadour," as the late Vernon Duke called him, practices what is probably the most intimate and delicate form of live entertainment extant. It is the art of singing (and often accompanying oneself on the piano) witty or ironic or sad but never sentimental songs in a small room to a small group of people, and in such a way that the performer and his audience, generally only a few feet away, become almost one. (Mabel Mercer, the great *doyenne* of the form, often sits at her listeners' table and sings to them, and she remembers long ago carrying this attention to its ultimate in a noisy Parisian *boîte* by singing into her customers' ears through a small megaphone.) Every member of the audience comes to believe that a song is being sung to *him*, and the performer, who can look directly into his listeners' eyes, feels that he is singing only to the listener he happens to look at. The songs are as important as their delivery. They are, as often as not, out-of-the-way tunes by the likes of Cy Coleman or Ivor Novello or Noël Coward or Cole Porter or Rodgers and Hart. They may have a small but steady currency, they may have long since been forgotten, they may never have been known at all because of having been dropped from a movie or Broadway show before it opened, or they may have been written only for the performer who is singing them. They must be sung immaculately, in an offhand, transparent way, so that the singer, his diction clean glass, lights up his materials with meanings their composers may never have thought of. Café singing, or at any rate Bobby Short's way of singing, is unencumbered by the theatrics of opera or rock, by the quaintness of folk singing, by the confinements of jazz singing, and by the mealiness of old-style pop singing. It is singing stripped to its essentials—words lifted and carried by the curves of melody.

Short's achievements as a performer are all the more remarkable when one considers his equipment. He has a baritone that is frequently plagued by laryngitis. He has a rapid, almost querulous vibrato, and he sometimes slides past or stops short of the note he is after. His piano playing is so unfettered it is usually accelerando—a tendency that is beautifully disguised by his accompanists, Beverly Peer (bass) and Dick Sheridan (drums), who invariably keep in perfect rhythmic step. But everything in Short's style miraculously balances out. His free sense of time gives his numbers a surprised, bounding quality, his vibrato makes his phrase endings ripple like flags, his laryngitis lends his voice a searching, down sound, and his uncertain notes enhance the cheerfulness and abandon he projects. His appearance is deceptive as well. He is slight—five feet nine, with a thirty-inch waist and small, demure feet. He has an oval face, a button nose, and vaguely apprehensive eyes, all of which do battle with an engulfing mustache. But three attributes work in wondrous concert for him. He is a faultless and inventive dresser (he is a regular on the best-dressed lists), he has a warm, princely bearing, and he has a stunning smile. The resulting impression, as one meets him, is of a tall, poised, and irresistibly attractive man.

I first met him early one afternoon at his apartment on the eighth floor of Carnegie Hall. Short has lived there twelve years. It is the sort of place old New Yorkers covet—a small, reasonable, soundproof triplex. No sound comes from outside, nor does any sound escape, so Short can sit before the baby grand in his living room at three in the morning and pound and shout with perfect propriety. The small foyer on the first floor contains a desk, a big Queen Anne armchair, a bicycle, and a staircase. A turn-around kitchen opens off it. The living room, at the top of the stairs, is two stories high, with a vaulted ceiling and a row of high windows facing north. At one end are a small bar, a bathroom, and a second set of stairs. These lead to a spacious balcony, which serves as Short's bedroom. A bedroom window faces a small roof, where his cats, Rufus and Miss Brown, are aired. The furnishings are high-class Camp. A heavy glass-topped coffee table rests on a zebra-skin rug, and on the rug, beneath the table, are two metal lizards —one gilt, one brass. A pair of big daybeds, which are covered with bright African-looking material and leopard-skin pillows, flank the table. Near the foyer stairs are a huge wooden lion, a stolid eighteenth-century Italian refectory table, and one of those roofed-in wicker wing chairs that still haunt old summer cottages in East Hampton and on Naushon Island. An antler chandelier hangs in the living room, and it is echoed by a Teddy Roosevelt leather chair with tusks as arms. Pictures of every description jam the walls, and the window side of the room is lined with books and bric-a-brac.

When I arrived, Short, who occasionally models, was posing for a *Harper's Bazaar* sketch. He was wearing an orange-and-white cashmere turtleneck, tan slacks, and low, buckled boots, and for the drawing he had added a square-cut puma-skin coat with an otter collar, designed by Donald Brooks for Jacques Kaplan. And he had on a cowboy hat. He was leaning against a support of the balcony, his hands in the coat pockets, and he looked melancholy and distant.

The diminutive Chinese girl who was sketching him said something. "It *is* a fantastic apartment," Short said. His voice was light, melodic, yet husky. "I was away when they decided to tear down Carnegie Hall, and I guess I didn't really realize what was going on, so I didn't panic. A lot of the people who lived here did, and they moved out, and when the building was saved they had a hell of a time getting back in." He cleared his throat unavailingly. "I've had *this* bout of laryngitis for weeks. Every morning I get on my bike and pedal over to my doctor on the East Side. He sprays me and makes bad jokes and I pedal back, but it doesn't get any better. But then it doesn't get much of a chance. At the Café Carlyle, where I work, it's three shows a night, six nights a week. And I can't just lay off for a week or two. My responsibility is to the Carlyle. I have to be on time and I have to do everything with grace, even when I feel like saying to hell with it, when it's like pulling teeth to get myself up from my early-evening nap and shower and shave and dress and get downstairs and into a cab. The romance of being a supper-club singer! I still do private parties as well. It's extra money for Dick Sheridan and Beverly Peer, and I find myself asking a lot of money. Sometimes I'm whisked down to '21' between shows to play for someone's birthday, and I've been flown to Hobe Sound and the Caribbean. And not long ago I was invited to perform at the White House when the Nixons gave a party for the Duke and Duchess of Windsor. It cost me a thousand dollars, what with new clothes and transportation and all, but I was delighted I could *afford* to go. I would have been a very upset boy had I been invited and not had the money. But the Carlyle is the middle of my life. In fact, I'm hopelessly associated with it. Bobby Short of the Carlyle, despite there still being people in New York who prefer to think of me as their secret, their discovery. I started there in 1968, and in a peculiar way. George Feyer, the pianist, had been in residence for twelve years. He took off two weeks that summer, and Peter Sharp, who owns the Carlyle, asked Ahmet and Nesuhi Ertegun of Atlantic Records who to get as a replacement. They said, 'Get Bobby Short.' I did my best to make those two weeks as successful as anything I'd done, and when Feyer's contract ran out they offered me half a year. Feyer found a better deal elsewhere, and I work there now eight months of the year. It's physically impossible to work more than that, and anyway it doesn't make sense for me to be so available that I lose my attraction value."

He shed the fur coat and, leaning back on one of the daybeds, struck a new pose, his hands clasped behind his head and his feet on the coffee table. A tall, thin, lugubrious-looking man in blue denim work clothes came in.

"How was your weekend, Wendell?" Short asked him.

"I'm not feeling so well. A cold."

"Are you congested? Well, I've got just the pill for you. It's the same one the astronauts took. Take one now and one tonight." Wendell went upstairs, put leashes on the cats, and took them out on the roof. Wendell cleans and cooks and does odd jobs for Short three days a week.

"I think the Carlyle is probably one of the last places in the world where you can drink tea with your pinkie comfortably out. It attracts royalty. It's not unusual to have a baroness or a princess around, and Jacqueline has been in with Aristotle Onassis. So has Mrs. Palm Beach Garner, Mrs. Winston Frost, and Bunny Mellon. My dressing room, which is on the fourth floor above the Café Carlyle, is really one of the maids' rooms that the hotel provides for the servants such people generally travel with. But you can come into the Carlyle wearing practically anything. It is big enough and elegant enough and grand enough not to be affected by unusual attire among its patrons. I'd been to the hotel several times before I worked there, and I was always treated beautifully. I must deal with the people who come solely to see Bobby Short. They make all sorts of complaints, written and verbal. 'Mr. Short didn't sing at all during his first show last night,' or 'Mr. Short finished his second set ten minutes early.' My God! And if I sing too many Negro songs, the Negro patrons get self-conscious and the whites think I'm being militant. Imagine Bessie Smith's 'Gimme a Pigfoot' being considered militant! Everyone who sings in a café has to have something about him that says, 'Come close but not too close.' But people often get too close, too pully on you. Beverly and Dick and I have been together for ten years, and we have accumulated a lot of friends. But we must think of ourselves as caterers at a party. After all, the waiters and bartenders can't get drunk, and I can't sit down with friends between shows and have a quart of champagne or six whiskeys. It takes some stuff to remember your place so long as you're earning a living, and I'll always have to earn a living. If I get overly friendly, the audience thinks, 'Oh, it doesn't matter. We know him so well that we don't have to listen!'

"The people who come to hear me are a mixed bag, and they range in age from eighteen to seventy-five. A lot of them are rich, but I have lived among the wealthy and bizarre so long that their ways don't bother me. I also get professional football players, and Leontyne Price, who is a great friend. Alice Faye and Bart Howard and Arthur Schwartz come in, and Craig Claiborne was there a while ago with a lady from Texas who's a billionairess. The clergy come in, and so do neighborhood ladies, who can walk safely home together. The whole clutch from Elaine's comes in, including Jack Richardson and Norman Mailer. Norman even wrote a poem about me once. Let me see if I can find it."

Short took a book from the bookcase and handed it to me. The poem, "Boîtes," is in a Mailer miscellany, "Cannibals and Christians," and it is a Vachel Lindsay blank-verse eulogy in which Short is called "divine," a "Prince of the Congo," "darkest delight," "blackbird," and a "King of the Congo."

I asked Short about the poem. "God!" he said. "It's too obviously a matter of social climbing, isn't it—being called a prince of darkness, or whatever it is? But musicians come into the Carlyle, too—people like Miles Davis and Cy Coleman and Cannonball Adderley and Joe Williams and Marian McPartland. And a lot of fashion people, but they have followed me all my career—the designers and the models, the manufacturers. Senator Javits and his wife are regulars, and there are a lot of French people, and I speak French to them, of course. And there have been a good many young people, including rock groups. They give one hope. People say that graciousness is finished, but it isn't. My people respect graciousness. They are ready to be gracious and they respond to graciousness."

The girl finished her sketches. She and Bobby packed the fur coat in a box, and she staggered out with it under one arm and her drawings under the other. Wendell shouted up the stairs that a bottle of champagne had exploded in the freezer. Short slapped his forehead. "Oh dear! That's terrible. That's the worst thing I've *ever* done. I put that in there last night before some friends came, but they drank something else and I forgot about it. Is it bad, Wendell?"

"Yes, it's in little pieces. After I clean up, do you want me to go out and get a roast or something?"

"All right, and some Boston lettuce and orange juice."

Short went over to the bar and poured a ginger ale. "I only eat once a day, at lunch," he said. "I can't eat before I work. If I do, I can't breathe when I sing, or else all the wine and cheese come up. Sometimes I go somewhere fancy for lunch—that's my treat for the day—or I cook something here. When I'm not working, I can put together a decent bœuf bourguignon for six or eight people. After they leave, I strip off all my clothes and go down to the kitchen and wash up. It takes me a couple of hours, but it's the best therapy in the world."

A radio, which had been playing when I arrived, began a Duke Ellington tune.

"I got to know the Ellington bandpack in the early forties," Short said, "when I was living in Los Angeles and was more or less adopted by Harold Brown, a pianist and the brother of Lawrence Brown, Ellington's trombonist. The band would come to the Coast—and those parties! They went on until eight or nine in the morning. All the liquor you could drink and all the available girls in town and Art Tatum playing the piano in a corner. I've been unswerving since then—a lifelong devotee. Some of those things Duke wrote in the late thirties and early forties—they're mind-bending. I haven't seen the band since last summer, when they were at the Rainbow Grill, that great glassed-in place up above the city. It was a total New York night. My date was an English girl, a fan of mine, and the Duke had a thing going. Everybody was there. Tony Bennett. Sylvia Syms. They both sang. Then someone saw me. I told them to go away and shut up, but Duke got me up there, and I chose 'Rose of the Rio Grande,' simply because I wanted to hear Lawrence Brown's great solo on it. He played it, and I found out later that Duke and Lawrence had had words earlier that night, and Lawrence had told him, 'No solos tonight.' It was a great compliment."

Short looked at his watch. "I have to go down to the photography department at Macy's to get an old picture of my mother restored." He handed me a dark oval photograph, torn and faded—a pretty woman with long hair and deep, faintly smiling eyes. "It will be in my book, which I just finished the transcript of the other night, at two-thirty in the morning. It's about the first seventeen years of my life— my life as a show-biz kid. Imagine *me* writing a book for an established firm like Dodd, Mead. My mother is remarkable. She's eighty-three and lives with my oldest sister, Naomi, in Danville, Illinois, where I was born. Mother was tiny, never weighing more than a hundred and fifteen pounds, and, as you can see, very pretty. When I was a kid she worked all day, and when she wasn't at her job she was at church or in a P.-T.A. meeting or trying to keep her house in order. She was a domestic, as most of her friends were, and she worked from seven-thirty in the morning until early evening. She was ambivalent. Her pride drove her out to work all day, using every avenue of strength she had, but then when I was ten she'd let me go and play the piano and sing in the local roadhouses—provided she knew the mother of someone in the band. She let me do this when she wouldn't allow a jazz record or a blues record in the house and when she thought it un-thinkable to go into show business, which was considered a one-way road straight to Hell, thanks to the Puritanical nonsense the Negroes borrowed from the whites. But it was the Depression and things were very rough, and I know that the three or four dollars I brought home on Saturday nights were used to pay the gas bill or buy clothes and books for us children. Mother never cracked more than ten dollars a week as a domestic, and here I could make almost half that in one night's work. I think she respected me for it.

"I was born the ninth of ten children. There were never more than seven of us alive at once. My mother and father came from Kentucky, but they met in Danville. It's about a hundred and twenty-five miles south of Chicago, and it hovers close to the Indiana line. It was the best of all possible places to be poor in the Depression—in a small town where there were no racial pressures. There was a small colored population and an old colored section, but the town was at least superficially integrated. We lived in a newer section, where there were whites. Very often I was the only Negro in my class. I never knew Father terribly well. He was slender and had a marvellous mustache, which was balanced by a tonsure that I inherited. He went through eight years of school, and then his father sent him to four more at Frankfort College, which was more like a high school then. His father was not wealthy, but he owned farms here and there. He'd been born at the end of slavery, but he was a freedman. My father had a talent for mathematics, and he was brilliant at speedwriting. He had gifts that could have made him a much greater man than he was. He held a number of white-collar jobs, civil-service jobs. He ran for justice of the peace in Danville, and he won. But he liked the coal mines. When the Depression hit, he went back to Kentucky to the mines. He sent us money and came to see us twice a year. But the mines were his Waterloo. I was about nine or ten when he died."

Miss Brown shot down the stairs from the bedroom, leaped up on the pillows on the daybed, and lay there watching Rufus, who was creeping along the base of the bookcase. "Rufus!" Short shouted. "Stop it!" Rufus slid across the floor on his belly, his eyes on Miss Brown. "Go on! Enough! Scat!" Rufus catapulted up the stairs and disappeared under the bed. Short picked up a handful of pistachio nuts from a bowl and began to open them.

"There was a piano in our house, as there was in every house then, and I taught myself to play and sing. I listened to Ivie Anderson and to Bing Crosby, and once in a while I'd get a good hot radio program from Chicago, and bands like Fess Williams' and Walter Barnes' came through town. I left Danville for the first time when I was eleven and a half. A couple of booking agents came through and heard me sing and play, and they took me off to Chicago—with my mother's permission, of course. I lived on the West Side with a Catholic family from New Orleans, which appealed to my mother, and I went to a Catholic school. When I left Danville I had no idea what image I projected. There I was, a child sitting in tails at the piano and singing 'Sophisticated Lady' and 'In My Solitude' in a high, squeaky voice in astonishing keys. The lyrics meant nothing to me, and they must have sounded strange to other people coming out of a child's mouth. So I changed and sang things like 'Shoe Shine Boy' and 'It's a Sin to Tell a Lie.' But I could not find it within me to believe that I *was* a child. And I didn't like being a child, because I couldn't stand the patronization connected with childhood. Moreover, it was never in me to be the best colored singer or the best colored student. I simply wanted to be the best singer and the best student. But I have a respect for my race that might surprise some of the people who discovered just six months ago that they are black. I was brought up in such a way that doesn't allow any head-hanging. There is nothing about me that can be called nonwhite, but I consider myself fortunate because I'm not so well known that people accept me only for my fame. I'm not sophisticated about the comings and goings of the revolutionaries today. I suspect that many of them are out for their own gains—financial, political, whatever. A long time ago I discovered that the best advertisement for a minority is that member who, without being Uncle Tom, takes the time to mesh with whatever exists socially. He makes it that much easier for the next member who comes along.

"That winter, I worked mostly around Chicago. I did some broadcasting over N.B.C., and a lot of so-called 'club' dates at places like the Sheraton Hotel. I'd be part of one-night shows that included an orchestra, tap-dancers, and other singers. I became the colored counterpart of Bobby Breen. I got thirty or thirty-five dollars for each club date, but of course I had to buy clothes and pay tuition and give something to the family I lived with. When I finished school in June of 1937 I was twelve and a half. But I didn't go home. I went East. New York wasn't easy, because I started there from scratch, performing all times of day and night for bookers. But I worked at the Frolic Café, over the Winter Garden Theatre, at La Grande Pomme, and at the Apollo in Harlem. The audiences at the Apollo were used to Pigmeat Markham and Butter Beans and Susie and Moms Mabley, and I was obviously a downtown act. They didn't care about my white tie and tails. All they wanted was to be turned on. They probably all had kids my age at home who danced and sang anyway.

"The New York thing came to an abrupt end early in 1938. I suddenly realized that there I was—a kid with two years of show biz and all the mannerisms of an adult—and I didn't like it, so I went back to Danville and stayed there four years, until I finished high school. It was a funny adjustment to make at first. I had come off what was regarded as the big time. My mother said I couldn't work for tacky people in tacky places after working in grand hotels and grand theatres for grand people. So I didn't work for the first year, but I began to feel the economic pressures and I went back to work in earnest. I had more pizzazz by then, and I was a professional. I sought out the best hotels and taprooms around Danville, and after a while I became solvent and could dress myself properly and even indulge myself. I finished high school in 1942, and a month later opened at the Capitol Lounge in Chicago. The rage was boogie-woogie. I thought it was cheap. I made up my mind there was something better. I had heard Hildegarde on records, and of course she was the queen then. She had the slickest night-club act of all time. It was produced down to the last sigh. Even down to a blue spotlight that brought out the color in the red roses that invariably stood by her piano. She would record whole Broadway scores, and she sang Vernon Duke and Cole Porter and the Gershwins and Noël Coward, and through her I became aware of the Broadway kind of score, of the mystique of the Broadway musical.

"In 1943 I went to the Beachcomber in Omaha, where I worked for a week opposite Jimmy Noone, the New Orleans clarinettist, and for a week opposite Nat Cole. Nat and I became friends and remained friends until he died. He was a sly, funny man, and he'd sit in the back room and watch me—a smart-aleck nineteen-year-old—performing out front, and he'd laugh and say, when I came off, 'What are you *doing* to these people?' I got a job in Los Angeles with Mike Reilly—'The Music Goes Around and Around and It Comes Out Here' Reilly—in the Radio Room. He had a comedy band, and they threw flounders at the audience, and that sort of thing. I first heard there about Mabel Mercer and Cy Walter, and I became deeply immersed in Rodgers and Hart. And Don McCrae, who is really Don Redman and who wrote 'Practice Makes Perfect,' came to my house with a huge stack of out-of-the-way songs and told me to learn them. My job at the Radio Room ended a couple of months later. Another comedy band had come in, and the act involved smoke pouring out of the top hat the leader wore. The smoke was flour, and it spewed out all over me, and I was in black tie. After the first show I refused to go back on, and I was dismissed. I worked around, mostly at private parties for fifty dollars a night, and at the old Trocadero Ballroom, filling in for Dorothy Donegan. Then I got a gig in Milwaukee, where I appeared opposite the Art Tatum trio, with Tiny Grimes on guitar and Slam Stewart on bass. Tatum will always be my idol, and it was marvellous to get to know him. He had the same sort of sly humor that Nat Cole had. He enjoyed pretty ladies and he drank a *lot* of beer. There was no condescension, and in a strange way I think he even admired me, even though he never talked about music. But it always astonished me that for the most part the people who came to hear him didn't really know what they were hearing."

Short jumped up. "Macy's awaits me." He reappeared ten minutes later. He was wearing a sensationally well-tailored Glen-plaid suit. His shoes were dark, his shirt was a pale blue, and his modestly wide tie was navy with white polka dots. We went over to Seventh Avenue and he flagged a cab. He conducted his business at Macy's in a sparkling way, as if *he* were waiting on the saleslady. In the cab he had told me that he had gone from Milwaukee to the Chase Hotel in St. Louis, where Hildegarde was the main attraction. It was the first time he had seen her work. Her manager heard him and called Herbert

Jacoby, who, along with Max Gordon, owned the Blue Angel in New York. Jacoby went out to St. Louis and asked Short to come to the Blue Angel the following spring. "Eddie Mayehoff was on the bill," Short said on the escalator. "And Irene Bordoni and Mildred Bailey, and of course I was just the opener. For a long time I thought my engagement at the Blue Angel was not successful, but I learned later that Jacoby and Gordon often cancelled new acts after the first night. I stayed for a full four weeks. I shared a dressing room with Mildred Bailey, and I got some interesting insights into her. Despite that enormous *poitrine* and her barrel shape and those toothpick legs, she was very vain. She had a lovely face and beautiful skin, and she'd sit at her dressing table in front of the mirror the whole time between shows, fixing her face and staring at herself. We talked constantly, but she never once took her eyes off herself and looked at me."

We came out into Herald Square. Short suggested that we walk up to Brooks Brothers, where he wanted to look at some dress shirts and pumps. "I met Mabel Mercer, too, for the first time, and Bart Howard, who gave me a lot of his songs. I longed to belong to Mabel's intimate circle, and I knew I had to come back to New York one day on a more permanent basis. Mabel has worked as viciously hard as I have. She has always sung in small places without microphones, and she thinks microphones are abominable. Mabel is much more fragile than I. She is, as we know it in America, the outstanding personage of our kind of art. When I first met her, the thing that struck me was her repertoire. I was involved in the same pursuit, and it was true serendipity. Even when she sang a song I knew, it came to be totally fresh. I can't think of any singer who is true to himself who has avoided being influenced by Mabel Mercer. People have accused me of stealing from other performers, but that's nonsense. What one does is absorb the *feeling* generated by a great singer like Mabel. She is an enormously private person, and I'm flattered that we have a friendship.

"After the Blue Angel I went back to California and worked off and on on Monday nights for three or four months at the Haig, a kind of a shack on Wilshire Boulevard across from the Ambassador Hotel. It was run by a show-biz nut named Johnny Bernstein, and he kept bringing me obscure show tunes. Between him and Don McCrae, my repertoire became sizable. The periods in between my stints at the Haig were very poor. I lived with Harold Brown and his wife. They fed me and slept me and even gave me pocket money, or I wouldn't be here today. Then I got a job at the Café Gala. It was in a big house on Sunset Boulevard which had been bought by the Baroness d'Erlanger for Johnny Walsh to sing in. He was a tall, fantastically handsome Irishman with white hair and beautifully tailored clothes, and he had the largest repertoire I'd ever heard. The Gala was the most chic club in California, or the West, for that matter. It was always filled with ex-New Yorkers, and you'd see Lena Horne and Lennie Hayton and Monty Woolley and Cole Porter. Walsh sold the Gala to a man named Jim Dolan. He gave me a one-week contract, but I stayed from July of 1948 to the fall of 1951. I became the mainstay, announcing shows and playing interim piano. Felicia Sanders worked there, and Bobby Troup and Dorothy Dandridge and Stella Brooks and Sheila Barrett. Eventually, a neon sign appeared on the roof: 'Jim Dolan Presents Bobby Short.' I acquired a new apartment and met all sorts of people high up in the movie business, and international people. I fell into a velvet-lined rut. In fact, one night Olga San Juan turned to Leonard Spigelgass at the Gala and said, 'Who is this Bobby Short? Why isn't he in films, why isn't he making a lot of records?' Spigelgass replied, 'He's too chic.' And that was the truth. I had become the young colored boy who was all chic and who dined at the Café Jay, which sat just twenty, fifteen of them invariably the biggest Hollywood stars, and that was as far as I could go. People kept telling me, 'Go to New York, Bobby. Get out of here and go to New York.' I knew I wasn't ready for New York, but I did go to Paris, first class, by plane."

At Brooks, Short tried on some pumps. "Do you see that lady sitting over there with the man?" he said. "She's Erika Lund, and she worked at the Gala when I was there. I still sing one of her songs." They greeted each other warmly, and he told her to stop by the Café Carlyle. Old Home Week continued at the shirt counter, where the dapper, middle-aged salesman told Short he had once been with Young & Rubicam and that he used to go to the Beverly Club at Lexington and Fiftieth to hear him. Short looked pleased, bought six shirts, and told *him* to stop by the Carlyle.

Short and I went over to the Algonquin and he ordered a beer. "I just love this place," he said. "It's an oasis in this mad city. Well, the rest of that year in Paris was insane. I worked for Spivy and I worked at the Embassy Club in London several times. I had an atelier in the most fashionable *arrondissement* in Paris. I had a maid, a private French tutor, I ate well, and when I was in London I bought all the clothes I could. Then it was back to L.A. and the Gala, and in the beginning of 1954 I met Phil Moore, the arranger and composer, and he became my manager. He figured out how my act could be enlarged, controlled, polished. The first thing he did was to put me in a room in Los Angeles with Larry Bunker, the drummer, and Rollie Bundock, the bassist. We made a tape and Phil sold it to Nesuhi and Ahmet Ertegun. Then I was flown to New York by Dorothy Kilgallen, as a birthday present for her husband, Dick Kollmar. The record came out, Dorothy paved the way in her column, and I got the job at the Beverly Club. I went on to the Red Carpet, Le Cupidon, and back to the Blue Angel, where I had top billing and made a thousand dollars a week. I worked the Living Room, the Weylin Hotel, and the Arpeggio. During the summers I went back to California for short stints, and to Florida for the first time, and Chicago. Early in the sixties, after I'd been here at the Sheraton-East, the old Ambassador Hotel, Herbert Jacoby and a rich friend and myself took over a room on East Fifty-fourth Street and called it Le Caprice. Herbert had always coveted an *haute-cuisine* French restaurant, which Caprice was, and my trying to cater to an eating clientele instead of a drinking one didn't make it. We lasted a year and three months. Then came the heavy time for Mr. Short. I hadn't taken any salary at all for the last three months at the Caprice, and I had gone through all my savings. I was on my uppers. During the summer of 1965 I didn't work in New York at all except for occasional weekends, and I ended up in Provincetown and Cleveland. But that winter I was lucky enough to have a standup part in the 'New Cole Porter Revue,' down at Square East in the Village. A while after that I got a job in the upstairs room at L'Intrigue over on West Fifty-sixth Street. I handled my own lights, I seated guests. It fed my cats, paid the rent, and kept me alive. For the next few years I subsisted in Boston at Paul's Mall, at the Living Room here, and at places like the Playboy Club in London. The nightclub business was not what it had been."

Short yawned. "Nap time. Why don't you stop by the Carlyle tonight? The first show is around nine-thirty, but don't come to that. It's always awful—cold, stiff, empty. It was a nice walk. Thank you."

The Café Carlyle is a small, oblong room (it seats under two hundred) on one side of the Madison Avenue entrance of the Hotel Carlyle. A tiny sit-down bar is concealed behind pillars, and against the opposite wall, on a low dais, is a grand piano. There are banquettes around the other walls, which are covered by murals, and the center of the room is taken up by a dozen tables. It is a dark, dowdy, comfortable place. I arrived at nine-thirty, convinced that Short was incapable of anything cold or stiff, and I was right. He appeared, resplendent in a dinner jacket and pleated white shirt, and sat down in semi-darkness at the piano, flanked on one side by Dick Sheridan and on the other by Beverly Peer. No lights went on; he simply started to play. He looked solemn and detached and private, as if he were playing for himself late at night in his living room. It was a graceful, flowing display. He did a Gershwin medley, "Perdido," the theme from "Exodus," a blues, and several other tunes. His style bears a loose, enthusiastic resemblance to Art Tatum's—it is florid and arpeggioed and slurred—and by the time he had played ten or so tunes a considerable head of steam had been built up. The lights went on, and he began to sing Cole Porter's "Let's Fly Away." It was immediately clear that it would be a difficult night. His laryngitis was compounded by a faulty microphone, and the crowd was noisy. During his third song he stopped abruptly when new arrivals began loudly "*Comment-ça-va*"ing the people at the next table. Looking over their heads with a slight smile, his hands resting on the raised keyboard cover, he waited until the room subsided, and then began precisely where he had left off.

After the last number he greeted several people, then sat down at my table. He mopped his face and ordered a glass of ice water and hot tea with honey. The headwaiter apologized for the microphone; the repairman had promised to come but had not. Short smiled and croaked, "I know. I know. Phil Moore told me that it really doesn't matter what a performer does. It's a question of how many dishes the busboys drop and of whether or not the microphones work. And it's up to the audience, too. When you get a bad one, you work harder and harder and sing louder and louder to compensate, and *they* talk louder and louder to compensate for you. But a bad microphone is like playing with a drunken drummer. If I were on a stage, removed, it would be different, but I'm practically within touching distance of everyone here. On top of that, I know most of them. Those are Shaker Heights people over there, and the group that came in and made all the noise includes Liza Minelli's estranged husband, and back against the wall is Geraldine Stutz, of Bendel, and her husband. Of course, one night you come in and the piano is in tune, the boys feel wonderful, I feel wonderful, and the audience is rotten. Another night, I feel perfectly rotten and the audience sits there as though they were in church. You must never be angry or uptight in the gut; you have to be free and loose. Singing itself is such pure expression. The human sound is the most touching in the world; it's exemplified by someone like Ray Charles. He has that kind of getting inside a song and finding something that the composer himself didn't know was there. And a good performer can't be carrying on emotionally when he sings. You simply can't sing well with a lump in your throat. Take 'I Still Believe in You.' It has one of my favorite lyrics of all time. It's by Rodgers and Hart, and was dropped from a 1930 show called 'Simple Simon' before the show opened. I first heard Charlotte Rae sing it, and I've known it for a year, but for a long time I could not bring myself to sing it without breaking up. Finally, I absorbed the song, and now I can do it."

Geraldine Stutz went by, and Short stood up and spoke to her, then poured more honey in his tea.

"I guess I have several hundred songs in my repertoire, and when I'm requested to sing a song I've never sung in my life I find that I suddenly know all the words, and we figure out a key and we're off. I can sing songs I haven't sung in ten years, and the only ones I ever have to brush up on are things I sang as a child. Actually, I wish I *could* push some of the lyrics I've got in my head out and replace them with newer material, but that's an occupational hazard; you become a kind of singing Smithsonian. I'm interested in all kinds of *good* songs. Sometimes the lyrics grab me, sometimes the song itself. It's not often that the marriage is perfect. But the Gershwins can be counted on, and Cole Porter made both ends work. Rodgers and Hart were brilliant. Vernon Duke wasn't always fortunate enough to find good lyricists. Yip Harburg was good with him, and so was Ira Gershwin. But I don't think Vernon was easy to work with. I love Harold Arlen and Johnny Mercer, and when they collaborated on the score of 'St. Louis Woman' it was almost too much of a good thing. Johnny Mercer displays a homespun façade in his work, but he's capable of turning out a truly sensational lyric. I worship Fats Waller, but I feel inadequate with his material. But I do all the Ellington and Strayhorn I can pick up. I get into Noël Coward and Ivor Novello, among the English songwriters. My thinking English friends bring them over to me. I prefer Coward to Novello; his songs hold up beautifully. I feel almost intellectual when I sing one. It's just like reading a Huxley novel. I like some of the things that Charles Trenet and Jean Sablon sang in the thirties and forties in France. English songs tend to be sentimental, but French songs are unique—tough, and the thirty-two-bar form be damned. But it is the Americans who excel at writing popular songs. You can go anywhere in the world and hear American songs."

For his second show he sang a dozen songs, among them a fascinating, meditative "I Can't Get Started," with lyrics that included such surprising, ingenious turns as:

When J. P. Morgan speaks I just nod,
"Green Pastures" wanted me to play God,
But you've got me downhearted, etc.

and

The Himalayan mountains I climb,
I'm written up in *Fortune* and *Time,*
The Siamese twins I've parted,
Still I can't get started, etc.

Then came a couple of Burt Bacharach songs, a swinging "Nashville Nightingale," a slow Stella Brooks blues, the Bessie Smith "Cake Walkin' Babies," and a long, intense reading of "Bye Bye Blackbird" that equalled any other version I've ever heard. In the fast numbers his tempos raced in all directions, his face took on a strained, almost diabolical look, he reared back and shouted, and he often ended a song by flinging his right hand out, leaping to his feet, and standing statue-still, his eyes fixed high on the back wall of the room. For slow ballads the lights were lowered and he sang quietly, his voice husky and small, his accompaniment full of soft tremolos and runs. The audience came around quickly, and by the time he had finished "Blackbird" there wasn't a murmur in the room.

He rejoined me and ordered more tea with honey, and I asked him about the songs he'd just sung, a couple of which I'd never heard before. " 'You Better Love Me' is from 'High Spirits,' which was based on 'Blithe Spirit,' and 'Sand in My Shoes' is from 'Kiss the Boys Good-bye,' the 1940 Loesser-Schertzinger thing. It was never a terribly successful song, but it's the most requested thing I do. That 'Can't Get Started' I love. Ira Gershwin wrote lots of stanzas, and he's a nifty one for going back and rewriting his lyrics years later. Did I do 'By Strauss'? That was from a 1936 revue, and it was by the Gershwins. Bert Lahr and Beatrice Lillie were in it, and Vernon Duke wrote his 'Now' for it. It was, I believe, first recorded by George Byron, the tenor who married Eva Kern, Jerome's widow. It was on the General label, and Byron's pianist on the date was Bobby Tucker. A voice coach who took a shine to me in Hollywood in the early forties introduced it to me. Then I did a couple of Bacharachs. He's a nice man, and his parents are saints. He's tall and she's tiny, and they're deliciously proud of Burt because he's made it so big. 'Nashville Nightingale' was a Gershwin number written in the late twenties. Vernon Duke gave me it, too. He never pushed any of his own songs, but he would sit with me for hours and push everybody else's. He came to New York once with fourteen unknown Gershwin tunes and wanted me to record them immediately, but unfortunately nothing came of it. 'It Never Entered My Mind' was from 'Higher and Higher,' a 1940 Rodgers and Hart effort, and I think I first heard Shirley Ross sing it on an old Blue Seal Decca. The 'Bye Bye Blackbird' is a little different, because I interpolate part of 'I'm a Little Blackbird Looking for a Blue-bird.' "

Short looked up. The room was packed, and the lobby outside the glass entrance door was filled with people waiting for tables. He smiled. "I better get up to my maid's room and change."

1970

All Dressed Up
and No Place to Go

I receive a telephone call not long ago from an Al St. Clair inviting me to the fifth annual Mobile Jazz Festival. St. Clair, who lives in Mobile and is a member of the festival committee, says that he has read a piece I have written on the gloomy state of jazz and that I might be cheered by the festival, which is devoted wholly to high-school and college jazz bands. The festival is small, nonprofit, and run on a competitive basis by a handful of young jazz-minded Mobilians. This year twelve high-school bands will compete, as well as fourteen big and small college groups from nine states, most of them Southern. The judges will include Thad Jones (cornet), Larry Ridley (bass), and three Mobilians—Mundell Lowe (guitar) and the brothers Al and Urbie Green (piano and trombone). St. Clair says that the music has been imposing in past years, and should be even better this year. I accept.

My trip a few days later, on a Thursday, is par for the course. We are an hour late taking off (no plane), and when we stop in Atlanta the end of the left wing slams into a parked food truck. The truck jumps several feet, and a football-size hole is opened in the wing. We are transferred to another airline and another plane, on which I run into Jones and Ridley. Jones, who is tall, thickset, and funny, is a C.B.S. staff man in New York as well as a co-leader of the Thad Jones-Mel Lewis big band, and Ridley, who is younger, smaller, and equally funny, has played a college gig with George Wein's band the night before in Maine and has been travelling ever since. A cloudburst keeps us on the runway for an hour, and we arrive in Mobile four hours late. St. Clair, a patient, quiet man, meets us (he has kept tabs on us, mysteriously, by "calling the computer" in Atlanta) and drives us to the Admiral Semmes Hotel, where the judges meet briefly and are given mimeographed sheets on which they are to grade the categories of Selection, Rhythm, Interpretation, Blend, Precision, and Dynamics. They are also to choose three big-band winners and three small-band winners, and they decide this year to disregard appearances and "presentation," on the basis that the music is what matters. A sliced-turkey-and-baked-potato dinner is held in the hotel for the festival committee, the judges, and the directors of the college bands. I sit between Lowe and Lee Fortier, the director of the Southeastern Louisiana College band. Lowe, who is in his late forties, is gracious and easygoing and lives in Los Angeles, where he is a free-lance composer and arranger. He gave up on New York five years ago, he says, and doesn't understand why he hasn't lived in California all his life. He and Fortier, who is about the same age, appear to have known each other in the old days when Fortier was a trumpeter with Woody Herman and Hal McIntyre. Fortier is earnest and fast-talking. "I still play an occasional gig," he says. "I subbed for Al Hirt at his place in New Orleans three years ago, but those days on the road are gone for me. I have two daughters and a son and I've put down my roots. I've got a bachelor of music and a master of music from L.S.U., and I'm the musical director at Broadmoor High, which is in Baton Rouge. I started the first high-school stage band in Louisiana nine years ago, and before that I had an all-parish band. I also direct the stage band at Southeastern, which is over in Hammond. The kids I teach in high school have good taste, and they're very choosy. They have to join the concert band first, and we draw the stage band from that. They listen to jazz and they like good rock. I remember one of them bringing me a record by Blood, Sweat, and Tears before the group was anyways known nationally, and saying, 'What do you think of *this?*' I played a lot of jazz for them—Buddy Rich, the Thad Jones-Mel Lewis band, Don Ellis, Woody, and the old Basie band. And Charlie Parker and Clifford Brown and Coltrane. I play the old Basie records for time. That's the kids' biggest hangup—time—and I'm a nut on the subject. And I recommend Jerry Coker's fine paperback, 'Improvising Jazz.' Most of the emphasis in the stage band is on ensemble, but every once in a while a bunch of us sit around with our horns and get some blues going. I write some chords on the blackboard and we go around from instrument to instrument and change key and go around again, and they learn a little about improvising. The kids love the stage band. I could call a rehearsal any time of day or night and they'd be there. And when they graduate they come to me and say, 'Man, I hate to leave high school,' because they may be going to study medicine or engineering at a college where there isn't any stage band. It isn't easy for those that decide to stay in music. It's mostly studio work after college, or teaching, but maybe rock will be the way out. Last year a bunch of the kids had a rock band with four or five horns and solos and they really had something going."

By eight o'clock we are in the new Municipal Theatre, which has fine acoustics. James Brown is holding forth next door in the Municipal Auditorium, and there are two basketball games on television tonight. Brown and basketball are big in Mobile, and the house is only half full. The judges are seated in a transverse aisle at a table with student lamps. They have their heads together and are laughing. Their faces are lit from below and they look like cowpunchers around a fire. The Glassboro Lab Band from New Jersey opens the proceedings, which are devoted to the first half of the college groups. It is nineteen-strong and weak in the knees rhythmically, but it has a good pianist and an interesting bass trombonist. The Ray Fransen Quintet from Loyola is made up of trumpet, alto saxophone, guitar, bass and the leader on drums. The bass player is black—the first for the evening. The group plays Eddie Harris's "Cryin' Blues" in a tight, swinging, Horace Silver way. Fransen is an excellent drummer, and his soloists are commendable post-bop performers. The University of Alabama Stage Band has thirty pieces, and it includes one Negro (on organ) and four girls. It is a show band with almost no solos, and it too has rhythmic problems. The Butler-Farmer-Jackson Pack—alto, tenor, and baritone saxophones, trombone, piano, bass, and drums—is out of Southern University and is all black. The saxophonists reveal admiration for John Coltrane, and the group moves capably, in the manner of the Herbie Hancock sextet. The Morehead State University Stage Band from Kentucky is surprising. The drummer is tough and sounds like the old Don Lamond, and there is a wild alto saxophonist and flutist named Brad Jones. In a complicated number, "Concertino," a trombone, a trumpet, and an alto saxophone move to one side of the stage, where they solo and play ensemble figures, and are answered by the rest of the band. The gimmick works. The Louisiana State University New Orleans Combo is led by Ben Smalley, a trumpeter and flugelhornist, and has piano, bass, and drums. Smalley, who is diminutive, plays with a sweet, florid precision. The group does "Here's That Rainy Day," "On the Trail," and a Brubeck number. Smalley would have little trouble in any New York or Los Angeles studio. The evening is closed by the University of Southern Mississippi Jazz Lab Band. It hustles, and in one number three soloists play at once, and in another four French horns appear and the saxophone section doubles on a total of twenty instruments. Like the two groups just ahead of it, it is all white.

After the concert St. Clair drives me to a party at Bill Lagman's house. Live oaks, mossy and thick-trunked, clasp hands across the streets, and the antebellum houses sit back on their plots, their big, elegant windows staring through porches and columns. They are 1830 New England houses, grown fat in an easy climate. Lagman, St. Clair tells me, has led a dance band for thirty years in Mobile and is on the festival committee. A year or two ago his musical faithfulness was rewarded with the Mr. Mobile Music Award. The guests are mainly involved with the festival. A fine buffet offers shrimps remoulade. After a while Mundell Lowe, Thad Jones, and Al Green gather in a small room off the kitchen, where there is an upright piano. Lowe has his guitar and Jones his cornet, and Green, a constantly smiling man who taught his extraordinary younger brother, Urbie, sits down at the piano. A local bassist appears. It is the best possible way to hear jazz, and the music is easy and affecting. Jones plays with startling freshness, and Green is a good late-swing pianist. Lowe, who does not perform much anymore, settles slowly into his instrument, and the muscles around his mouth reflect his pleasure. There are blues and ballads, and Lagman gets out his trumpet and joins in. He has the gentle, old-lady tone of the old New Orleans trumpeters, and the contrast between him and Jones, who has a brilliant tone and a nervous, punching attack, is marvellous. I wish that the kids could be there.

I have a late breakfast on Friday with Chuck Suber, the publisher of *Down Beat*. He is an intense, unassuming man in his late forties, and he has spent a good deal of the past fifteen years travelling the country and helping to put the high-school and college stage-band movement on its feet. He hands me a six-page brochure he has written, "How to Organize a School Jazz Festival-Clinic." It is terse and enthusiastic and exhaustive. He talks in much the same way: "Generally, the first music teachers in the public schools in this century were Sousa men, displaced when concerts in the parks and such began to give way after the First World War to the Model T and the movies. The next wave of teachers was made up in large part of dance-band men displaced after the Second World War, when the big bands began to disappear. Gene Hall, an inspired leader and teacher, organized the first college stage-band course in 1947 at North Texas State. He coined the euphemism 'stage band' simply because the terms 'jazz band' and 'dance band' were not acceptable in academic circles. Concurrently, jazz musicians were studying at the Westlake College of Music on the Coast, and in Boston at the Berklee School of Music, which has now become a four-year college with an enrollment of nine hundred and fifty. The first high-school stage-band festival was held in Brownwood, Texas, in 1952. There were nine or ten bands. I was there, and it excited me tremendously. Gradually, Gene Hall graduates began fanning out—getting jobs in high schools and colleges, starting stage bands, fighting for recognition—and their students did the same thing. The Farmingdale High School Dance Band from Long Island, with Marshall Brown as its director, appeared at Newport in 1957, and became the first high-school jazz band to gain national recognition. In fact, it was something of a sensation. The next year the International Youth Band, which had kids from all over Europe and the U.S.A., was another Newport success. By 1960 Stan Kenton was hiring sidemen from North Texas State, and the thing had mushroomed. Fifteen or sixteen thousand high schools of all kinds now have stage-band courses, and there are sixty-two regional high-school festivals, some of them with as many as a hundred and twenty-six competing groups. Six colleges offer majors in jazz, or the equivalent of it, and four hundred and fifty colleges have accredited jazz courses. There is also a loose federation of a dozen or so college festivals, held, among other places, in Hamden, Connecticut, and Notre Dame, Little Rock, the University of Utah, San Francisco Valley College, and here in Mobile. Each sends a winning big band, combo, and vocalist to the National Collegiate Festival. The first such festival was held in Miami Beach in 1967, and the fourth one will be given in Urbana, Illinois, in May."

I ask Suber where this flood of musicians hopes to work after college.

"That's the great problem. Some will try and make it on the road and some will wind up in the studios, but most of them will probably go into teaching, which of course results in a kind of closed-circuit, self-perpetuating system. Another problem is with the blacks. Integration has been slow, and many of the black schools, still hung up on the Negro-middle-class distaste for jazz, have nobody to organize and teach stage bands. But the whole program, despite the cul-de-sac conditions in jazz these days, is well worth it. It teaches the kids about a great, unique form of music. It teaches them a little about improvisation. Most important, it teaches them a valuable form of self-expression in an increasingly repressive and unoriginal society."

Suber is a judge at the high-school competition this afternoon. We get to the Municipal Theatre just before one-thirty. A dozen bands are scheduled. All are from Alabama, with the exception of the Starliners from Bowie, Maryland, and the Holy Cross Stage Band from New Orleans. It is only the second time the Mobile Festival has included a high-school competition. The house, which is nearly full, is made up largely of the relatives and friends of the musicians. Giggling and squirming are constant, and now and then a row of kids, uprooted by winds of enthusiasm, rises, flows down an aisle, and subsides in another row—pigeons suddenly clouding the air and settling fifty feet away. Solos, numbers, and sets are cheered wildly, and when each band finishes, its members file into the audience and sit in a clump. Feeling relieved and possibly heroic, with the eyes of a grateful audience riveted on them, they whisper and elbow one another. If the succeeding band sounds uncertain, the whispering becomes a steady counterpoint, but if the new group is obviously superior they grow still, amateurs digging old pros. Some of the bands are out of tune, some sag rhythmically, and many are marching bands in disguise. They play Neal Hefti, Marshall Brown, Stan Kenton, Blood, Sweat, and Tears, and the Beatles. The afternoon is a tossup between the Holy Cross Stage Band and the Murphy High Band from Mobile. Both play the Beatles' irresistible "Hey Jude," but Murphy High, warmed by the bosom of local pride, brings the house to a boil. The last group is un- believably old-fashioned ("That Old Black Magic," "I'll Be Around"), and provides a calming anticlimax.

I fall into an ironic reverie, remembering the music scene in my high school in the early forties. We had a band, or, rather, we had two bands—a ten-piece "big" one, which played dreary stock arrange- ments of the "Johnson Rag" and "Stardust," and a splinter Dixieland group. But it was an underground operation. We had no teacher or director. We were allowed to use a rehearsal room in the basement of the school chapel only when it was not occupied by the longhairs or the marching band. We provided our own arrangements, our own instru- ments, and even our own raison d'être, by giving illicit, well-attended jam sessions in the chapel basement. (During them, the resident music teacher, high-domed and wearing trousers invariably six inches too short, would poke his head in, and if he didn't throw us out would smirk and slam the door. The glee club, which he directed, was warmly received at neighboring girls' schools.) Most of the musicians were terrible, but the exceptions were memorable. There were a couple of flashy drummers patterned on Gene Krupa, a bass player with the power of Wellman Braud and the precision of Jimmy Blanton, and a musing, gentle cornettist who could play all of Bix Beiderbecke. There was also a tenor saxophonist from Maine who, though he couldn't speak two coherent sentences, played exactly like Lester Young. But those were champion times. We *were* Krupas and Blantons and Youngs, and since jazz had reached one of its peaks, our idols were almost al- ways within sustaining reach. Now jazz has grown lean and withdrawn, but every backwoods high school has a *Good Housekeeping* approved jazz band with school-supplied instruments, arrangements, practice halls, and teachers. A huge army of potential professionals, all dressed up and no place to go.

Another dinner is given before this evening's concert, at which the remaining college groups will play. The festival committee and the judges attend the dinner, and the judges are presented with miniature silver tankards. St. Clair takes me through the Municipal Auditorium on the way to the theatre. It is almost the size of the Houston Astrodome and is packed with dining Shriners. The music tonight at the festival is, by and large, several notches above last night's. The Jacksonville State University Band plays Buddy Rich's version of the Beatles' "Norwegian Wood," and there is a fine, bursting trombone solo in "Summertime." The next group, a quintet from the University of Florida, is made up of semi-ringers, for its members are graduate students. They pump sternly through a couple of free-for-all "new thing" numbers and sound like an Archie Shepp ensemble minus the humor. The Loyola University Jazz Lab Band, which I have heard about for several years, plays four swinging, precise numbers, one of them Don Ellis's difficult "In a Turkish Bath." It has a Negro bassist. Ray Fransen is on drums, and he makes everything cook. It is the best band we have heard yet. Some comic relief follows. The University Debs, hailing from Ball State University in Indiana and made up of eight very assorted girls accompanied by a rhythm section, yoohoo their way through a milky gospel number, some soft rock, and an imitation blues. The Louisiana State University Jazz Lab Band, which boasts the second Negro performer of the evening, is built mainly around the trumpet and flugelhorn of Ben Smalley. A nine-piece group, the Texas Southern University Contemporary Jazz Ensemble, has two whites and seven blacks, and is the first really integrated band at the festival. It is expert. It plays one long three-part number that suggests George Russell. The last band of the evening, Lee Fortier's Southeastern Louisiana College Stage Band, is every bit as good as a Woody Herman band, and three of its numbers, arranged and/or written by an alumnus, Joe Cacibaudia, are fascinating. They are full of satisfying, teeth-grinding harmonies, a variety of rhythms, and subtle dynamics.

The competition is over, and the judges retire to a dressing room to choose the winners. There is a good deal of badinage, some of it salty. The University Debs are awarded a special prize, since they are in a class by themselves. Not surprisingly, Morehead, Loyola, and Southeastern sweep the big bands, while Ray Fransen's Loyola group, the University of Florida Quintet (the grad students), and Texas

Southern (the integrated group) take the small-band honors. Suber and his compeers have already named the Holy Cross band the winner of the afternoon. Tomorrow night all eight winners will give a display program.

Off to another party with St. Clair, this one at a doctor's house, where a Dixieland band made up of local businessmen is to perform. The living room is built around an indoor garden with small trees, and the music is paunchy and purple-faced. A stocky man in his late thirties tells me that he acts as the group's bandboy. He says the band doesn't take itself seriously. I note the standing microphones in front of the band, the bank of recording equipment beside it, the stacks of tape, and the glistening instruments. Thad Jones sits in against his will—a cheetah pursued by hippos. Suber and I talk of the times when his father, who was head of Local 802 in New York, took him to the Savoy Ballroom to hear Chick Webb.

On Saturday morning I learn that someone got brutish with Thad Jones at the end of last night's party, and that, on top of that, his horn has been stolen from his hotel room. It is not the horn but the mouthpiece that matters. A trumpeter builds his chops around his mouthpiece, and adjusting to a new one is like starting a new career. I wander over to the theatre, where rehearsals are in progress, to talk with Ray Fransen, who seems the most confident and gifted musician in the festival. I notice that Mobile, like all old Southern towns, comes in warring parts. I'm in the middle of town, but I pass a sagging antebellum house and a field-size lot full of knee-high grass and gap-toothed shrubbery. Beyond the house I can see the twelve-story Admiral Semmes and the thirty-three-story First National Bank Building. The celebrated Mobile azaleas are in bloom, but the sour, noxious odor that rolled over the town yesterday, compliments of Mobile's two paper mills, still hangs in the air. Blacks seem to make it all right in the public places, but there haven't been many at the parties, and a member of the festival committee has told me that when the leaders of N.O.W., a civil-rights group, were invited to the festival, one of them told him that they would attend, so long as they didn't get "rained on" in the Municipal Theatre. The town cherishes its past, but one of its chief diversions is listening in on police calls.

I find Fransen backstage. He is compact and round-faced and bearded. He is also articulate, outspoken, and out of step with his generation, for he has a strong sense of tradition. "I was born in New Orleans, and I've lived there all my life. No one in my family plays an instrument, but I was always exposed to music—to Cole Porter and Gershwin and even Art Tatum. When I was a kid I was real fat and introverted, and I used to stay home and listen to the old people's radio station, WWL. My father's a Nicaraguan. He's a dentist and damned good, and I guess it was he who, if he didn't lead me into music, allowed me into it. He loves music as art and he loves manual dexterity. I started lessons on drums six years ago, and on the side I played in rock groups. Both experiences dragged me. I went the whole rudimental route in the drum class, but drum rudiments are just like scales—a means to an end and not an end. I got tired of rock drumming quick; I didn't want to blow my eardrums out. Anyway, that's changing. The rock musicians are stretching out their numbers and getting into solos and other instruments than guitars. I consider myself a percussionist. I've learned most of the percussion instruments, including timpani and vibes. I'm going to do graduate work in ethnomusicology, but my prime interest is in being a performer. I'm not interested in amassing a fortune, but rather than prostitute myself musically I'd sell shoes. Fortunately, with my background, I could probably get a job in a symphonic organization or in jazz or with certain rock groups. The reason the kids ignore jazz is partly because they associate it with parents, with a different era. It's supposed to be acquainted with brothels, and brothels are out. But when they *do* listen, they hear the excitement. I took my quintet into a small beer lounge on campus a while back, and at first nothing happened. Then it caught on and now the place is packed. But the kids are denying roots. They only want what's now. They say, I don't want to study Dixieland, but I say, Man, you don't have to *study* it, just know what it is. The past is there for a cat to take what he needs from it. Paul Desmond listened to Lester Young and Gil Evans to Brahms, and they wouldn't be what they are if they hadn't. I listen and steal from everybody—Gene Krupa and Sidney Catlett and Chick Webb—and recently I've been listening to Joe Morello and Buddy Rich and Grady Tate. That's the drag about my generation—tossing everything out and replacing it with nothing. It's ridiculous. Everybody hates what's going on, but nobody has any solutions."

There aren't many surprises at tonight's performance. A lot of new material is brought out, though, including numbers by Charlie Mingus, Luis Bonfa, and Clifford Brown, and the Ball State Debs have new hairdos. Everyone plays well. For some reason, the trophies are handed out after the theatre has emptied, but it is good to see the three hundred or so kids cheering the winners and keeping their disappointments to themselves. The judges make the awards—all except Thad Jones, who flew home earlier today.

1970

Night Clubs

I. The Gordon House

Night clubs, those womblike houses of illusion that came down to us from the eighteenth-century London pubs by way of Parisian cafés and the New York speakeasies, were long considered by the perspicacious as warm retreats where, the world safely locked out, one could laugh and weep and eat and drink while absorbing a unique and delicate culture, and, particularly in New York, as well-paying, highly exacting finishing schools whose best graduates have gone on to firm up Hollywood and Broadway and television. Among the graduates of the last twenty years alone are Barbra Streisand, Andy Williams, Nichols and May, Pearl Bailey, Carol Burnett, Harry Belafonte, Andy Griffith, Diahann Carroll, Phyllis Diller, Shelley Berman, Aretha Franklin, Miriam Makeba, the Smothers Brothers, Dick Gregory, Woody Allen, and Alan Arkin. (And this list does not in any way diminish the countless jazz musicians, folk singers, cocktail pianists, magicians, puppeteers, and divas emeritae who, because of their lack of mass appeal, have remained perennial, endlessly rewarding night-club undergrads.) There were excellent reasons why night clubs were rigorous training grounds. Most good clubs were small, and few performers can get away with fluffing a lyric or fudging a gag or singing flat in front of an audience sitting within kissing distance. Nor, since most night-club patrons tended to be habitués, can he repeat himself three shows a night, six nights a week. Moreover, the iron law of put-up or shut-up was in constant effect, for the customer was paying more for his evening, pound for pound, than for any other kind of entertainment. But night clubs, despite their humanistic virtues, have for some time now been dying out. Television, biting the hand that has so winningly fed it, is the chief cause. It pays its performers more than any night club (the Las Vegas and Miami night spots, which pay plenty, are pre-digested carnivals rather than night clubs), and it offers Streisand and Griffith and Burnett and Bailey absolutely free—all of which raises an unavoidable irony: Where will television, which has no farm system, get new, young talent when its present stars grow old?

These considerations led me to look up the two men who, between them, have invented and operated the three most imaginative and enlightening of all New York night clubs—Max Gordon (not the theatrical producer but "the other Max Gordon," as he is sometimes called), the owner of the Village Vanguard, which is not only one of the best American night clubs, past or present, but is probably the oldest (it opened in 1934, at 1 Charles Street in Greenwich Village, and a year later moved a couple of blocks north to where it is now) and Barney Josephson, the owner of the still lamented Café Society Downtown and Café Society Uptown which flourished between 1938 and 1948.

I went to see Gordon first. He is unique on several counts. He is, as he is fond of saying, "probably the oldest night-club owner in the world." He is also, in a field that has long been harvested by the underworld, absolutely honest. He pays his performers, who rarely fall below the B level, decent wages, and he charges his customers decent prices for decent booze and food. (To be sure, he has, he says, paid a mysterious monthly "protection" fee to one man for thirty-six years. What with inflation, it was recently raised from two to three dollars.) He has, as well, been a ceaseless, high-class experimenter. At one point in 1948 he owned the Vanguard, and in partnership with Herbert Jacoby, probably the premier promoter of supper clubs, owned the Blue Angel and Le Directoire. And among the more uncommon acts he has hired were Lenny Bruce, the young and unknown Thelonious Monk, John Carradine, and a band made up of nothing but bass fiddles, as well as put on a series of evenings in the Vanguard called "Speak Out" in which a panel of such lions as John Simon and Archie Shepp and LeRoi Jones belabored the audience and was belabored in turn to such memorable effect that the entire proceedings were printed in a monthly jazz magazine. Above all, Gordon, in a quicksand business, is indomitable. He has not only shepherded a wife and two daughters through the vagaries of New York life but has steered the Vanguard through innumerable financial and emotional storms, the "darkest" being the night in the early sixties when, Con Edison having removed its meter from the club that morning, the show went on by candlelight.

Gordon, a diffident dresser, does not resemble a white-on-white night-club operator. (All he said, after trying on a handsome new Brooks Brothers suit in front of his mirror, was "Gee, I don't know.")

He is short and slightly bent and gnomish. His hands and feet are child-like, and he is dominated by a large head, which in turn is dominated by a broad brow and heavy white receding hair. His eyes are sad, and prunelike wrinkles course down his face. (When the comedian Joe Frisco visited Gordon's first club, the Village Fair Coffee House, in the early thirties, he pointed to Gordon and asked a friend, "Who's that miserable guy by the door? He looks like the Wailing Wall in Jerusalem.") But Gordon, like many hesitant, inward-gazing people, glows. His Solomonlike visage is constantly ruffled by smiles and laughter, and if he gets excited his voice, which creaks when he breaks one of his occasional long silences, booms. He is a funny, astute, dreaming man who shrugs off victory and laughs at defeat, and who invariably treats the weaknesses in others with respect. He is, not surprisingly, a pithy social observer. "When I first rode the New York subways late at night in the twenties," he has said, "they were full of Jews. Now they're full of blacks." One of his many admirers has said of him, "If I had to spend the rest of my days on a desert island and could take just five people, Max would top the list."

Gordon lives in an airy, high-ceilinged apartment on East Seventy-ninth Street with his wife, Lorraine, and his daughters, Rebecca and Deborah. One girl is in school, the other in college, and Mrs. Gordon, in addition to being a fervent supporter of the Women's Strike for Peace, manages a smart poster gallery around the corner on Seventy-eighth Street. When I stopped in at the apartment late one morning, Gordon was still in his bathrobe and pajamas. "I get home at two or three," he said. "I discovered a long time ago that you can't run a club *in absentia*. People are apt to tap the till, and anyway the customers need you, the performers need you. I feel guilty about the hours I keep because of Lorraine, but then I don't go down to the club till ten or so in the evening, and she has her job and her causes. We've lived here twelve years. Two years ago the building was coöpted, but we didn't buy. A lady named McDonald bought the apartment. We've never seen her and I don't know if she's seen the apartment. It worries Lorraine that she might throw us out. But it doesn't bother me—the places I've lived in. When I came to New York in 1926 I lived in furnished rooms. I must have lived in twenty or more of them, and they were mostly in a complex, a rabbit warren owned by a man named Albert Strunsky. The N.Y.U. Law School is there now. The side facing Washington Square had big studios where fancy people paid seventy-five dollars a month, but we lived on the other side, in rooms with hall toilets, for six dollars a week. There was no central heating, just gas heaters, and you took your life in your hands if you went to sleep in the winter and left the gas on. Strunsky was a marvellous man. He'd known Jack London, and he loved creative people. You could always owe him money. He looked like an Irishman, with his beet face and polished scalp. A cousin, Simeon, was an editorial writer with the *Times,* and another relative, Anna, was a Yiddish writer. I think one of his daughters married Ira Gershwin. Strunsky was always around, and when someone asked him where his beautiful wife was, he'd say, 'Oh, Palm Beach.' Lorraine and I were walking down the street a while ago, and there was an old sofa, all broken down and gaping, sitting by the curb. It made me laugh. It was authentic Strunsky period.

"I'd come to New York from Portland, Oregon, ostensibly to go to Columbia Law School. I was raised in Portland, but I was born in 1903 in Svir in Lithuania. I was the third of four children. My mother brought us over to Providence, Rhode Island, in 1908. My father had already established himself in the dairy and delicatessen business. I remember him churning butter in the window of his shop, and going for rides on Sunday in a surrey with a fringe on top. We spoke Yiddish at home, but my Yiddish fell away. I have no memory of the lack of English. I can't read Yiddish now, although I speak it haltingly, and I probably could enjoy a play in Yiddish. We stayed in Providence several years. Then my father moved to Portland, and we followed him. He became a kind of peddler, and he'd go out to the eastern part of the state and buy furs from trappers. He used a horse and wagon first, and then he had a Ford pickup truck. We were poor, and we hustled as children. I sold papers, and we'd save all kinds of boxes during the year and sell them for people to sit on at the Rose Festival parade. Mark Rothko, the great painter, was related to us, and we sold papers together. We talked about it on the phone the day before he committed suicide, just a little while ago. I couldn't understand him doing that. He had a big studio, a home, money. When I went to the funeral his elder brothers were there, and I asked them why they had let Mark sell papers and run the streets when they already owned a drugstore. They shrugged and said, 'What did we know in those days?' My mother and father were separated off and on when I was growing up. I never knew why. My father worked hard, and he was a good, gentle man. But my mother was hard-bitten. She was not a happy woman. She had a goiter and a heart condition. But she had that Jewish drive to educate her children, and I think I broke her heart when I didn't become a lawyer. When I was in high school I hung around with people who read novels and poetry, and I never studied. But I went to Reed College in Oregon, and when I was a junior I got fed up. I wanted to get away, to lash out, so I matriculated at Stan-ford and then ran out of money. I got a job in an all-night cigar store, saved some money, and went back to Reed and graduated. I only lasted at Columbia six weeks. I lived on the campus for a while after I'd dropped out, and I got to know the intellectuals, like Gus Solomon, who's a federal judge in Oregon, and Furner Nuhn, who contributed to the *American Mercury*. Then I moved down to Strunsky's. I didn't know what I wanted to do. All I knew was that work was unworthy of me. What *was* worthy I didn't know. So I wouldn't work until I really had to, and then I'd get a job in a mail-order place, running an addressograph machine or licking envelopes. When I tired of one place I'd go to another, or if I had scraped enough money together I'd lay off a couple of months. I spent my days in the Public Library and my nights at Paul's on Wooster Street or Sam Johnson's on Third Street. I stayed up until three or four in the morning and slept until two or three in the afternoon. Paul's and Sam Johnson's were coffeehouses with poetry. Eli Siegel, who has a movement called Aesthetic Realism now, ran Sam Johnson's. He'd won the *Nation* poetry prize in 1925 for 'Hot Afternoons Have Been in Montana.' There would be poetry readings and lots of discussion groups, and I met people like Joe Gould and John Rose Gildea and Harry Kemp and Max Bodenheim, whom I'd read in college. There was a lot of drinking—wine, or alcohol mixed with the essence of juniper. It was Prohibition that did that. The minute repeal came, everybody went on the wagon. Gildea was a wonderful man. He married an East Side girl, and he'd come to the Village in tails and stay three days. He improvised poetry for drinks, and some of it was marvellous. I don't think he ever published anything. I remember taking him home and walking under the Sixth Avenue 'L' on a freezing winter night while he spouted this great poetry at the top of his lungs. I took Joe Gould home, too. Malcolm Cowley would give him piles of books to review, but he read very fast, skipping a lot, and his reviews were short and sketchy. Harry Kemp, whose poems you can find in the old anthologies, was a huge, heavyweight strapping guy. A big, real, impossible man. He'd had an affair with Upton Sinclair's wife, and in 1922 he published "Tramping on Life," a very successful autobiography. He followed it with "More Miles," but that flopped. He ran Harry Kemp's One-Act Playhouse, where Clifford Odets started as an actor. Kemp lived on the dunes at Provincetown, where he helped start the Provincetown Playhouse, and when he came to town he'd look for me in the coffeehouses and he'd shout, 'Max! Where are you? I have a new poem to read to you!' and crush me with an embrace when he found me. I was enchanted with Provincetown when I went up there later in the thirties. Kemp would roar down Commercial Street, talking, talking, talking, and it was like the Village, only with water."

Gordon went out to the kitchen and made a pot of tea. "I'm not much at this sort of thing," he said when he came back, "but it's real tea and it's hot." He lit a big cigar. It made him look top-heavy. He puffed for a while, his eyes narrowed against the smoke, and then put the cigar down and took a sip of tea.

"In 1929 I went home. It was frustration and fatigue, and I went home to recharge my batteries. I stayed four or five months and came back in November of that year and drifted into my old life of odd jobs with mail-order outfits and writing for little puff magazines. By this time I had vague visions of being a writer. For the puff magazines, which were a racket, we'd pick out people of the second and third echelon who had been in the news and write congratulatory biographies, about three hundred words or so, and then call them up and read them what we'd written and ask them how many copies they wanted at thirty-five cents a throw. I also wrote a humorous essay which had to do with a *schnorrer,* a Yiddish word for a phony promoter. It was printed in the *Menorah Journal,* which was edited by Eliott Cohen, who later edited *Commentary.* Albert Halper, the novelist, was in the same issue, and I noticed a while ago that he's just published an autobiography. I knew I wasn't a writer, but I also knew I had to be *some*thing. I had got to the point where I was sick worrying about my mother, about what she was thinking of me. People didn't have contempt for their parents then, and this guilt was engulfing me. Ann Andreas, who was a good friend of mine, saved me. She suggested I start a decent coffeehouse, since Sam Johnson's and Paul's had gone downhill. My sister had moved to New York, and between us we raised four or five hundred dollars. I found a half basement on Sullivan Street that seated about seventy-five. I think it's a fraternity house now. We opened in the latter part of 1932, and we called it the Village Fair Coffee House. We served tea and coffee and sandwiches and setups. The waitresses wore pajama-type pants, and it was the sort of place where they'd sit and talk with the customers if they were invited to. But it was all very innocent. The poets, who were always looking for new places, started coming in, and I hired Ivan Black, the press agent, as a master of ceremonies and a bouncer. I fed him and give him five bucks a week, and he organized everything. He was a newspaperman and a poet and he read his own stuff, including a risqué parody of Joyce and Gertrude Stein that had run in *Transition.* I came across a reprint of it the other day in an old file, and, you know, it's pretty funny. It's called 'Mister Weirdy at Home.' "

Gordon shuffled some papers and handed me the reprint. It begins:

At that time he was constipaching, ins aferment outs abloat, his faceskin a ptomaine green Oily. He was about to write his gratest poem. Pianowing was his livelihoodway and even more his life-leewayhoot but when he got leadbelly he verscript. He put on a Beethovenfrown as browclasp. He dipt his pen and poised.

"It really went over big, and when he'd finish, Ivan would call on poets in the audience to read. They'd get food or liquor or fifty cents. Graham Norwell, a Canadian painter, did the murals in the place. He was a wonderful, handsome man, but he'd lost his teeth and he was a drunk. I paid him in gin. Once, when he had an exhibition of his stuff over in Brooklyn, he went to the opening, and he looked so awful—I think he'd dyed his hair orange—that they wouldn't let him in. We had other entertainment besides the poets. The late Michael Field's wife danced to records, and so did the painter Oronzo Gasparro. Maggie Egri sang Hungarian folk songs that she said she had learned at her mother's breast in Joplin, Missouri. She was a real, bona-fide witch. I used to stand on the side and wonder what it all meant, and yet in a way I was part of it, too. After a while, things got sort of drunken and evil-seeming. Uptown people started coming down so they could say they'd bought John Rose Gildea a drink, and a lot of the poets became more interested in the bottle than they were in conversations about life and literature. Then, unbeknownst to me, one of the waitresses got caught trying to sell liquor to a cop in plainclothes, so they put a cop on the premises every night, and there he sat in his uniform, and it put a pall on the place. I could have given him twenty-five dollars and he would have gone away, but I didn't know enough. The place had been jammed every night, but in a month's time it was empty, and we closed. We'd been running a year."

Gordon stood up, cigar in mouth, and stretched. "I've got to get down to the club. There are some orders coming in, and my day porter is sick. We can have a bite on the way at the old Charles on Sixth Avenue." Ten minutes later he reappeared, housed in a dark suit and a lively tie. We walked to Park Avenue and found a cab.

"I was out of work for a while," Gordon said. "Then I put in six weeks running a place for a mob underling named Frankie Starch. He wasn't doing any business in the place he had, and he asked me to come in as a partner at thirty-five dollars a week. I changed the name of the place to the Village Fair Coffee House, and all the same poets and painters appeared, but it wasn't the same, because Starch and his friends were always around. I couldn't handle them. They were a tough bunch, and Starch kept referring to the poets as 'creeps.' I was eating in an all-night cafeteria after work one night and one of his hunkies found me and said, 'Frankie wants to see you.' Oh, boy, I thought. But all he wanted was to fire me, which he did. The last time I saw him, years ago, he was running a newsstand on Sixth Avenue and Third Street. I'd saved a hundred and fifty dollars, and I borrowed another fifty from a friend at Columbia, and in February of 1934 I found another basement place, at 1 Charles Street. Jack Delaney, the Village pub keeper, had had it one time, and I rented it for twenty-five dollars a month. It didn't have a stick of furniture, but I knew Frances Bell, from Provincetown. She had a place there called the White Whale, and she had another one in an old blacksmith shop on Barrow Street. It had brick walls and belly stoves and it was so cold—that was the winter when the temperature hit twenty below in New York—you couldn't pick up the silver. She gave me a bunch of barrels—big ones to stretch planks between for tables, and smaller ones to sit on—and I gave her a due bill for seventy-five dollars. I can't remember why, but I called the place the Village Vanguard, and a lot of the old crowd, including Gasparro and Maggie Egri and such, came back. After a year or so we moved, not losing a night's business, to the present Vanguard. It had been a speak called the Triangle Gardens. It was bigger—I could only seat forty or fifty at the old place—and it seemed to me that moving there would be like growing up. Then the damnedest thing happened, and it really shook me up. I got arrested and spent a night in jail. Someone had written obscene graffiti on the men's-room wall, and there is a crazy New York ordinance that holds a cabaret owner responsible for such things. I had to go to court in a paddy wagon, and when the judge heard from the cop why I'd been arrested and that I'd spent the night in jail, *he* was astonished and dismissed the case. But I've never forgotten the experience. There must be twenty coats of paint on the bathroom walls at the club, and the only things I don't wash off or paint over are scribblings like the one I found the other day: 'Roland Kirk is a nice cat.' "

Gordon ordered a Scotch-and-soda at the Charles, which is spacious and plush and emblazoned with paintings of nudes. He settled back and waved his hands in front of him. "This place always reminds me of one of my worst disasters—a fancy ice-cream parlor I opened in 1955 on Fifty-eighth Street near the Paris Theatre. My partner was Michael Field, and we called it Maxfield. The name was almost the only good thing about it. Michael had been a pianist before he got into his cooking school and his cookbooks, and he was a friend from the old days. The idea for the place was mine, and Michael was crazy about it. I wanted a place that would maybe cost ten thousand and that *looked* genuine, but he wanted it to *be* genuine. So we put in a mosaic floor, like the one in the men's room in Penn Station. We found an old Mazda-bulb sign for outside. All the tables and the counter top were marble. I think it took fourteen men to lift that counter into place. The chairs were old ice-cream-parlor chairs, the walls were red velvet and had hand-carved figures on the moldings, and the chandeliers were brass. It was a beautiful place, and it had beautiful food. Michael insisted we make our own ice cream, and he made all the desserts. I never saw so much cream in my life. But beauty is skin-deep, and underneath everything was wrong. We'd spent thousands and thousands and thousands. The floor alone cost thirty-five hundred and the sign twelve hundred, and all that marble was real. Those genuwine ice-cream-parlor chairs were so uncomfortable you couldn't sit in them for more than twenty minutes. We'd found these old glasses for the ice cream in a place down in the Bowery, but they were so heavy you could barely lift them, and they were so big they wouldn't fit into the dishwasher until we had special trays built. The prices were too high. People came around from Bergdorf's for a cup of coffee—*fresh* coffee, never more than twenty minutes old—and it would cost them twenty-five cents, and they'd hit the ceiling. We stayed open until one or two in the morning trying to catch the late crowd, but we didn't have a liquor license. And then the union started giving us trouble. It turned out that I had to run the place because Michael was so busy with his other interests, and at the time I had the Vanguard *and* the Blue Angel to worry about. I'd get to Maxfields at ten every morning absolutely pooped. I told Michael I couldn't put so much time in, and he said he couldn't spare any more, and shortly afterward he walked out and I never saw him again. The place is a Shelley's luncheonette now."

Gordon downed a second Scotch, neat, and ordered bay scallops. "My other great disaster took place ten years before, and the only difference was that it happened on *East* Fifty-eighth Street. Barney Josephson's Café Society Uptown had started doing poorly, and Herbert Jacoby and I bought it from him for seventy-five thousand, renamed it Le Directoire, tossed everything out, redecorated, and maybe spent another seventy thousand. At first it went like a house afire. We had Kay Thompson and the Williams Brothers, and there were literally lines around the block every night. But she left, and Abe Burrows came in, then Pearl Bailey, then Mata and Hari, and everything changed. We charged so much money that people got mad and stayed away, and the reason we charged so much was that when we redecorated we had somehow managed to reduce the seating capacity from three hundred and fifty to one hundred and thirty-six. Business got worse and worse, and finally, after eight months, we gave the place back to Barney for five thousand and got out. We'd poured everything from the Blue Angel into it, and it's a wonder that didn't fold, too."

Gordon speared some scallops with his fork and pushed them through his tartar sauce. "The food isn't bad in this old place. These are honest-to-God bay scallops, not the chopped-up haddock that you get most places. At the time of Le Directoire, Jacoby and I had already been in business five years at the Blue Angel, which was on Fifty-fifth between Third and Lexington. He had managed the Ruban Bleu before that, but there was some sort of ruckus and he had walked out. He started coming down to the Vanguard to watch the acts, and we talked. He wanted to open a place, but he didn't have any money, and he asked me to come in as a partner. I put down five thousand, and he borrowed five thousand. It was a strange relationship. Jacoby had run places in Paris, and I guess he had more to do than anyone else with establishing the supper club over here. He's a man of taste and some background and he's also a snob, but I was just a downtown Village boy who got dressed up to go uptown. So at first I had to defer to him in many ways. He did the emceeing, at which he was good, and he did the booking, which tended to follow a delicate, almost esoteric line. The very first show included a French singer, Madame Claude Alphand, and an Ecuadorian baritone, who was terrible, and Sylvia Marlowe, the harpsichordist. The décor reflected Jacoby, too, with its gray velvet walls and rosettes and pink crystal chandeliers. And so did the food. We had a French chef, our own pastries, and Mme. Romaine, the omelette lady, came in every night to cook omelettes for supper. I don't know whether it was ego or what, but as time went on I started making booking suggestions, and it turned out that we tended to agree on most acts. We held auditions one afternoon a week, and eventually the Blue Angel had such a reputation that anyone who had worked there could get a job in any room in the country. In fact, there were acts who'd say they had worked with us when they hadn't, and we'd get verifying calls from bookers and club owners all over the country.

"It's hard to believe now some of the people who worked at the Blue Angel, the acts we helped start off—Josephine Premice, the dancer, and comedians like Kaye Ballard and Carol Burnett and Alice Pearce and Wally Cox and Orson Bean and Phyllis Diller and Shelley Berman. Woody Allen, too, who was so nervous when he started he shook like a leaf, and Nichols and May. There were dozens of singers.

Some were established, like Mildred Bailey and Maxine Sullivan, but most were starters, like Andy Williams and the Inca Trio, which had that fantastic soprano, Yma Sumac, and Martha Wright and Pearl Bailey and Bobby Short and Harry Belafonte and Barbra Streisand. Jacoby doted on French acts, and there were nights at the Blue Angel when I never heard a word of English. Irene Bordoni was an oo-la-la French singer and Odette Myrtil was a French comedienne, and there was an amazing act, Les Mains d'Yves Joly, who used their fingers as puppets. There were a lot of English comedians, and one, Douglas Byng, was nerve-racking. He kept twitching his head and looking at his shoulder, as if some sort of bird was sitting there, and he talked so fast I couldn't understand a word. And, of course, there were a great many people—and this is one of the sad things about show business—who performed and did nothing and disappeared. The Blue Angel was a quality room, and we did a good business until we began to feel the pressure from television, in the late fifties. Business dropped off, as it did everywhere. Jacoby got restless, anxious. He wanted to turn the place into a full-time restaurant. We dickered, and I found some buyers from Chicago who were interested in taking over his share, but he couldn't make up his mind, and finally I bought him out for fifteen thousand in cash and a twenty-thousand-dollar mortgage. I changed the acts a little, bringing in Nipsy Russell and Clara Ward, the gospel singer, and Max Morath, the ragtime pianist. But everything looked musty and dusty to me. I couldn't stand the rosettes on the walls, and the floor had got tacky. We were doing fairly well, but the place needed new blood, a new face. After a year or so I said the hell with it, and in the spring of 1964 I sold the works to the Living Room people. It was time for me to go back downtown where I belonged. I'd been neglecting the Vanguard and it wasn't doing well."

Gordon lit a cigar, and we walked over to the Vanguard. It is in the basement of a triangular, two-story building that faces Seventh Avenue and is wedged between Eleventh Street and Waverly Place. The door needs paint, and the awning is tattered and worn. It's the sort of entranceway you could pass at an amble and miss. I followed Gordon down narrow, steep stairs and under a low arch that has probably cracked some of the most distinguished heads in the world. The main room of the Vanguard is, like the building it is in, triangular, and is fifty or sixty feet long. At its apex there is a small bandstand, and its base is flanked by a coatroom and the bar. Behind the bar are the washrooms and a small kitchen. Banquettes line the walls of the main room, and there are a dozen tiny tables. The place didn't look like the

Hollywood version of an empty night club. The chairs, instead of being stacked upside down on the tables, were exactly where their last occupants had left them, and the floor was littered with cigarette butts. It was cold, and the room smelled like a cave.

"I've got to get someone in here to clean up," Gordon said. "I never get spooked when I'm here alone, but I can't stand the cold." He turned on a small gas heater by the bandstand, and we went into the kitchen. It was clean and compact, with two big black stoves, a sink, a worktable, a small wooden desk, and a couple of chairs. Gordon sat down at his desk in his hat and coat and made a couple of telephone calls. "My office, my home, my palace," he said when he had finished. "This place has been like a love match to me. I've probably spent more time in it than anywhere else. I've even slept here, stretched out on a couple of tables. I've learned that if you're good to the Vanguard, the Vanguard will be good to you. And I learned that when we moved here. The entertainment then was pretty much catch-as-catch-can. Ivan Black had taken a job over at the Four Trees, which later became Café Society Downtown, and Eli Siegel replaced him as master of ceremonies. He never drank, so I had to pay him, and he recited Vachel Lindsay at the top of his voice. He wasn't everybody's favorite, but he kept things in hand. In between poetry readings I played a phonograph for dancing, and we had a lot of itinerant entertainers. They floated all over the Village—operatic baritones, comedians, piano players—and they'd come in and perform and people threw money at them. On Christmas Eves the Almanac Singers would come in and everybody would join them singing. Pete Seeger and Woody Guthrie were in that group. I began to look for acts to put in, and what I wanted was something that would comment on the social and political scene. There was a girl who used to hang around at this time, and her name was Judy Tuvim, which is Hebrew for 'holiday.' She was answering telephones with Orson Welles' Mercury Theatre. She brought down Adolph Green, and he brought in Betty Comden, who was a student at N.Y.U. They were part of a group that had been rehearsing uptown called Six and Company, and I hired them for Sunday nights for twenty-five or thirty dollars. They did a lot of topical stuff, like our selling the Sixth Avenue 'L' to the Japs so that they could make bombs to blow up the Chinese with. They changed their name to the Revuers, and they were so good that the whole town started knocking at the Vanguard door. It got so crowded people had to sit on the floor. So they began performing six nights a week, and they were with me a year. I could have kept them five years, but they were offered more money by the Rainbow Room, and it was a step up for them. They spawned a lot of imitators, but none had that same fresh young quality, that quickness and sparkle. Folk singers started getting big, and Josh White and Leadbelly came in as a team, and I had Burl Ives and Richard Dyer Bennett and Pete Seeger. I also began hiring jazz groups, like a marvellous trio with Zutty Singleton and Eddie Heywood and Albert Nicholas. I had calypso groups, and Professor Irwin Corey, the comic, first came in 1945. And, by God, he was back with me last week. By this time the Blue Angel was going strong, so we began trying out acts here first and then sending them uptown. That happened with Eartha Kitt and Pearl Bailey and Josephine Premice and Harry Belafonte. Eddie Heywood had brought Pearl Bailey to me, which was often the way I got my best acts, like Aretha Franklin, who was brought here by Major Holley, the bassist. Pearl was a band singer, but she was already doing her thing of switching from singing to talking in the middle of a number, and I encouraged her to do it. I had established a room that was free and easy, and I think *she* felt free and easy. Then somewhere in 1957 I switched almost completely to a jazz policy, even though I still had acts like the Kingston Trio and Mort Sahl and Nina Simone and Miriam Makeba and Lenny Bruce. I never *did* get completely used to Bruce. The four-letter words stuck to me like burrs, the way they still do when I find them on the printed page."

There was a banging at the street door. "That'll be the Coca-Cola man," Gordon said. "I have to let him in. The door upstairs never used to be locked, and people would wander in all afternoon—singers, comics, musicians, looking for jobs. But I got mugged on the stairs about a year and a half ago, so I keep it locked now." Gordon returned, and there was a tremendous *thump-thump-thump* as the delivery man eased his dolly down the stairs. Gordon paid him in cash and sat down.

"I probably have the smallest staff of any place this size in New York. My bartender has been with me twenty years, and there's my day porter. I have a couple of waiters who come and go, and my sister Sadye helps out. She'll be in in a while, so that I can go uptown for a nap. People sometimes ask me who decorated the place. The answer is nobody. It decorated itself. It hasn't changed much. The stage used to be where the bar is now, and a Refregier protégé did the original murals. I remember a horse playing a piano. But the walls crumbled, and the murals with them. People don't seem to care much about eating in basements, so the food end has never been very important. The most ambitious I ever got was when I hired a chef who said he'd studied cooking in Paris. I auditioned him by bringing five or six friends down, and he cooked a beautiful meal. I bought a whole bunch of those utensils for eating snails with and special bowls for onion soup. All that stuff is still packed away in here somewhere. His first night, fifty or so people ordered dinner. The orders kept coming into the kitchen, but nothing came out. The waiters stood around, and when the food was finally ready it was either overdone or under-done or cold. He didn't know what the hell he was doing, but when dinner was over, out he went into the room in his chef's garb, perspir-ing and covered with gravy stains, and said, 'Well, how was every-thing, folks?'

"The worst time for the Vanguard came in the early sixties. I had to sell our car and the little place we had built out on Fire Island. One of my girls was there visiting a friend last summer, and they went by our old house and the friend told her it's still called 'the Gordon house.' One of the axioms of the night-club business is that you have to have somebody to lean on for money. Like the man who lent me the fifty dollars to open the first Vanguard in 1934. He lent me ten thou-sand during the bad days in the sixties, and a week ago I paid him the last fifty dollars. I've never been much of a businessman, but we've taken in some money at times. When I could still afford Miles Davis, he'd bring in nine thousand a week. Money is a funny thing. A lot of musicians have borrowed from me—twenty-five, fifty, a hundred—and most of them pay it back. The ones who don't, though, will pay me, say, half, and then usually I don't see them for a long time. When they show up again, I think, He still owes me twenty bucks, but I don't say anything and he doesn't say anything, and after a while the unpaid money just seems to disappear, as though it had never existed. It's amazing how money can vanish like that. Business has picked up in the last year or so. The kids are coming in, and they aren't so different from the way we were in the late twenties. And I get a lot of blacks, so I only use strong black acts like Elvin Jones and Roland Kirk and Pharaoh Saunders. The Bill Evanses and Gary Burtons and Mose Allisons just don't do anything for the Vanguard anymore. And the Thad Jones-Mel Lewis big band is in its sixth year of Monday nights. They jam the place, they keep me going. A lot of people sit in, like Ray Charles, when he's around, and last week there were so many visiting musicians in this kitchen I could hardly get in the door. It's like the old jam sessions Harry Lim ran here one night a week in the forties. Of course, I'll never retire. How could I? I couldn't live on Social Security. When my present lease is up, I'll renew it for another ten years."

There were steps on the stairs. "That'll be Sadye now," Gordon said.

II. The Happiest Days of My Life

Barney Josephson, who is sixty-nine, still cherishes and grows elo-quent over what he wrought at Café Society Downtown and Café Society Uptown thirty-three years ago. His intent was simple and revolutionary: to present first-rate but generally unknown Negro and white talent to integrated audiences in honest, attractive surroundings. The performers at the clubs were as often as not discovered by Josephson or by the critic John Hammond, who provided the musical talent, and the list is astonishing. Among the singers were Sarah Vaughan, Billie Holiday, Mildred Bailey, Lena Horne, Kenneth Spencer, Lucienne Boyer, Joe Turner, the Golden Gate Quartet, Patti Page, Josh White, Burl Ives, Big Bill Broonzy, Susan Reed, and Kay Starr. Among the comedians were Imogene Coca, Zero Mostel, Jimmy Savo, Jack Gilford, Jim Backus, Carol Channing, and Jim Copp. Among the dancers were the Kraft Sisters and Pearl Primus. And among the musicians were Frankie Newton, Red Allen, Bill Coleman, Teddy Wilson, Art Tatum, James P. Johnson, Albert Ammons, Meade Lux Lewis, Pete Johnson, Edmond Hall, Lester Young, Sidney Catlett, John Kirby, Eddie Heywood, Vincente Gomez, Django Reinhardt, Hazel Scott, Mary Lou Williams, Cliff Jackson, and Ellis Larkins. The surroundings in which this galaxy revolved were remarkable. Café Society Downtown at Sheridan Square was in a comfortable, L-shaped basement (capacity two hundred and ten) decorated with funny murals by the likes of Adolf Dehn, Sam Berman, Ad Reinhardt, and Abe Birnbaum. The Uptown was on Fifty-eighth Street between Park and Lexington, in what is now the Fine Arts Theatre. It was an airy, two-story amphitheatre (capacity three hundred and fifty), with surrealistic murals by Anton Refregier. The bandstand was at the rear, and it was flanked by tiers of banquettes and tables that descended to a dance floor. A balcony with more tables ran along the back of the room. There were floor shows at both clubs at nine, twelve, and two, and a typical one at the Uptown included several numbers by Teddy Wilson's band (Joe Thomas, trumpet; Edmond Hall, clarinet; Benny Morton, trombone; John Williams, bass; Sidney Catlett, drums), one of them a flagwaver built around a long and invariably ingenious Catlett solo; half a dozen rushing, helter-skelter piano solos by Hazel Scott, who liked to jazz up Bach and "In a Country Garden"; Jimmy Savo's inimitable pantomime; and the loose-boned gospel songs and spirituals of the Golden Gate Quartet. In effect, three concerts, or recitals, were offered every night, and each was different. Between the shows, which lasted about an hour, one ate and danced—not to an intermission trio but to Wilson's great band. Both clubs were congenial, clean, and pressureless. One could sit at the bar, nursing a single beer, for an entire evening. And parents actually *sent* their children to them unchaperoned for such state occasions as birthday parties and graduation parties. The food was important. It was fancier at the Uptown, partly owing to the fact that this club brought in a different sort of trade and partly owing to Josephson's mysterious belief that "people at Downtown just didn't pay much attention to eating, because they were in a basement." (Vide Max Gordon.) There was no cover charge in either club, and the minimum—a dollar or two—included food and/or drink. At the Uptown, the table d'hote dinner ranged from two dollars and a quarter (creamed chicken) to four seventy-five (prime sirloin steak). The service made both eighteen-year-olds and seventy-year-olds comfortable. "Many of the people who came to my clubs were like Eleanor Roosevelt," Josephson has said. "She had never been in a night club in her life, and she never went to another one."

I had heard nothing of Josephson for years, and when it was announced, not long ago, that the equally elusive pianist Mary Lou Williams would be playing at a place in the Village called the Cookery and that it was owned by Josephson, I went down one afternoon to visit him. The Cookery, on the northeast corner of Eighth Street and University Place, is a spic-and-span restaurant furnished with plain, wood-topped tables and an omelette bar and decorated with Refregier hangings and murals. The prices are reasonable, and both cheeseburgers and steak all' pizzaiola are on the menu. Josephson was sitting at a table with his wife. She is intense, wiry, and fast-moving; Josephson is easy-going. He wears glasses, his cheeks are pink, his hair is white, and he looks like the late Ed Wynn. He speaks softly and quickly, laughs a lot, and is an effortless monologist. And he doesn't look a day over fifty.

Mrs. Josephson departed soon after I sat down, and Josephson began to talk. "I couldn't have been more bored with this business when I met my present wife, Gloria, thirteen years ago," he said. "This Cookery has been here seventeen years, and I've had three others uptown that were either unprofitable or were in buildings that were torn down. I live in the apartment house upstairs—right over the candy store, you could say, like the immigrants who roomed in the back of their shops and turned down the heat under their soup when the little bell out front rang and they had to go see who was in the store. Gloria's a Brooklyn girl and a lawyer. She would come here for dinner, but we never went out. Then one evening I was at the cashier's desk by the window and I saw her going by with her briefcase. I ran out and asked her to have a drink at the steak place across the street. We had a drink at the bar and we had dinner, and I asked her to marry me. We went out every night for three weeks, and two weeks later we were married. I'd been single nine years, and this time marriage took. Right away we gave a series of Friday-night parties for thirty or forty in our flat upstairs, and Gloria cooked the dinners. They had hot and cold first courses, hot and cold entrées, and each meal was different. I'd married a great cook! She began giving my chef recipes on her way to work, and if they were successful they were added to the menu. Then our two boys, Edward and Louis, who I consider my greatest achievements, came along, and eventually I suggested that she learn the practical end of the business. I'm twenty-one years older than Gloria, and what would happen if I went? Managers rarely work out, and selling a business like this isn't easy. She thought that was sensible, and she's never practiced law since."

The restaurant was a third full, and most of the patrons were single women, or children refuelling on their way home from school. The atmosphere—calm, dignified, efficient—was familiar, and suddenly I recognized it. Both Café Societys had the same cool, even when they were jammed and jumping.

Josephson called a waitress and ordered two Cokes. "I can't get over having Mary Lou Williams working for me again," he said. "She was at the Downtown for five years, and although she was never an overpowering attraction, she had a devoted coterie. Her coming back happened in the damnedest way. A young Jesuit named Peter O'Brien called me and said he had spent a lot of time recently with Mary Lou Williams, and could he come and see me? He did—in fact, he came several times—but he never mentioned just what he had on his mind. I found him a charming man, and if I were an important Catholic layman I'd tell the Pope to keep an eye on him. Then O'Brien appeared with Mary. I hadn't seen her for twenty years. From time to time she had called me, generally about someone she knew who was in trouble, but never about herself. Well, out it came: 'If I could only work for you again, Barney'—in that funny, chuckling way she has—'the happiest days of my life were at the Downtown.' She wasn't interested in cash, she said. She just wanted to work, and—well—she'd been getting seventeen hundred plus a week when she finally left me. I thought about it and looked into it and found I didn't need a cabaret license as long as there were no more than three instruments, all stringed. She brought along a bassist, Michael Fleming, and they opened soon after. I can't get over watching my old Cookery patrons watching her, and I can't get over how many of my Café Society customers have come in.

"The way I first got into the night-club business was far stranger. My parents came over from Latvia in 1900, and I was born two years later in Trenton. There were already two girls and three boys. My father was a cobbler and my mother a seamstress. When I was eight or nine months old my father stepped on a rusty nail and gangrene set in, and it was fatal. My mother was left with six children and no money. She went to work for a ladies' tailor, and an Irish lady who had twelve or thirteen children of her own took care of me during the day. My oldest brother, David, worked in a shoe store, and my oldest sister in a sweatshop, making ladies' silk bathrobes. We lived in an apartment so small one of my sisters slept in a closet. But my mother was a very frugal woman, and in time she had enough money to buy a house. It had four floors and cost a thousand dollars. It even had a bathroom, and the bathroom had a copper tub that David painted white every spring. When I got out of high school, David, who now had his own shoe business, told me that since we already had two brothers who were lawyers and I didn't look like medical material, I had better go into the shoe business with him. He had a keen sense of style. If he picked out a hundred pairs of shoes, they were *all* good. But he always overbought. He showed a profit—but in inventory, not cash. So along came the Depression, and there we were, with all those Whitehouse & Hardy shoes and seventy-five thousand dollars in accounts receivable. We went broke. My brother eventually started up again, but I didn't want any more of being an owner, so by the mid-thirties I was clerking in a shoe store in Atlantic City. I made forty dollars a month, lived in a four-dollar room, and ate my meals across the street in Bayliss's drugstore. But all this time I had the notion of starting a night club in the back of my head.

"When I worked for my brother, I used to go to the Marbridge Building on Herald Square, where all the shoe manufacturers showed their wares. I was an out-of-town buyer, so I was taken out to night clubs. I liked what I saw, at least from a business point of view. A café restaurant has no inventory. The food turns over every day and the liquor once a week. And it's a cash business, or it was before credit cards and charge accounts. I had been to Europe in the early thirties and had visited the political cabarets, where there was very pointed satire. And I'd seen Gypsy Rose Lee doing a political strip tease at fund-raising affairs in New York for the Lincoln Brigade. I conceived the idea of presenting some sort of satire and alternating it with jazz music. But there was an even more important reason why I wanted to start a club. My fondness for jazz often took me to places like the Cotton Club in Harlem to hear Ethel Waters or Duke Ellington. Well, the Negro patrons were seated at the back in a segregated section— in a *Harlem* night club! And I'd been to the Kit-Kat Club in the East Fifties, which had all-black entertainment, plus black help, and yet not a Negro was admitted to the place. Until junior high I had gone to school with nothing but other Jews and the Irish. The first day I walked into class I saw a black boy sitting at a desk. The desk you picked became your desk for the year. Nobody had taken a desk near him, so I did, and we became great friends. And later I argued in a debate against military training in schools. I lost the debate, but afterward eight or ten boys got me in a corner and beat me up for what I'd said. So all those things were in my background, and New York in the mid-thirties echoed my feelings. It was the time of the labor organizers and the Ladies Garment Workers' show called 'Pins and Needles' and the W.P.A. Art Movement and 'The Cradle Will Rock.' I wanted a club where blacks and whites worked together behind the footlights and sat together out front. There wasn't, so far as I knew, a place like it in New York or in the country."

Two skinny, shy, dark-haired boys who turned out to be Josephson's tumbled in the restaurant door and stopped at the table. They said they had taken the subway all the way from school on the upper West Side and hadn't got lost once. Josephson laughed. "Go and eat. Go and eat," he said. "Your mother's in the back.

"I made my decision early in 1938. I quit my job in Atlantic City and, with just seven dollars and sixty cents to my name, borrowed six thousand dollars from two friends in Trenton. I had found a shuttered-up basement in Sheridan Square. The liquor license was twelve hundred, the cabaret license a hundred and fifty, and the rent two hundred, and out the money began to go. And there was the decorating. I didn't want mirrors and draperies and velours. I wanted art. Sam Shaw, a painter and photographer, brought some of his W.P.A. Art friends in to do some murals—Adolf Dehn, William Gropper, Sam Berman, Gregor Duncan, and Abe Birnbaum. I paid them two hundred dollars each and gave them due bills of a like amount for food and liquor. Some of those due bills went on for years, too. I didn't tell them what to paint, only· that the place would be called, in a tongue-in-cheek way, Café Society. Clare Boothe Luce had suggested it, through some mutual friends, and it fitted into my satirical scheme. A couple of girls on *Vogue* who had given me all sorts of ideas suggested we have a doorman but that he be dressed in a raggedy coat and white gloves with the fingertips out. They also suggested we find an Elsa Maxwell type who'd ride a scooter up and down the aisles. We did have the doorman for six or eight months, but we never found the right Elsa Maxwell. But the greatest help to me was John Hammond. He built my first band around the trumpet player Frankie Newton, and he brought in Albert Ammons and Meade Lux Lewis, the boogie-woogie pianists. And three weeks later he told me I had to have still another boogie-woogie pianist, Pete Johnson, but that Johnson only came with Joe Turner, the blues shouter. Jack Gilford was my first comedian. He'd been a stooge for Milton Berle at vaudeville houses like the Palace, where he was planted in the audience to shout insults at Berle onstage. John brought in the Golden Gate Quartet soon after, and they made the blood rush up my arms, which brought the goose pimples out when they sang—and here I was a disbeliever—'As they were driving the nails in His feet/ You could hear the hammer ringing in Jerusalem's streets.' We opened on December 18, 1938. Village people came, and so did uptown types and the college kids. On Friday nights the place looked like Princeton, Yale, and Harvard rolled into one. It was a grand success, but I was losing money. I simply didn't know enough about this sort of merchandising. By the end of the first year I was twenty-eight thousand dollars in the hole. It became a holding operation, paying out two hundred here and three hundred there to my creditors. I began to think that I had opened the club in the wrong part of town, that I should move uptown. I found a place on Fifty-eighth Street which had changed hands a lot and been burned out by some mugs trying to collect fire insurance. My press agent, Ivan Black, sent out a release saying that Café Society was so successful I was opening an uptown branch. Actually, I planned to dump the original club, but when people heard about the uptown club the crowd doubled downtown and I suddenly began making money. Café Society Uptown opened on October 8, 1940. A waiter I had stopped by to see me the other day, and he'd come across the menu for that night. It offered shrimps and oysters and clams, celery and olives, a couple of soups, a two-inch prime filet mignon with mushrooms, two vegetables, a choice of potatoes, and dessert. The price on the card was a dollar fifty! Uptown had cost me almost thirty thousand dollars to put in shape, all of it borrowed, but it started making money immediately, and by the end of that year I had paid off every cent."

The lights in the Cookery dimmed for the start of the dinner hour. Several groups of people came in, and Josephson excused himself to seat them. A headwaiter carried a huge poinsettia from the back of the restaurant and put it on one end of the omelette bar. Next to the bar was a brand-new grand piano. Josephson finished seating a family of five, then sat down. "That plant adds a little festivity to where Mary sits. She didn't want a Steinway, she wanted a Baldwin. I'm renting it, and if I decide to buy it the rent money goes toward the purchase." Josephson laughed. "I've got some accountant, and she's having fits over all this. 'You bring this piano player in here and it's doing nothing but costing money,' she says to me. 'Thirty dollars for that plant and nineteen dollars for the piano tuner each time he comes, and now he's coming *twice* a week. Next thing, you'll be out of business, with all your music.'

"I moved the Downtown show to the Uptown when it opened, and brought new people in Downtown. Mary took Hazel Scott's place, and Ida Cox came in for Billie Holiday. Teddy Wilson went Uptown and Eddie Heywood came in Downtown. In time I had a steady floating company of musicians and comedians and dancers and singers that moved back and forth between the clubs and that worked on a nearly permanent basis. It was a new concept in night clubs, and it gave the performers a sense of security most of them had never had before. It also gave them time to try out new routines and ideas. Hazel Scott was with me for seven years and the boogie-woogie boys, as we called them, for over four. Billie and Lena Horne stayed a year, and so did Jack Gilford. Jimmy Savo, who hadn't worked for ten years, stayed for three. People like Suzy Reed and Josh White were in and out for years, and so was Mildred Bailey. I don't know how I had this in me, but I learned how to shape talent, how to bring a performer's best out. I even costumed them, and I'd find myself in Bergdorf's with some cute new little singer and saying to one of those gray-haired salesladies, 'I'd like this young lady gowned.' Lena Horne was one of my first projects. She had worked in the line at the Cotton Club, and I first heard her, at John Hammond's suggestion, when she was singing with Charlie Barnet's band at the Paramount. She was beautiful, stunning, but it was hard to tell whether she could really sing or not. But I hired her, and at her first rehearsal I noticed that all her movements and routines were done in Latin rhythms, which were very big then. It didn't look right. I asked her if she was a Negro, and she bristled and said yes. I told her she could pass for anything, and she blew up. 'I don't dig you,' she said, and I said, 'Lena, there are dozens of nice Jewish girls from Brooklyn doing the Latin routines. Let me present you as a Negro talent. There won't be another like you for ten or fifteen years.' I got her singing blues and things like 'Summertime,' but she didn't have any contact with the audience because she wasn't putting feeling and meaning into what she sang. She would close her eyes when she sang or look at the ceiling. So I said to her, 'I know about white people and the Negroes and that most Negroes cannot look white people in the eye. Is that why you never look at your audience? Don't be afraid of them.' I sat at a ringside table, and when she looked at the ceiling I'd make signals. And I went over the lyrics of her songs, pointing out their meanings. Finally, she got to the point when she sang a blues of making people stand up and shout.

"Suzy Reed was the first Joan Baez—a beautiful girl with long reddish hair and a simple, direct manner. I made her keep her hair straight, told her not to wear makeup, and dressed her in little-girl frocks. At her first rehearsal she came out with a hop, skip, and jump and said, 'This is a zither.' I shouted, 'That's it, that's it! Don't ever change a thing!' And when she skipped out there in front of the audience and said, 'This is a zither,' she had them. I don't know whether it was because nobody had ever seen a zither before or whether it was the peaches-and-cream way she said it. I got Josh White to sit on a high stool when he sang, and I dressed him in open-necked shirts. He was a terror with the girls, and when they saw that neck—all muscles and tendons—they wanted to bite it. Of course, there were people I missed and people I nearly missed. I missed out on Pearl Bailey altogether. She struck me as a bit of a Tom, and I never hired her, but I know now I was being over-sensitive. And I almost didn't get Pearl Primus, a great dancer. She brought some records to her audition, but she looked so awful I made an excuse about the phonograph being broken and asked her to come back another time. She started to cry. I excused myself and pretended to fuss over the phonograph. She put on a record, took one fantastic leap, and that was it. John Martin of the *Times* ranked her with Ted Shawn and Martha Graham. I had my share of busts, generally with singers who, though I'd give them months of vocal lessons, just couldn't sing. Sarah Vaughan didn't work out, but for different reasons. I kept her six months, but people couldn't understand her singing—all the strange twists and turns she did with her voice—and she still didn't know how to get herself up right. Carol Channing was a bust, too. She sang and did impersonations of society dowagers and her special number was supposed to be a take-off of Ethel Waters in 'Cabin in the Sky.' It struck me the wrong way, and I asked her not to use it. She felt I'd cut the heart out of her act, and she went ahead and did it anyway, so I fired her. Jim Backus flopped. He had another man with him, and I think they had a radio show, but nobody listened to them at the club. But I was beginning to learn that although performers fail at one thing it doesn't mean they aren't good at something else. So I was always very careful not to hurt people at my auditions, especially because I never forgot a story Bernie Bernard told me. He was a Hollywood agent who had booked vaudeville talent in the Midwest. Two men auditioned for him, and he told them their act wouldn't go. He looked at one of them and said, '*You* have some possibilities, but your partner is impossible.' The next day the one he had spoken to came back, very upset, and it turned out his partner had just hung himself. When I was convinced a performer had gifts, despite negative audience reactions, I stayed with him. Jack Gilford started slowly and he used to beg me to let him go, but I refused, and one night his time came. It was at the two-o'clock show. Ammons and Johnson and Lewis and Billie Holiday were doing a benefit somewhere, and Joe Turner hadn't showed up, so all we had were the band and Gilford. He asked me what in God's name he was supposed to do. I told him he had to go on. The place was only half full, but a table of six or eight people had just come in. I'd been in enough places where the last show would be cancelled under such circumstances, but anyway Gilford, who was also the master of ceremonies, introduced the band, and they did their production numbers. Then he said, 'I would now like to introduce Albert Ammons, but Albert Ammons isn't here.' He got a laugh. Then he sat down at the piano and went into this beautiful pantomime with his great rubber face and made you *believe* he was Albert Ammons, by his motions and by scrunching up the back of his neck so that it looked like Ammons' rolls of fat. Then he did Meade Lux Lewis. Sometimes Lewis would start to fall asleep when he was playing, and I'd have to get someone to poke him, so Jack sat there nodding and swaying, and it was perfect. He did Billie and Johnson and Joe Turner and his own act, and the next day I had a call from one of the latecomers. It was Jed Harris, the David Merrick of the time, and he wanted Gilford for a revue called 'Meet the People' that he was bringing to New York from California. Gilford joined it, and it was a great success. His Broadway career had begun. And do you know what he does every year on December eighteenth, the anniversary of Downtown's opening? He sends me a telegram, wishing me well, and it doesn't matter where in the world he is.

"I also had a hand, in a roundabout way, in getting a girl named Betty Perske started. She was tall and thin and had a deep voice, and she used to hang around Downtown all the time by herself. I didn't care for single girls in the club, but I found out that she lived over on Barrow Street with her aunt, and I told my headwaiter to keep an eye on her. There was something special about her, and one night she told me she wanted to act. I said I'd arrange a meeting for her with Jack Shalitt, a talent scout for Howard Hughes. That was the last I saw of her. Time passed, and one evening Shalitt came in with a long face and asked me if I'd seen *Life* magazine that week. I had and I was delighted. There was a nine-page spread on Zero Mostel. I had hired Zero in the early days at the Downtown, when none of the uptown operators would touch him. Shalitt said, 'No, no, I don't mean that. I mean the girl on the cover. We didn't get her, we missed her.' I didn't recognize the girl or her name. Shalitt said she was Betty Perske. She *had* gone to Shalitt, and he'd sent pictures of her to Hughes. He wasn't impressed, and when Mrs. Howard Hawks saw them on his desk one evening at a dinner party and asked if she could show them to *her* Howard, Hughes said fine, and Hawks signed her and changed her name to Lauren Bacall."

Now the Cookery was full, and Josephson asked me if I'd like some dinner. I ordered a petit pissaladière and the steak all' pizzaiola and a demi-carafe of red wine. It was eight o'clock, and Mary Lou Williams sat down at the piano. She was in a dark blue gown and her hair was parted on one side, débutante fashion. She looked around in a bemused way, rubbed her hands together, said something to her bassist, and started "My Blue Heaven." Her playing was sure and inventive and utterly relaxed. There was no microphone, but her long, graceful melodic lines moved easily through the room. She sounded, in fact, as if she were playing for friends in her living room. "Yesterdays" went by, and it was followed by a rocking boogie-woogie number and a fast "Blue Skies." Josephson was smiling and his cheeks were flushed. "She's playing better now than she was thirty years ago," he said. The set ended; Miss Williams greeted Josephson and sat down with Peter O'Brien.

"I got along very well with my performers, and they with me," Josephson said. "I always paid people at scale or better, and the highest salary I paid was thirty-five hundred a week. I also managed a lot of my performers for free when they went out to Hollywood and such. But no matter how well we got on, surprising things happened. I had an iron law at both clubs that there was to be no marijuana. When Billie Holiday was with me she'd get in a cab between shows and drive through Central Park, smoking. One night she came back and I could tell by her eyes that she was really high. She finished her first number and I guess she didn't like the way the audience reacted. Performers often wear just gowns and slippers, no underwear, and at the end of the song Billie turned her back to the audience, bent over, flipped up her gown, and walked off the floor." Josephson laughed. "I asked her backstage what in heaven's name she thought she was doing, and she just mumbled and slammed the dressing-room door.

"It had become the custom by the time Eddie Heywood came into the Downtown for the bandleader to double as m.c. Heywood stammered. He told me he was afraid people would laugh at him, and I told him not to worry. The first night was pretty bad, the next night better, and in a week there was only a trace. It must have had something to do with the intimacy of a microphone, and possibly also my confidence in him. Anyway, a couple of weeks later he explained that he was classified 4-F because of his stammering and that he was due for a medical review and could he quit emceeing for a few days until his stammer returned? He did, his 4-F status was renewed, and that night he announced shows again. One of the most surprising things also happened during the war, but it was at the Uptown. Jimmy Savo had a marvellous silent act in which he'd stop at a ringside table and pick up a customer's pack of cigarettes—this when cigarettes were so scarce. He'd take out a cigarette and, breaking it in two, light one half and put the other half in his pocket—all the while bowing and smiling to the owner of the cigarettes. Then he'd move to another table, still carrying the pack, and offer each of the people a cigarette, and keep this up until the cigarettes were gone. He'd return the empty pack to its owner, again bowing and scraping. He was in the middle of his act when a British sailor jumped up and grabbed a microphone and announced in a Cockney accent that he was going to sing a famous British Navy song about the time a British sailor floored 'that black nigger Jack Johnson.' Big Sid Catlett was sitting up there on the bandstand with his arms folded, and suddenly he picked up his drumsticks and began this tremendous thundering. The rest of the band joined in and the sailor was drowned out. The place was packed with servicemen, and they were outraged that one of them had been insulted, and there was nearly a riot. Afterward, I told the sailor that the word 'nigger' was not appreciated at Café Society Uptown, and he said he never knew there was anything insulting about the word and that he had black friends all over the world. It's a wonder more things didn't happen in those days. Like the time John Hammond and his wife came for dinner at the Uptown with Paul Robeson. Robeson and Mrs. Hammond danced. The headwaiter told me that the people at table forty-one would like to see me. There were two couples at the table, and one of the men said, 'Do you allow niggers to dance with white women in this place?' 'Sir,' I replied, 'we do not use that word in here. Furthermore, there is a law in this state against discrimination, and we abide by it. But it's still a democracy and you have a right not to like what you see.' 'Well, we don't like it at all,' he said. They walked out, but I made sure they paid their bill in full, even though they had just begun their shrimp cocktails."

Mary Lou Williams was playing again, and Josephson turned to watch her. Five minutes went by, and he turned back to me. "In the late forties, with both clubs going full steam, my life turned inside out. My brother Leon, who was working for me, was subpoenaed by the Un-American Activities Committee, which was headed by J. Parnell Thomas, the gent who later served time for misusing government funds. Leon was an avowed Communist and he refused to answer any questions, on the ground that the Committee was an illegal tribunal. He was cited for contempt, tried, and found guilty. His case was appealed to the Supreme Court, which refused to hear it, and he served ten months in prison. I think he may have been the first person to go to jail for contempt of the Committee. It was front-page stuff, and since no one knew who Leon Josephson was, he was always mentioned in the papers as the brother of Barney Josephson, the owner of Café Society Uptown and Café Society Downtown. The Hearst press—Pegler and Kilgallen and Lee Mortimer and Winchell—took off, and the innuendo, the guilt-by-association, began. Pegler devoted a column to Leon implying that he was a drug addict, and the last line was 'And there is much to be said about his brother Barney.' Just that, no more. So I was the brother of a Communist drug addict, I allowed Negroes in my clubs, I had introduced inflammatory songs like 'Strange Fruit' and 'The House I Live In,' and on and on. It ruined my clubs. Three weeks after the first uproar, business at the Uptown dropped forty-five per cent. I was determined not to give in to such viciousness, and I kept going for almost a year. But I had already lost ninety thousand dollars, so I sold both clubs, and by 1950 I was out of the night-club business and flat broke. I've only been into the Uptown once since it's become the Fine Arts Theatre, and that was to see 'Riffifi.' But all I could see were Teddy Wilson and Jimmy Savo.

"Part of the reason I started a place like the Cookery was that I could be unknown, anonymous, and that's the way it's been. But this morning I ran into one of my old neighborhood customers, a lovely lady who has been eating here since we opened. She stopped me outside the supermarket and said, 'Mr. Josephson, you have made our world, our city a little bigger and a little better by bringing Mary Lou Williams into the Cookery, and I thank you.' That made me feel marvellous."

1971

Mingus at Peace

Charles Mingus, the incomparable forty-nine-year-old bassist, composer, bandleader, autobiographer, and iconoclast, has spent much of his life attempting to rearrange the world according to an almost Johnsonian set of principles that abhor, among other things, cant, racism, inhibition, managerial greed, sloppy music, Uncle Tomism, and conformity. His ingenious methods have ranged from penny-dreadful broadsides to matter-of-fact punches on the nose. The results have been mixed. They have also been costly, and have landed Mingus on the psychiatric couch and in Bellevue (self-committed), lost him jobs, and made him periodically fat. ("I eat out of nerves.") At the same time, Mingus' experiences have been steadily distilled into a body of compositions that for sheer melodic and rhythmic and structural originality may equal anything written in Western music in the past twenty years. (Their content has been equally fresh, for they have included, in the Ellington manner, everything from love songs to social satire.) These experiences have, as well, been reflected in his playing, which long ago elevated him to the virtuosic ranks of Picasso and Buddy Rich and Nabokov. But now Mingus has taken another step. He has written a book about himself—"Beneath the Underdog: His World as Composed by Mingus" (Knopf).

The book, which was edited by Nel King, is impressionistic and disembodied (it has almost no dates), and has at least a taste of all the Minguses. It is brutal and dirty and bitter. It is sentimental and self-pitying. It is rude and, in places, unfair (the curt handling of the great Red Norvo). It is facetious and funny. It is awkward and unerringly right, and it is the latter when Mingus' fine ear is receiving full tilt. Duke Ellington's verbal arabesques have never been captured better:

[Juan] Tizol [an Ellington trombonist] wants you to play a solo he's written where bowing is required. You raise the solo an octave, where the bass isn't too muddy. He doesn't like that and he comes to the room under the stage where you're practicing at intermission and comments that you're like the rest of the niggers in the band, you can't read. You ask Juan how he's different from the other niggers and he states that one of the ways he's different is that HE IS WHITE. So you run his ass upstairs. You leave the rehearsal room, proceed toward the stage with your bass and take your place and at the moment Duke brings down the baton for "A-Train" and the curtain of the Apollo Theatre goes up, a yelling, whooping Tizol rushes out and lunges at you with a bolo knife. The rest you remember mostly from Duke's own words in his dressing room as he changes after the show.

"Now, Charles," he says, looking amused, putting Cartier links into the cuffs of his beautiful handmade shirt, "you could have forewarned me—you left me out of the act entirely! At least you could have let me cue in a few chords as you ran through that Nijinsky routine. I congratulate you on your performance, but why didn't you and Juan inform me about the adagio you planned so that we could score it? I must say I never saw a large man so agile—I never saw *anybody* make such tremendous leaps! The gambado over the piano carrying your bass was colossal. When you exited after that I thought, 'That man's really afraid of Juan's knife and at the speed he's going he's probably home in bed by now.' But no, back you came through the same door with your bass still intact. For a moment I was hopeful you'd decided to sit down and play but instead you slashed Juan's chair in two with a fire axe! Really, Charles, that's destructive. Everybody knows Juan has a knife but nobody ever took it seriously—he likes to pull it out and show it to people, you understand. So I'm afraid, Charles—I've never fired anybody—you'll have to quit my band. I don't need any new problems. Juan's an old problem, I can cope with that, but you seem to have a whole bag of new tricks. I must ask you to be kind enough to give me your notice, Charles."

The charming way he says it, it's like he's paying you a compliment. Feeling honored, you shake hands and resign.

Mingus' relationship with jazz critics has been surprisingly amiable, and the lumps landed on them in the book are pretty funny. A party is given for Mingus when he first arrives in New York from the West Coast around 1950. No matter that the critics named were never in the same room at the same time in their lives, or that at least two of them were still in college and unpublished. Mingus is talking to Dizzy Gillespie:

> "Man, that's a lot of talent, don't you dig it? I see Leonard Feather, he's a piano player. There's Bill Coss and Gene Lees— they sing, I heard. Barry Ulanov must play drums or something, dig, with that *Metronome* beat. Martin Williams can play everything. I can tell by the way he writes. Put Marshall Stearns on bass and let Whitney Balliett score and John Wilson conduct. Let all them other young up-and-coming critics dance. How would you like to review that schitt for the *Amsterdam News?*"

(There are, for the record, other Mingus liberties in this passage. Feather does play piano, and Lees, and perhaps Coss, sing, but so do Williams and the unmentioned Wen Shih. The late Marshall Stearns played C-melody saxophone, and this writer plays drums. And Nat Hentoff, who is mentioned elsewhere in the book, once studied classical clarinet. To my knowledge, Wilson and Ulanov are non-performers. Finally, jazz critics, wallflowers all, rarely dance.) But the best parts of the book deal with Fats Navarro, a brilliant, concise trumpeter who died at the age of twenty-six in 1950. He tells a young and ingenuous Mingus what it is really like to be a jazz musician:

> "Mingus, you a nice guy from California, I don't want to disillusion you. But I been through all that schitt and I had to learn to do some other things to get along. I learned better than to try to make it just with my music out on these dirty gang-mob streets 'cause I still love playing better than money. Jazz ain't supposed to make nobody no millions but that's where it's at. Them that shouldn't is raking it in but the purest are out in the street with me and Bird and it rains all over us, man. I was better off when nobody knew my name except musicians. You can bet it ain't jazz no more when the underworld moves in and runs it strictly for geetz and even close out the colored agents. They shut you up and cheat you on the count of your record sales and if you go along they tell the world you a real genius. But if you don't play they put out the word you're a troublemaker, like they did me. Then if some honest club owner tries to get hold of you to book you, they tell him you're not available or you don't draw or you'll tear up the joint like you was a gorilla. And you won't hear nothin' about it except by accident. But if you behave, boy,

you'll get booked—except for less than the white cats that copy your playing and likely either the agent or owner'll pocket the difference."

That's worthy of Mayhew's annals of the London poor.

After I read the book, I looked Mingus up to see how he was handling his new career. We met late on a Sunday night in a restaurant on West Tenth Street a week or so before his book was published. Mingus was dressed in an unusually conservative dark suit and tie, and he was in his middle state. That is, he was neither thin nor huge; he was, as they used to say in the two-pants-suit days, portly. A Charlie Chan beard was arranged carefully around his mouth, and he looked wonderful. The last time I had seen him, a year before, his face had been gray and puffy; he had not played a note for two years, and he was very fat and had a listless, buried air. Now he was sitting at the bar sampling a tall white drink. "Ramos gin fizz," he blurted out. "Milk or cream, white of an egg, orange flower water, lemon juice, gin, and soda water. I used to drink ten at a sitting in San Francisco." Mingus talks in leaping slurs. The words come out crouched and running, and sometimes they move so fast whole sentences are unintelligible. It is an obstacle he is well aware of, for later in the evening he delivered a lightning two-or-three-sentence volley and said, "Did you understand what I just said?" I admitted that I had got about sixty per cent of it. Slowing to a canter, he repeated himself and I got almost a hundred per cent. Mingus finished his Ramos fizz and ordered a half bottle of Pouilly-Fuisse and some cheese. He pronounced the name of the wine at a dead run, and it came out "Poolly-Foos." "We went down to the peace demonstration in Washington this weekend to play, and it was a drag," he said. "They've never had any jazz at these things, and it seemed like a good idea, but we never did play. My piano player didn't show, and my alto sax couldn't make it, so we only had four pieces, and it wouldn't have made any sense going on like that. I went to bed right after I got back this morning. I hadn't been to bed in two nights. I can't sleep at night anyway, but I do all right with a sleeping pill in the day. I even had a wonderful dream just before I got up to meet you. I had everything under control. I was on a diet and losing weight all over the place, and I felt *so* good. But a dream like that is worse than a nightmare. You wake up and the real nightmare starts."

Mingus asked the bartender if he could get some lobster and was told that the kitchen had closed. "Maybe they got some across the street in that steak house," Mingus said. He told the bartender to keep the rest of the wine—that he'd be back right after he'd eaten. We crossed the street and went down some steps into a dark, low, empty room. Mingus moved lightly but gingerly and, squeezing himself into a booth, ordered lobster tails, hearts of lettuce, and another half bottle of Poolly-Foos.

"My book was written for black people to tell them how to get through life," he said. "I was trying to upset the white man in it—the right kind or the wrong kind, depending on what color and persuasion you are. I started it twenty-five years ago, and at first I was doing it for myself, to help understand certain situations. I talked some of it into tape recorders, and that girl in the white Cadillac in the book, she helped me type it up. But I wrote most of it in longhand in the dark backstage or on buses on huge sheets of score paper. The original manuscript was between eight hundred and a thousand pages. It went up and down, what with parts of it getting lost. I started looking for a publisher more than ten years ago. Things hadn't loosened up yet, and a lot of them looked at it and it scared them. It was too dirty, it was too hard on whitey, they said. McGraw-Hill finally bought it, but they put it on the shelf for a long time. Then Knopf got interested and bought it from McGraw-Hill."

Mingus asked the waitress for a glass of water. She was young and blond. "Say, you my same waitress? It's so dark in here you look like you keep changing." Mingus leaned back and smiled his beautiful smile.

"I'm your waitress," she said, putting a hand lightly on his left arm. "Are you Jaki Byard?"

"Jaki Byard? Jaki Byard? He's my piano player. He's a super-star now. I'm glad you my same waitress. Now, bring me that glass of water, please. Then I got hold of Nel King, who wrote a movie I was in, and she put the book in shape. It took her a year and a half. A whole lot of stuff has been left out—stuff about blacks wearing Afros because they're afraid not to, and skin-lighteners, and my wife, Celia. There was a lot about her in there, but she didn't want to be in the book, so I left her out. I wrote it a b c d e f g h at first, but then I mixed up the chronology and some of the locations. Like that party when I first came to New York in the late forties. It didn't take place at any apartment in the East Seventies but over at the old Bandbox, next to Birdland. The critics were there, and they didn't stop talking once. They kept right on even when Art Tatum and Charlie Parker sat in together for maybe the only time in their lives. It was the most fantastic music I ever heard. Tatum didn't let up in either hand for a second—*whoosh-hum, whoosh-hum* in the left, and *aaaaaaaaaarrrrrrrrr-hhhhhhhheeeeee* in the right—and neither did Parker, and to this day I don't know what they were doing."

I said I had particularly liked the passages in the book dealing with Fats Navarro.

"Yes. Those are the best part of the book. I loved Fats and I could hear his voice in my head the whole time I was writing him down. But that's just my first book. It's not an autobiography. It's just me, Mingus. My next book will be my life in music."

Mingus finished his lobster tails and wine and we went back across the street. He telephoned his manager, Sue Ungaro, and arranged to meet her in ten minutes at a Japanese restaurant at Twelfth Street and Second Avenue. It was almost one o'clock. Mingus emptied his bottle of wine and we took a cab across town. The restaurant was shut, and Mrs. Ungaro was nowhere in sight.

"We better walk over to her place, maybe meet her on the way," Mingus said. The street was deserted, but he reached into a coat pocket and took out a big East Indian knife and, removing its scabbard, held it at the ready in his left hand. "This is the way I walk the streets at night around here. I live down on Fifth Street, and we got so much crime I'm scared to be out at night." We passed St. Mark's in the Bowerie and headed west. I mentioned that Peter Stuyvesant was buried beneath the church.

"Yeh? That the Stuyvesant of Stuyvesant Casino?"

Mrs. Ungaro was putting some trash in a garbage can in front of her building. She is a pretty, slender strawberry blonde, and she was wearing bluejeans, clogs, and a short, beat-up raccoon coat.

"They closed," Mingus said, pocketing his knife. Mrs. Ungaro said she'd still like something to eat. We took a cab to the Blue Sea on Third Avenue and Twenty-fourth Street. It was closed. Mingus told the driver to make a U-turn, and we went down to a small bar-and-grill on Tenth and Third. We sat in a semicircular booth under a jukebox loudspeaker. Mrs. Ungaro ordered a hamburger and salad and Mingus asked the waitress, who was wearing enormous false eyelashes and a black knitted see-through pants suit, for a dish of black olives and some Poolly-Foos.

"Poolly what?" she said, moving her lashes up and down like a semaphore. "I don't know. I'm just helping out tonight, because I've known these people a long time."

The manager, a short man in shirtsleeves with gleaming glasses and a big paunch, said they had Soave Bolla. A half bottle in a straw basket was put in an ice bucket on the table. Mingus scrunched it down in the bucket and piled ice cubes carefully around its neck.

He looked at Mrs. Ungaro and smiled. "It's been five years, baby. You know that?" She nodded and took a bite of hamburger. "Sue wrote in for the Guggenheim I just got. I want to write a ballet with the money—an operatic ballet. I've had it in my head for years, like I had the book in my head. It'll have to do with Watts, where I was born and raised, and I want Katherine Dunham to choreograph it. I know her very well, and we've talked about it a long time. But getting the Guggenheim wasn't as easy as filling out forms. I had to carry about fifty pounds of music over for them to see. If I don't finish the ballet this year, I'll apply again."

"Charles wants to put together a seventeen-piece band," Mrs. Ungaro said. "And he wants to use some of the Guggenheim money, but they won't allow it. It's only for composition."

"If I do finish the ballet, I'll apply anyway so that I can write some chamber music. That's what I started out doing years and years ago, and I want to go back to it. I've been teaching all winter, one day a week, at the state university at Buffalo. The Slee Chair of Music. They invited me, and I've been teaching composition to about ten kids. They're bright, and they get their work done on time. I used some of my own pieces, showing them how to work with a melody and no chords or sets of chords, and no melody or just a pedal point, to give them a sense of freedom. But I feel sorry about jazz. The truth has been lost in the music. All the different styles and factions went to war with each other, and it hasn't done any good. Take Ornette Coleman." Mingus sang half a chorus of "Body and Soul" in a loud, off-key voice, drowning out the jukebox. It was an uncanny imitation. "That's all he does. Just pushing the melody out of line here and there. Trouble is, he can't play it straight. At that little festival Max Roach and I gave in Newport in 1960, Kenny Dorham and I tried to get Ornette to play 'All the Things You Are' straight, and he couldn't do it."

Mingus took a sip of wine and made a face. "I don't know, this doesn't taste right."

"Maybe it isn't cold enough," Mrs. Ungaro said.

Mingus fished out his knife, deftly cut the straw basket off the bottle, and put the bottle back in the ice. The waitress appeared and said: "Everything fine, honey?"

"The wine doesn't taste right. It's not cold enough."

The waitress took three ice cubes out of the bucket and plopped them in our glasses and splashed some wine over them.

"Hey, that'll make it all water," Mingus said, seizing the bottle and jamming it back in the bucket.

"I'm just helping out, sir, like I said."

"She'll make the reputation of this place," Mingus mumbled.

I asked Mingus what he thought about the black militants, reminding him of the electric evening at the Village Vanguard when he had not only tongue-lashed the predominantly white audience for twenty minutes but had publicly fired and rehired Jaki Byard.

He laughed. "Man, I'm a single movement."

"The Panthers have been to see Charles," Mrs. Ungaro said, "but he won't go along with them."

"I don't like to see the blacks destroying this country. It's a waste of time. The militants have nothing to sell. And that's what this country does best—sells. Makes and sells things to the world. But the militants don't sell *nothing*. All the black pimps and black gangsters know this, because they *have* something to sell, like the king-pimp Billy Bones in my book. Man, he made millions of dollars around the world. The black people don't like themselves to begin with. You've got all these variations of color and dialect. You've got terrific economic differences. You never hear anything from the wealthy blacks, but they don't like the militants. Some of them been working at their money seventy-five years, in real estate or whatever, and they not about to let the militants come and take it away for something called freedom. Hell, what's freedom? Nobody's free, black or white. What's going to happen is there will be one hell of a revolution and it'll be between black and black. Like the big trouble in Watts, when the blacks were ready to shoot the blacks. It all started when a truckload of militants arrived and started throwing bombs into the black stores and such. Well, man, the shop owners—and I grew up with a lot of them—got upset and came charging out with guns, and by this time the truck had moved on and the white cops had arrived and saw all these blacks standing around with guns and started shooting *them,* and that was it."

Mingus leaned back, out of breath. The manager passed the table and Mingus asked him if he had any fresh fish. The manager went into the kitchen and came back with a handful of cherrystones. Mingus looked surprised. He ordered half a dozen on the half shell, and some vintage champagne.

"No vintage," the manager replied. "I got a bunch of vintage in last week and it was dead and I sent the whole mess back. I'll give you regular. Piper Heidsieck."

The clams arrived and Mingus coated each one with lemon juice and cocktail sauce and about a teaspoonful of Tabasco. "Hell, a while back, I took my daughter to Columbia to hear What's-His-Name, Eldridge Cleaver, and right away all I heard him saying was mother this and mother that. Well, I didn't want my daughter hearing that. That's vulgarity no matter if the man is right or wrong. I left. I took my daughter and left right away."

Mingus looked relaxed and content. In fact, he looked as if he had finally got the world straightened around to his liking. The talk wandered easily along between jukebox selections, and Mingus and Mrs. Ungaro discussed astrology (Mingus: "My birth date is four/two-two/two-two. The astrologists have never been able to get over that"), weight problems (Mingus: "Man, I get to this size and it's painful. My arms hurt all the time up here from banging against the rest of me"), the effects on the stomach of too much vitamin C, the sorrows of drug addiction, and the fact that Mingus suddenly has more "visible, taxable" money than ever before in his life.

The lights started to go out. It was almost four o'clock. Mingus went to the men's room, and Mrs. Ungaro said: "I don't really like Charles' book, and I've told him. I think the sexual parts are too savage, and I think that Charles himself doesn't really come through. It's the superficial Mingus, the flashy one, not the real one." Mingus reappeared and the waitress let us out the door. " 'Night, now," she said with a couple of semaphores. "It's been a real pleasure serving you."

Two nights later I went to the Village Vanguard, where Mingus was opening with a sextet for a week's stand. It included Lonnie Hillyer on trumpet, Charlie McPherson on alto saxophone, Bobby Jones on tenor saxophone, John Foster on piano, Mingus, and Virgil Day on drums. Mingus the musician is a tonic to watch. Like all great professionals, his husk remains visible while the inner man disappears completely into his work. He becomes a massive receiver-transmitter, absorbing every note played around him and then sending out through his bass corrective or appreciative notes. The result is a constant two-way flow which lights up his musicians who, in turn, light up his music. A successful Mingus number invariably suggests a transcontinental train rocking and blazing through the night.

Whenever he has felt out of sorts in recent years, Mingus has taken to offering lacklustre medleys of bebop numbers or Ellington tunes, completely ignoring his own brilliant storehouse of compositions. But at the Vanguard he brought out refurbished versions of numbers I hadn't heard him play since the fifties, among them "Celia" and "Diane." They were full of his inimitable trademarks—long, roving melodies, complex, multipart forms, breaks, constantly changing rhythms, stamping, howling ensembles, and the raw, against-the-grain quality he brands each of his performances with. Most of them were also done in Mingus' customary workshop manner. When a number would start hesitantly, he would rumble, "No. No, no," and stop the music. Then the group would start again. Sometimes there were three or four false starts. In all, I heard half a dozen long numbers, and they were exceptional. Mingus soloed briefly just once, on a blues, but everything was there, and there were also rewarding moments from Bobby Jones, who nearly split open Sy Oliver's decorous little band in its première a year ago, and from Foster, a mad pianist who easily mixes rumbustious gospel chords and steel-spring arpeggios. Mingus, dressed in a short-sleeved shirt and tie, sat on a tall stool and played, and he looked as serene and compact as he had on Sunday.

At the beginning of the following week, I went to see a Mingus I had not known existed—the Establishment Mingus. Knopf was giving a publication party for "Beneath the Underdog," with music. It was held in a couple of boxlike, orange-carpeted rooms in the Random House building on East Fiftieth Street, and when I arrived, about halfway through, it was jammed, and Mingus' sextet, with a ringer on bass, was playing "Celia" at close to the one-hundred-decibel level. There were more blacks than whites, and I spotted Mingus, again dressed in a dark suit and tie, talking with a lady of precisely his proportions. It was like seeing Sidney Greenstreet and Eugene Pallette porch to porch. Nat Hentoff and Murray Kempton were closeted in a corner, and Nesuhi Ertegun, heading toward them, said he hadn't seen Hentoff in ten years. Ornette Coleman, dressed in a glistening black silk mandarin suit, told me he had just completed a piece for eighty musicians that sounded just like his playing. Nel King said that Mingus' book had been a lot of work and that perhaps her being a woman was a help in managing his tempestuous moods. Mayor Lindsay, who had been invited, hadn't arrived, but Max Gordon, a Mingus supporter from the early days, had. He was standing with Mingus and Sue Ungaro and a tall, slender youth in a beard, straw hat, and cowboy boots. Mrs. Ungaro was still in her bluejeans and clogs. "Meet my son, Charles, Jr.," Mingus said. He poked Charles, Jr. in the stomach. "*He* doesn't have any weight problem. And look at his beard! I can't grow any more than what I have on my face." Mingus asked his son if he had read his book.

"Listen, I haven't even *seen* it yet," Charles, Jr., replied. "Besides, I've been working on my play."

I told Mingus that one of the minor but unavoidable axioms of the literary life was that children never read their parents' books, and cited as an example H. Allen Smith's son, who once admitted to me that he had never cracked a single book his renowned father had written. Mingus grunted. Nel King approached and told him she wanted him to meet someone, and I asked Mingus before he was towed away how he liked the party.

"It's strange, man," he said.

1971

Index

Index